T0125032

DEMOCRATICK EDITORIALS

Essays in Jacksonian Political Economy

Wm Leggett

DEMOCRATICK EDITORIALS

Essays in Jacksonian Political Economy by WILLIAM LEGGETT

Compiled, Edited, and with a Foreword
by Lawrence H. White

Liberty Fund
INDIANAPOLIS

This book is published by Liberty Fund, Inc., a foundation established to encourage study of the ideal of a society of free and responsible individuals.

The cuneiform inscription that serves as our logo and as the design motif for our endpapers is the earliest-known written appearance of the word "freedom" (*amagi*), or "liberty," It is taken from a clay document written about 2300 B.C. in the Sumerian city-state of Lagash.

 All inquiries should be addressed to Liberty Fund, Inc., 8335 Allison Pointe Trail, Suite 300, Indianapolis, Indiana 46250-1684. This book was manufactured in the United States of America.

Frontispiece photo courtesy of the Library of Congress.

Library of Congress Cataloging in Publication Data

Leggett, William, 1801–1839.
Democratick editorials.

Includes bibliographical references and index.
1. United States—Economic policy—To 1933—Addresses, essays, lectures. 2. United States—Politics and government—1815–1861—Addresses, essays, lectures. I. White, Lawrence H. (Lawrence Henry). II. Title.
HC105.L43 1984 338.973 83-24893
ISBN 0-86597-036-X
ISBN 0-86597-037-8 (pbk.)

16 15 14 13 12 11 10 09 08 07 C 6 5 4 3 2
16 15 14 13 12 11 10 09 08 07 P 6 5 4 3 2

CONTENTS

PART THREE

Abolition Insolence

PART FOUR
The Division of Political Classes

PART FIVE
The Principles of Free Trade

PART SIX

Literary Property

FOREWORD

Ten years after Thomas Jefferson's death, in 1826, an outspoken young editor in New York City was reformulating and extending the Jeffersonian philosophy of equal rights. William Leggett, articulating his views in the columns of the New York *Evening Post, Examiner,* and *Plaindealer,* gained widespread recognition as the intellectual leader of the *laissez-faire* wing of Jacksonian democracy.

LEGGETT'S LIFE

William Leggett was born April 30, 1801, in Savannah, Georgia. His father, Abraham, a revolutionary war veteran, had moved the family shortly after the war from Westchester County, New York, first to Charleston, South Carolina, then to Savannah. When William was about four years old, the family returned to New York.[1] At the young age of fourteen he entered Georgetown College but was forced to withdraw the following year when his father's business failed. In 1819 he moved with his family to the Illinois frontier, where his first writings—poems—appeared in the columns of a local newspaper.

In the fall of 1822 Leggett returned east to enter the United States Navy as a midshipman. During a tour of duty he contracted yellow fever, from which his health evidently never completely recovered. He also disagreed with his commander, leading to a court-martial trial. As a result Leggett resigned his

[1] Theodore A. Leggett, *Early Settlers of West Farms,* with additions by A. Hatfield, Jr. (New York: n.p., 1913), pp. 51–52; Abraham Leggett, *The Narrative of Abraham Leggett,* introduction and notes by Charles I. Bushnell (New York: privately printed, 1865), pp. v–vi. The area of West Farms has since been annexed from Westchester by the Bronx.

commission in 1826. While in the Navy he had continued his efforts at poetry, publishing a volume of works in 1825. He now undertook to support himself with literary contributions to New York newspapers and magazines and with some acting roles. The combination of the two pursuits soon led him to regular work as a theatrical and literary critic for two periodicals. In 1828 Leggett began his own weekly, *The Critic,* which ran for eight months. On its demise, William Cullen Bryant of the New York *Evening Post* took Leggett on as a critic.[2]

Leggett had no taste for politics when he joined the *Evening Post* in 1829. In fact, he accepted the job on the condition that he not be asked to write on the subject.[3] He achieved some importance as a theatrical critic, particularly in championing the Shakespearean actor Edwin Forrest. For our purposes, however, the important phase of Leggett's career had just begun. Within a year he had adopted wholesale Bryant's free-trade Jacksonian position and had begun authoring his own political editorials. In 1831 he became a partner. In June 1834 he assumed sole editorship of the paper upon Bryant's departure for Europe. Leggett soon brought financial difficulties upon the paper. His editorials antagonized heads of government agencies, who withdrew their patronage advertising. He later mused over the financial fate of the uncompromising newspaper editor: "He who strives to be a reformer, and to discharge his high trust with strict and single reference to the responsibilities of his vocation, will be sadly admonished by his dwindled receipts that he has not chosen the path of profit,

[2] Page S. Proctor, Jr., "William Leggett (1801–1839): Journalist and Literator," *Papers of the Bibliographical Society of America* 44 (July–September 1950), pp. 241–243; Richard Hofstadter, "William Leggett, Spokesman of Jacksonian Democracy," *Political Science Quarterly* 58 (December 1943), pp. 582–584; [William Cullen Bryant,] "William Leggett," *The United States Magazine and Democratic Review* 6 (July 1839), pp. 20–22.

[3] William Cullen Bryant, "Reminiscences of the 'Evening Post,'" in John Bigelow, *William Cullen Bryant* (New York: Chelsea House, 1980), pp. 326–327.

however much he may be consoled by knowing it is that of honour."[4]

After the fall of 1835 ill health forced Leggett to resign his duties for a year. Shortly after returning to work in the fall of 1836, he dissolved his partnership with Bryant to establish two periodicals of his own. The *Plaindealer,* begun in December, was a weekly sixteen-page journal of politics, news, and the arts. The *Examiner,* begun in May 1837, was a daily four-page newspaperwith a similar mix of contents. The *Plaindealer* was modeled after, and the *Examiner* named after, the London *Examiner,* which Leggett much admired. Both papers were composed and written by Leggett front to back. Both ceased publication in September, 1837. Though the papers evidently failed for financial reasons,[5] sickness again had caught up with the editor. Given the volume of his weekly word output during this period, it is no surprise that overwork should have taken its toll. The later numbers of the *Plaindealer,* with their tendency toward copious extracting from other publications, clearly show the strain. Yet in this journal, particularly in its early numbers, are to be found Leggett's best and most passionate writings.

After the failure of his papers Leggett lived in New Rochelle, New York, on the charity of his friend Edwin Forrest. An attempt was made to revive the *Plaindealer,* but Leggett's ill health caused the plan to be abandoned. Friends were eventually able to secure from President Van Buren—though he had been the target of sharp editorial attacks by Leggett—an appointment for Leggett as diplomatic agent to Guatemala in 1839. The voyage promised a healthful change of climate, but death came while he prepared to depart.[6]

[4] William Leggett, "The Newspaper Press," in *A Collection of the Political Writings of William Leggett,* selected and arranged by Theodore Sedgwick, Jr. (New York: Taylor & Dodd, 1840), vol. II, p. 199.

[5] James J. Barnes, *Authors, Publishers and Politicians* (London: Routledge & Kegan Paul, 1974), p. 267 n. 8.

[6] John Greenleaf Whittier, "William Leggett," in *Old Portraits and Modern Sketches* (Boston: Ticknor, Reed, and Fields, 1840), p. 232.

THE LOCO-FOCO MOVEMENT

The political currents of the Jacksonian era can hardly be detailed here, but William Leggett's important role should be indicated. He was not directly involved in party politics but, through his editorials, exerted a notable influence on the causes taken up by the democratic-republican followers of Andrew Jackson. Much of this impact was felt after his death. John Greenleaf Whittier in 1850 remarked of Leggett's pioneering efforts: "No one has labored more perseveringly or, in the end, more successfully, to bring the practice of American democracy into conformity with its professions."[7]

Leggett's editorials directly provided inspiration to the radical young democrats of New York. Among them, "the coming forth of his paper [the *Evening Post* under Leggett's editorship] was looked for daily with the most eager desire" to see "upon whom or what the [lightning] bolt [of his invective] had fallen." To them Leggett was "the champion of the cause." When his illness prevented his writing editorials, "the *Evening Post* was bereft of the mighty spirit which gave it power over men's minds, and it seemed as if the sun was standing still in the political world."[8]

When the radicals split off from the regular democrats to form their own party in 1835, Leggett's writings were themselves among the divisive issues. In September, 1835, Leggett was effectively excommunicated by the semi-official organ of the Jackson administration, the Washington *Globe,* for his criticism of federal officials and his defense of the rights of abolitionists. Early in October the Democratic Republican General Committee of New York, meeting in Tammany Hall, similarly censured the *Evening Post* for discussing the slavery issue and resolved to end the patronage of publishing its proceedings in Leggett's newspaper.[9]

[7] *Ibid.*, p. 218.

[8] F. Byrdsall, *The History of the Loco-Foco or Equal Rights Party* (New York: Burt Franklin, 1967 [Reprint of 1842 edition]), pp. 15, 22–23.

[9] See Leggett's editorials "Extremes Unite" and "The Committee and the Evening Post" in *Political Writings,* vol. II, pp. 70–76, 76–80.

At the Tammany Hall meeting of October 29, the radical wing unfurled banners emblazoned with various slogans and gave "heartfelt cheers" to a banner expressing support for Leggett's *Evening Post* as against the regular-democratic New York *Times*. The regulars unceremoniously sought to end the meeting by stomping out of the hall, shutting off the gas lamps as they departed, leaving the radicals to meet among themselves in the dark. Those remaining formed the splinter Equal Rights Party, more commonly known as the "Loco-Focos" after the brand of matches they used to light that first meeting. During the match-lit meeting the Loco-Focos adopted a resolution pledging support for the *Evening Post* and "the efforts of its talented editors."[10]

Leggett himself discouraged the formation of a separate party, urging the young radicals to seek reform within the existing party organization. In 1836 the party offered Leggett its mayoral nomination, but he declined it on grounds of poor health, financial troubles, and commitment to the paper in Bryant's absence. In the two-year lifespan of their party, Loco-Foco candidates never received more than five thousand votes in city elections. But the doctrines of the group—Leggett's doctrines—spread throughout the Democratic party of the northern states for the next two decades. To his followers Leggett was a martyr who had raised the banner of anti-monopoly reform. Among their tangible accomplishments may be counted the New York State Free Banking Act of 1838, the provision for a general incorporation law in the state's 1846 constitution, and, on the national level, the removal of federal government deposits from state banks by the Independent Treasury Act.[11]

[10] Byrdsall, *op. cit.*, pp. 26–27.

[11] *Ibid.*, pp. 34, 46; William Trimble, "Diverging Tendencies in New York Democracy in the Period of the Locofocos," *American Historial Review* 24 (April 1919), pp. 399–400, 416; *Idem*, "The Social Philosophy of the Loco-Foco Democracy," *American Journal of Sociology* 26 (May 1921), pp. 705–708; Hofstadter, *op. cit.*, pp. 593–594.

With the noteworthy exception of his late-blooming abolitionism, Leggett's views on questions of political economy underwent little or no fundamental change during his brief career. This is not surprising: he had become convinced of a powerful and consistent doctrine *ab ovo,* as it were, and had written his last editorial only eight years later.

The doctrine, from beginning to end, was one of equal rights—equal human rights to liberty and property. From these rights Leggett carefully derived his position on any given topic. For the most part Leggett spoke of these equal rights as natural rights, anterior to society and limiting the legitimate province of government. In his most systematic statement of political principles he grounded the legitimacy of government in a Lockean social compact whereby strictly limited powers—only those necessary for the protection of person and property—were delegated to government.[12] Yet Leggett was unwilling to extend the natural rights principle to cover every question. In a discussion of copyright law he explicitly founded his argument on a very different principle, the Benthamite principle of "the greatest good of the greatest number."[13]

These two strains of thought—natural rights and utilitarianism—coexist throughout Leggett's writings. His affinity for the English utilitarian Jeremy Bentham is evident from numerous quotations of his maxims, one of which appeared just below the masthead as the motto of the *Plaindealer:* "The immediate cause of all the mischief of misrule is, that the men acting as the representatives of the people have a private and sinister interest, producing a constant sacrifice of the interest of the people." Leggett shared with Bentham a concern for the welfare of the many, what Bentham called the "universal interest," as opposed to that of their rulers, the special inter-

[12] See "True Functions of Government" below, p 3.
[13] See "The Rights of Authors" below, p. 396.

est. Both advocated free markets, universal suffrage, and economy in government.[14]

Leggett cited several British economists besides Bentham, most importantly Adam Smith. Political economy and Jacksonian democracy were to Leggett "sister doctrines," both fundamentally libertarian in import.[15] The deepest roots of Leggett's thought lay not in British political economy, however, but in the natural rights tradition of American founding fathers Thomas Jefferson and John Taylor of Caroline. He quoted at length on one occasion from Taylor's *Inquiry into the Principles of the Government of the United States* (1814), lauding it as "one of the most democratic and at the same time most eloquent books ever written in this country."[16] He proudly claimed to be guided strictly by Jeffersonian principles: "The principles we maintain are those which were maintained by Jefferson. We profess to be a disciple of that great apostle of liberty, and if any article of faith is heterodox as tried by the standard he has furnished, let it be pointed out, and we promise to renounce it at once."[17] Leggett was fond of citing Jefferson to the effect that government's sole duty is to restrain men from injuring one another.

The equal rights principle meant to Leggett that the law may not discriminate among citizens, benefiting some at the expense of others. Few government programs could pass through this filter. Strict application of the equal rights principle thus led Leggett naturally to favor minimization of government powers. Every extension of the sphere of government action beyond the Jeffersonian night-watchman duties, in his

[14] Jeremy Bentham, "Lending Principles of a Constitutional Code For Any State" in *Bentham's Political Thought,* edited by Bhikhu Parekh (New York: Barnes & Noble Books, 1973), pp. 195–206. This first appeared in *The Pamphleteer* 44 (1823).

[15] See "The Sister Doctrines" below, p. 35.

[16] Leggett, "Banking," *Plaindealer* 39 (August 26, 1837), pp. 610–612.

[17] Leggett, "Democracy," *Plaindealer* 38 (August 19, 1837), pp. 593–595.

view, created a privileged aristocratic class at the expense of the productive laboring class.

THIS VOLUME

The editorials in this volume are organized under headings of those topics to which Leggett devoted the greatest attention. In putting together this collection, I have attempted to combine the best of the editorials that appeared in *A Collection of the Political Writings of William Leggett* (1840) with the best of his *Plaindealer* pieces that did not make that collection. Though there is fairly clear external evidence concerning the dates on which Leggett presumably wrote the *Evening Post* editorials, Bryant being in Europe, I have included only two *Evening Post* editorials that did not appear in the 1840 collection.[18] I have not included anything from the *Examiner*, since Leggett wrote virtually nothing of importance there that he did not later include in the *Plaindealer*.

In choosing among Leggett's political writings, I have rejected pieces dealing primarily with party disputes or personalities of the day. Other pieces from the 1840 collection have been omitted in the interest of avoiding repetition. The repetition that remains usefully indicates what Leggett most wanted to emphasize. Ellipses appearing in the editorials following indicate where deletions have been made of partisan invective or, more commonly, of long extracts from other publications. The content of those deleted extracts should be clear from Leggett's replies to them.

My foremost debt is to Walter E. Grinder of the Institute for Humane Studies, who years ago first suggested William Leggett to me as a figure deserving study. His guidance and encouragement since then have been invaluable. I also wish to

[18] For a list of those editorials see Proctor, *op. cit.*, pp. 252–253.

thank Axel Leijonhufvud, Joseph R. Peden, Linda Bandy-White, David D. Boaz, and D. Alexander Puig for their help, and Steve Wylie for his useful comments on a paper on Leggett I wrote several years back.

Lawrence H. White
Department of Economics
New York University

PART ONE

The Doctrine of Equal Rights

TRUE FUNCTIONS OF GOVERNMENT

"There are no necessary evils in Government. Its evils exist only in its abuses. If it would confine itself to *equal protection*, and, as heaven does its rains, shower its favours alike on the high and the low, the rich and the poor, it would be an unqualified blessing."[1]

This is the language of our venerated President, and the passage deserves to be written in letters of gold, for neither in truth of sentiment or beauty of expression can it be surpassed. We choose it as our text for a few remarks on the true functions of Government.

The fundamental principle of all governments is the protection of person and property from domestic and foreign enemies; in other words, to defend the weak against the strong. By establishing the social feeling in a community, it was intended to counteract that selfish feeling, which, in its proper exercise, is the parent of all worldly good, and, in its excesses, the root of all evil. The functions of Government, when confined to their proper sphere of action, are therefore restricted to the making of *general laws*, uniform and universal in their operation, for these purposes, and for no other.

Governments have no right to interfere with the pursuits of individuals, as guarantied by those general laws, by offering encouragements and granting privileges to any particular class of industry, or any select bodies of men, inasmuch as all classes of industry and all men are equally important to the general welfare, and equally entitled to protection.

Whenever a Government assumes the power of discriminating between the different classes of the community, it

Evening Post, November 21, 1834. Title added by Theodore Sedgwick, Jr. in editing *A Collection of the Political Writings of William Leggett* (1840).

[1] From Andrew Jackson's message to the Senate, July 10, 1832, vetoing the rechartering of the Bank of the United States.—Ed.

becomes, in effect, the arbiter of their prosperity, and exercises a power not contemplated by any intelligent people in delegating their sovereignty to their rulers. It then becomes the great regulator of the profits of every species of industry, and reduces men from a dependence on their own exertions, to a dependence on the caprices of their Government. Governments possess no delegated right to tamper with individual industry a single hair's-breadth beyond what is essential to protect the rights of person and property.

In the exercise of this power of intermeddling with the private pursuits and individual occupations of the citizen, a Government may at pleasure elevate one class and depress another; it may one day legislate exclusively for the farmer, the next for the mechanic, and the third for the manufacturer, who all thus become the mere puppets of legislative cobbling and tinkering, instead of independent citizens, relying on their own resources for their prosperity. It assumes the functions which belong alone to an overruling Providence, and affects to become the universal dispenser of good and evil.

This power of regulating—of increasing or diminishing the profits of labour and the value of property of all kinds and degrees, by direct legislation, in a great measure destroys the essential object of all civil compacts, which, as we said before, is to make the social a counterpoise to the selfish feeling. By thus operating directly on the latter, by offering one class a bounty and another a discouragement, they involve the selfish feeling in every struggle of party for the ascendancy, and give to the force of political rivalry all the bitterest excitement of personal interests conflicting with each other. Why is it that parties now exhibit excitement aggravated to a degree dangerous to the existence of the Union and to the peace of society? Is it not that by frequent exercises of partial legislation, almost every man's personal interests have become deeply involved in the result of the contest? In common times, the strife of parties is the mere struggle of ambitious leaders for power; now they are deadly contests of the whole mass of the people, whose pecuniary interests are implicated in the event, because the Government has usurped and exercised the power of legislating on their private affairs. The selfish feeling has been so strongly called into action by this abuse of authority as almost to overpower the social feeling, which it should be the object of a good Government to foster by every means in its power.

No nation, knowingly and voluntarily, with its eyes open, ever delegated to its Government this enormous power, which places at its disposal the property, the industry, and the fruits of the industry, of the whole people. As a general rule, the prosperity of rational men depends on themselves. Their talents and their virtues shape their fortunes. They are therefore the best judges of their own affairs, and should be permitted to seek their own happiness in their own way, untrammelled by the capricious interference of legislative bungling, so long as they do not violate the equal rights of others, nor transgress the general laws for the security of person and property.

But modern refinements have introduced new principles in the science of Government. Our own Government, most especially, has assumed and exercised an authority over the people, not unlike that of weak and vacillating parents over their children, and with about the same degree of impartiality. One child becomes a favourite because he has made a fortune, and another because he has failed in the pursuit of that object; one because of its beauty, and another because of its deformity. Our Government has thus exercised the right of dispensing favours to one or another class of citizens at will; of directing its patronage first here and then there; of bestowing one day and taking back the next; of giving to the few and denying to the many; of investing wealth with new and exclusive privileges, and distributing, as it were at random, and with a capricious policy, in unequal portions, what it ought not to bestow, or what, if given away, should be equally the portion of all.

A government administered on such a system of policy may be called a Government of Equal Rights, but it is in its nature and essence a disguised despotism. It is the capricious dispenser of good and evil, without any restraint, except its own sovereign will. It holds in its hand the distribution of the goods of this world, and is consequently the uncontrolled master of the people.

Such was not the object of the Government of the United States, nor such the powers delegated to it by the people. The object was beyond doubt to protect the weak against the strong, by giving them an equal voice and equal rights in the state; not to make one portion stronger, the other weaker at pleasure, by crippling one or more classes of the community, or making them tributary to one alone. This is too great a power to entrust to Government. It was never given away by the people, and is not a right, but a usurpation.

Experience will show that this power has always been exercised under the influence and for the exclusive benefit of wealth. It was never wielded in behalf of the community. Whenever an exception is made to the general law of the land, founded on the principle of equal rights, it will always be found to be in favour of wealth. These immunities are never bestowed on the poor. They have no claim to a dispensation of exclusive benefits, and their only business is to *"take care of the rich that the rich may take care of the poor."*

Thus it will be seen that the sole reliance of the labouring classes, who constitute a vast majority of every people on the earth, is the great principle of Equal Rights; that their only safeguard against oppression is a system of legislation which leaves all to the free exercise of their talents and industry, within the limits of the GENERAL LAW, and which, on no pretence of public good, bestows on any particular class of industry, or any particular body of men, rights or privileges not equally enjoyed by the great aggregate of the body politic.

Time will remedy the departures which have already been made from this sound republican system, if the people but jealously watch and indignantly frown on any future attempts to invade their equal rights, or appropriate to the few what belongs to all alike. To quote, in conclusion, the language of the great man, with whose admirable sentiment we commenced these remarks, "it is time to pause in our career—if we cannot at once, in justice to the interests vested under improvident legislation, make our government what it ought to be, we can at least take a stand against all new grants of monopolies and exclusive privileges, and against any prostitution of our Government to the advancement of the few at the expense of the many."

THE RESERVED RIGHTS OF THE PEOPLE

The President of the United States, in his last Message to Congress, has the following remarkable sentiment, which we shall make the subject of a brief commentary: "To suppose that because our Government has been instituted for the benefit of the people, it must therefore have the power to do whatever may seem to conduce to the public good, is an error into which even honest minds are apt to fall."

Whoever has watched with attention the course pursued by the General and State Governments ever since their first organization, must, we think, have been struck with the conviction that one of the great practical evils of our system arises from a superabundance of legislation. It is probable, nay certain, that putting the acts of Congress and those of the State legislature together, they amount to some thousands annually. Is it possible that the good people of the United States require to be hampered and pestered by such a multiplicity of fetters

Evening Post, December 13, 1834. Title added.

as this; or that they cannot be kept in order without being manacled every year by new laws and regulations? Every superfluous law is a wanton and unnecessary innovation of the freedom of action, and impairs the RESERVED RIGHTS OF THE PEOPLE. Let us inquire what these rights are.

All governments are originally instituted for the protection of person and property; and the people, in their formation, only delegate to their rulers such powers as are indispensable to these great objects. All the powers not thus delegated are retained by the people, and may be denominated their reserved rights. In defining the objects of government, all writers agree that they are those which we have just specified, namely, the protection of the rights of person and property. Whatever is necessary to these purposes, the people have given away, whatever is not necessary they have retained. Protect their persons and property, and all the rest they can do for themselves. They want no government to regulate their private concerns; to prescribe the course and mete out the profits of their industry. They want no fireside legislators; no executive interference in their workshops and fields; and no judiciary to decide their domestic disputes. They require a general system of laws, which, while it equally restrains them from violating the persons and property of others, leaves their own unimpaired.

For the attainment of these primary objects in the formation of government it can never be necessary to confer privileges on one class of a community which the others do not equally enjoy. Such privileges would be destructive of the great end of all governments, since they tend to create, or at least strengthen those inequalities of wealth and influence from which originate those dangers to person and property against which all governments were intended to guard. Such a course inevitably tends to increase the vigour of the strong, and the imbecility of the weak by comparison, thus exposing the latter to successful invasions of their rights of person and property.

Among the rights expressly reserved to themselves by the

people of the United States, was a complete equality of civil privileges. This right is inherent in every people, and when not expressly relinquished, remains with them as a matter of course. But in respect to the people of the United States, it is not merely tacitly reserved, it is guaranteed, and asserted, and recognized in the constitution of our general government, as well as in those of the states, as their great fundamental principle.

The only case in which the people of the United States have delegated to their representatives the right of interfering in their private business and pursuits is that of commerce, and the reason is obvious. Such a power was necessary in the government, to enable it to establish a uniform system of regulations and imposts, and to make commercial treaties with foreign nations. Without it there would have been no regular or permanent system of foreign trade; each man might make his own private arrangements without conforming to any rule and thus the government would be reduced to the alternative of either leaving our ships and commerce to their fate, or going to war to protect those whom it could not controul. And this power to "regulate" the pursuits of industry extends no further. It was not necessary to the purposes of a good government, in relation to any other class of the community, and was never conceded by them either virtually or verbally.

Yet if we analyse the course of legislation in the United States, ever since the adoption of the various constitutions of government, we shall find that legislative bodies have been regularly and systematically employed in frittering away, under a thousand pretenses, the whole fabric of the reserved rights of the people. Nine tenths of their legislation has consisted of infringements on that great principle of equal rights without whose eternal barrier no nation can ever long maintain its liberty. The representatives of the people have gradually usurped and exercised all the rights which, if our government was administered in its purity, would be left for the people to exercise. Their vocation has consisted, not in making general, but special laws; not in legislating for the whole, but for a small part; not in preserving unimpaired the rights of the people, but in bartering them away to corporations. Corporations for purposes of charity—for men cannot give to the poor unless they are incorporated; corporations for purposes of education—for children will not learn their A B C nowadays, unless under a system of exclusive privileges; corporations for spinning and weaving—for the wheel will not turn nor the shuttle go, unless they are incorporated—corporations for this, that, and for every purpose which the ingenuity of money making man can devise. Each one of these not only enjoys privileges denied to every other citizen, and of which none but monied men can partake, because the foundation of all these corporations is money, money, money; but each one of these also violates the reserved right of the great body of the people. It is either legislating away for a certain period, or forever, a part of their sovereignty, or it is interfering with the pursuits of individual industry, by raising up a rival fatal to its prosperity.

In this way our national and state governments have, until lately, been employed in filching away the reserved rights of the great body of the people, to give or sell them, to little knots of monied men, and thus enable them by the aid of certain privileges, to combine more successfully against individual rights and individual industry. The people were placed between two fires. On one hand Congress was establishing a great Bank, and giving away tens of millions to great corporations in all quarters; on the other the states were forging another set of fetters in the shape of all sorts of privileged bodies, each one ruling its little district; each one swallowing up the business of private individuals; each one prescribing the prices of goods and the rates of labour, and each one a rotten borough, returning members of Congress. At one time these rotten boroughs, like those of England, returned a majority of the members of Congress! Can we wonder then that protection and prohibition, internal improvements, and corporate privileges, were almost the only words heard in that honourable body? Can we wonder that the voice of the people was as the voice of one crying in the wilderness, and that but for the honest, fearless, high minded, and clear headed Andrew Jackson and his worthy counsellors, not a vestige of the reserved rights of the people would have survived the practical operation of the principle repudiated by that great and wise man, namely, "that because our government has been instituted for the benefit of the people, it must therefore have the power to do whatever may seem to conduce to the public good."

Under the sanction of such a principle, a government can do any thing on pretense of acting for the public good. It will become the mere creature of designing politicians, interested speculators, or crack-brained enthusiasts. It will gradually concentrate to itself all the reserved rights of the people; it will become the great arbiter of individual prosperity; and thus before we know it, we shall become the victims of a new species of despotism, that of a system of laws made by ourselves. It will then remain to be seen whether our chains will be the lighter from having been forged by our own hands.

OBJECTS OF THE EVENING POST

Those who only read the declamations of the opponents of the Equal Rights of the people, may be induced to believe that this paper advocates principles at war with the very existence of social rights and social order. But what have we asked in the name of the people, that such an interested clamour should be

Evening Post, January 3, 1835. Title added by Sedgwick.

raised against them and us? What have we done or said, that we should be denounced as incendiaries, striking at the very roots of society and tearing down the edifice of property? It may be useful to recapitulate what we have already done, in order that those who please may judge whether or not we deserve these reproaches, from any but the enemies of the equal rights of person and property.

In the first place, in designating the true functions of a good government, we placed the protection of property among its first and principal duties. We referred to it as one of the great objects for the attainment of which all governments were originally instituted. Does this savour of hostility to the rights of property?

In the second place, we maintained that all grants of monopolies, or exclusive or partial privileges to any man, or body of men, impaired the equal rights of the people, and was in direct violation of the first principle of a free government. Does it savour of hostility to the rights of property to maintain that all property has equal rights, and that exclusive privileges granted to one class of men, or one species of property, impair the equal rights of all the others?

As a deduction from these principles, we draw the conclusion that charters conferring partial or exclusive monopolies on small fractions of society, are infringements on the general rights of society, and therefore that the system ought to be abandoned as soon as possible, as utterly at war with the rights of the people at large. It is here that the shoe pinches, and here the clamour against us will be found to originate. Thousands and tens of thousands of influential individuals, at the bar, on the bench, in our legislative bodies, and everywhere, are deeply interested in the continuance of these abuses. Lawmakers, law-expounders and law executors, have invested either their money or their credit in corporations of every kind, and it is not to be wondered at that they should cry out against the abandonment of a system from whence they derive such exorbitant gains.

We are accused of violating vested rights when we ask, in the name of the people, that no more be created, and that all those possessing the means and the inclination, may be admitted, under general regulations, to a participation in the privileges which hitherto have been only enjoyed through the caprice, the favour, the policy, or the corruption, of legislative bodies. We never even hinted at touching those vested rights, until the period to which they had been extended by law had expired, and till it could be done without a violation of legislative faith. We defy any man to point out in any of our arguments on this subject a single idea or sentence that will sustain the charge of hostility to actually vested rights. Our opposition was prospective, not retroactive; it was not to present, but to future vested rights.

In attacking a course of policy in the future, do we make war on the past? In pointing out what we believe errors in former legislation, and recommending their abandonment in future, do we violate any right of property, or recommend any breach of public faith? Or, in advocating the equal rights of all, do we impair the constitutional rights of any? It might be well for the clamourous few who assail our principles and our motives with opprobrious epithets, which, though they do not understand their purport themselves, they mean should convey the most dishonourable imputations—it might be well for them to answer these questions before they resort to railing.

One of the greatest supports of an erroneous system of legislation, is the very evil it produces. When it is proposed to remedy the mischief by adopting a new system, every abuse which has been the result of the old one becomes an obstacle to reformations. Every political change, however salutary, must be injurious to the interests of some, and it will be found that those who profit by abuses are always more clamourous for their continuance than those who are only opposing them from motives of justice or patriotism, are for their abandonment. Such is precisely the state of the question of monopoly at this moment.

Under the abuses of the right to grant exclusive privileges to the few, which is a constructive, if not a usurped power, a vast and concentrated interest and influence has grown up among us, which will undoubtedly be seriously affected in its monopoly of gain from that source, by the discontinuance of their chartered privileges, when they shall expire by their own limitation. The admission of all others having the means and the inclination to associate for similar purposes, by destroying the monopoly at one blow, will in all probability diminish the prospect of future gains; and these will be still further curtailed, by at first restricting banks in their issues of small notes and in the amount of notes they are permitted to put into circulation, and finally by repealing the restraining law,[1] and throwing banking open to the free competition of the whole community. These may prove serious evils to the parties concerned; but it is a poor argument to say that a bad system should be persevered in, least a small minority of the community should suffer some future inconvenience. The magnitude of the evils produced by an erroneous system of legislation, far from being a circumstance in favour of its continuance or increase, is the strongest argument in the world for its being abandoned as soon as possible. Every reformation may in this way be arrested, under the pretence that the evils it will cause are greater than those it will cure. On the same principle the drawing of a tooth might be opposed, on the ground that the pain is worse than that of the tooth-ache, keeping out of sight the fact that the one is a lasting and increasing, the other a momentary evil.

It is the nature of political abuses, to be always on the increase, unless arrested by the virtue, intelligence and firmness of the people. If not corrected in time, they grow up into a gigantic vigour and notoriety which at length enables them to wrestle successfully with the people, and overthrow them and their rights. The possessors of monopolies and exclusive

[1] This law prohibited banks not expressly chartered by the New York State legislature.—Ed.

privileges, which form the essence of every bad government, pervert a long perseverance in the wrong, into a political right; abuses grow venerable by time; usurpation matures into proscription; distinctions become hereditary; and what cannot be defended by reason, is maintained on the ground that a long continuance of wrongs, and a long possession of rights, are equally sacred.

REPLY TO THE CHARGE OF LUNACY

The Bank tory presses originated the imputation of lunacy against the conductors of this journal, and the echoes of the Albany Argus have caught up the cry, and rung the changes upon it, until very possibly many of their readers, who do not read the Evening Post, may suppose it has some foundation in truth. One good-natured editor in Connecticut, we perceive, has taken the matter up quite seriously in our defence, and seeks to prove that we are not crazy in the full sense of the word, but only partially crazy, or suffering under a species of monomania on the subject of monopolies. We are infinitely obliged to our benevolent defender, and in return for his courtesy beg leave to assure him, that if our views on the subject of banks and corporations are evidence of the malady he imputes to us the disease is endemic in this state, and not even Governor Marcy's proposed magnificent lunatic asylum would be capable of containing one hundredth part of the monomaniacs who now go at large, and are generally supposed to be in the full enjoyment of their senses.

Evening Post, January 30, 1835. Title added by Sedgwick.

The charge of lunacy against an antagonist whose arguments are not refutable is neither a very new nor very ingenious device. Its novelty is on a par with its candour. It is a short and wholesale method of answering facts and reasonings, of which weak and perverted minds have ever been ready to avail themselves, and it has ever been especially resorted to against such as have had the boldness to stand forward as the asserters of the principles of political and religious liberty. Those who are unable to refute your arguments, can at least sneer at their author; and next to overthrowing an antagonist's doctrines, it is considered by many a desirable achievement to raise a laugh against himself. To be laughed at by the aristocracy, however, (and there are too many aristocrats who, to answer selfish purposes, rank themselves with the democracy) is the inevitable fate of all who earnestly strive to carry into full practical operation the great principle of equal political, civil, and religious rights. To escape "the fool's dread laugh," is therefore not to be desired by those who are ardent and determined in the cause of true democratic principles. Such derision they will consider rather as evidence of the soundness of their views, and will be inclined to say with John Wesley, "God forbid that we should not be the laughing-stock of mankind!"

But we put it to every reader seriously, whether, in all they have seen against the doctrines maintained by this paper on the subject of banks and corporations, they have yet found one single argument addressed to men's reasons, and tending to show that our views are wrong. They have read, doubtless, a deal of declamation about our ultraism and our Jacobinism; they have seen us called a Utopian, a disciple of Fanny Wright,[1] an agrarian, a lunatic, and a dozen other hard names. They have seen it asserted that we are for overthrowing all the cherished institutions of society; for breaking down the foundations of private right, sundering the marriage tie, and estab-

[1] Frances Wright (1795–1852), controversial feminist and communitarian reformer.—Ed.

lishing "a community of men, women, and property." But amidst all this declamation—amidst all these groundless and heinous charges, have they yet found one editor who had the candour fairly to state our views, and meet them with calm and temperate argument? If they have found such a one, they have been more fortunate than we.

While the principles which we maintain are subject to such constant and wilful misrepresentations, it may not be without use frequently to repeat, in a brief form, the real objects for which we contend. All our agrarian, utopian and anarchical views, then, are comprehended in the following statement of the ends at which we aim.

First, with regard to corporations generally: we contend that it is the duty of the legislature, in accordance with the principle of equal rights, on which this government is founded, to refrain, in all time to come, from granting any special or exclusive charters of incorporation to any set of men, or for any purpose whatever; but instead, to pass one general law, which will allow any set of men, who choose to associate together for any purpose, (banking alone temporarily excepted,) to form themselves into that convenient kind of partnership known by the name of corporation.

Second, with regard to banking: we contend that suitable steps should be immediately taken by the legislature to place that branch of business on the same broad and equal basis: that to this end, no more banks should be created or renewed; that existing banks should be gradually curtailed of their privilege to issue small notes, until no bank notes of a smaller denomination than twenty dollars should be in circulation; and that then the restraining law should be repealed, and the community left as free to pursue the business of banking, as they now are to pursue any business whatever.

We are not in favour of pulling down, or overthrowing, or harming, in any way, any existing institutions. Let them all live out their charters, if they do nothing in the meanwhile to forfeit them; and as those charters should expire, the very same stockholders might, if they chose, associate themselves together in a voluntary corporation, under the proposed general law, and pursue their business without interruption, and without let or hinderance.

The grand principle which we aim to establish is the principle of equal rights. The only material difference between the present system, and the system we propose, is that instead of exclusive privileges, or particular facilities and immunities, being dealt out to particular sets of individuals by the legislature, all kinds of business would be thrown open to free and full competition, and all classes and conditions of men would have restored to them those equal rights which the system of granting special charters of incorporation has been the means of filching from them.

All our Utopianism, Jacobinism, Agrarianism, Fanny Wrightism, Jack Cade-ism; and a dozen other *isms* imputed to us, have this extent, no more. It would argue that there was something very rotten in the democracy of the present day, if for entertaining and strenuously asserting such views, the conductors of a public journal, whose business and pride it is to maintain democratic principles, should be generally supposed to labour under mental derangement. If this is lunacy, it is at all events such lunacy as passed for sound and excellent sense in Thomas Jefferson. The sum of a good government, as described by that illustrious champion of democracy, is all we aim at—"a wise and frugal government, which shall restrain men from injuring one another; shall leave them otherwise free to regulate their own pursuits of industry and improvement; and shall not take from the mouth of labour the bread it has earned."

THE LEGISLATION OF CONGRESS

. . . .

Either the present number of representatives in Congress is necessary, or it is not. If the former, then a regular and general attendance is demanded of the members. If the latter, then it is an abuse to saddle the people with the expense of these supernumerary legislators, who spend their time in gallanting the ladies about the city of Washington, or flirting with them in the galleries of the two Houses. If their wisdom is essential to the welfare of the people, then the people who pay them have a right to its exercise: if it is not, it might better be employed on their own account at home.

The close of every session of Congress, whether short or long, invariably exhibits a vast mass of public business either not acted upon, or left unfinished, consisting not unfrequently of questions of great and general importance to the whole Union. This lamentable result may be partly owing to the annual increase of private claims not susceptible of judicial decision, and therefore brought before Congress as the only resort. If so, it would seem to be high time to make such a disposition of these matters as may allow ample time to the proper affairs of the nation; to those general laws which are of universal concern, and the neglect of which is felt in every part of the country.

The cause of this neglect of more important affairs, in the first instance, and this precipitate legislation on them afterwards, will be discovered in the unlimited indulgence of the rage for speech making—the *cacoethes loquendi*, which is the prevailing epidemic in Congress—added to that propensity to private, partial, and local legislation, which is becoming the curse of this country. Almost every member has his budget of

Evening Post, March 11, 1835. Title added by Sedgwick. Text abridged.

matters of this sort, in which the great mass of the nation has no concern whatever, and which he cannot die in peace without thrusting upon the attention of Congress, and urging with a pertinacity and verbosity precisely in proportion to their insignificance. In this way the people are borne down to the earth with public benefits and harassed with legislation, and there is some reason to fear that it will be discovered ere long that they cannot breathe without a special act of Congress.

"DO NOT GOVERN TOO MUCH," is a maxim which should be placed in large letters over the speaker's chair in all legislative bodies. The old proverb, "too much of a good thing is good for nothing," is most especially applicable to the present time, when it would appear, from the course of our legislation, that common sense, common experience, and the instinct of self-preservation, are utterly insufficient for the ordinary purposes of life; that the people of the United States are not only incapable of self-government, but of taking cognizance of their individual affairs; that industry requires protection, enterprize bounties, and that no man can possibly find his way in broad day light without being tied to the apron-string of a legislative dry-nurse. The present system of our legislation seems founded on the total incapacity of mankind to take care of themselves or to exist without legislative enactment. Individual property must be maintained by invasions of personal rights, and the "general welfare" secured by monopolies and exclusive privileges.

The people of the United States will discover when too late that they may be enslaved by laws as well as by the arbitrary will of a despot; that unnecessary restraints are the essence of tyranny; and that there is no more effectual instrument of depriving them of their liberties, than a legislative body, which is permitted to do anything it pleases under the broad mantle of THE PUBLIC GOOD—a mantle which, like charity, covers a multitude of sins, and like charity is too often practised at the expense of other people.

RELIGIOUS INTOLERANCE

Certain sectarian newspapers are doing all in their power to stir ill blood between the Protestant sects, particularly the Calvinists, and the Roman Catholics. The Journal of Commerce and the Commercial Advertiser lead the van in this warfare of bigotry and intolerance. It is strange that the world should not yet have learned, after so many lessons written in blood, that persecution inflames and combines those whom it aims to subdue and disperse. If political evil should ever come of the Roman Catholic religion in this country it will come in consequence of the exercise of that narrow and intolerant spirit which we are sorry to see so active among us. There are other religious sects whose predominance we should consider quite as unfriendly to the perpetuation of free institutions and the diffusion of human liberty. They whose creed prompts them, in this day and generation, to urge proscription of the Roman Catholics because they believe more or less or different from themselves, are, to say the least, quite as dangerous enemies of the principles of liberty as the Roman Catholics possibly can be.

Evening Post, March 21, 1835. Title added.

DIRECT TAXATION

No reflecting mind can consider the mode of raising revenue in this country for the support of the Government, in con-

Evening Post, April 22, 1834. Title added by Sedgwick.

nexion with the great principle on which that Government is founded, without being struck with the anomaly it presents. The fundamental principle of our political institutions is that the great body of the people are honest and intelligent, and fully capable of self-government. Yet so little confidence is really felt in their virtue and intelligence, that we dare not put them to the test of asking them, openly and boldly, to contribute, each according to his means, to defray the necessary expenses of the Government; but resort, instead, to every species of indirection and arbitrary restriction on trade. This is true, not only of the General Government, but of every State Government, and every municipal corporation. The General Government raises its revenue by a tax on foreign commerce, giving rise to the necessity of a fleet of revenue vessels, and an army of revenue officers. The State Governments raise their funds by a tax on auction sales, bonuses on banks, tolls on highways, licenses, excise, &c. The municipal corporations descend a step in this prodigious scale of legislative swindling, and derive their resources from impositions on grocers, from steamboat, and stage-coach licenses, and from a tax on beef, wood, coal, and nearly every prime necessary of life. This whole complicated system is invented and persevered in for the purpose of deriving the expenses of Government from a people whose virtue and intelligence constitute the avowed basis of our institutions! What an absurdity does not a mere statement of the fact present?

Has any citizen, rich or poor, the least idea of the amount which he annually pays for the support of the government? The thing is impossible. No arithmetician, not even Babbit with his calculating machine, could compute the sum. He pays a tax on every article of clothing he wears, on every morsel of food he eats, on the fuel that warms him in winter, on the light which cheers his home in the evening, on the implements of his industry, on the amusements which recreate his leisure. There is scarcely an article produced by human labour or ingenuity which does not bear a tax for the support of one of the three governments under which every individual lives.

We have heretofore expressed the hope, and most cordially do we repeat it, that the day will yet come when we shall see the open and honest system of direct taxation resorted to. It is the only democratic system. It is the only method of taxation by which the people can know how much their government costs them. It is the only method which does not give the lie to the great principle on which we profess to have established all our political institutions. It is the only method, moreover, in consonance with the doctrines of that magnificent science, which, the twin-sister, as it were, of democracy, is destined to make this country the pride and wonder of the earth.

There are many evils which almost necessarily flow from our complicated system of indirect taxation. In the first place, taxes fall on the people very unequally. In the second place, it gives rise to the creation of a host of useless officers, and there is no circumstance which exercises such a vitiating and demoralizing influence on politics, as the converting of elections into a strife of opposite parties for place instead of principles. Another bad effect of the system is that it strengthens the government at the expense of the rights of the people, induces it to extend its powers to objects which were not contemplated in its original institution, and renders it every year less and less subject to the popular will. The tendency of the system is to build up and foster monopolies of various kinds, and to impose all sorts of restrictions on those pursuits which should be left wholly to the control of the laws of trade. We are well satisfied, and have long been so, that the only way to preserve economy in government, to limit it to its legitimate purposes, and to keep aroused the necessary degree of vigilance on the part of the people, is by having that government dependent for its subsistence on a direct tax on property.

If the fundamental principle of democracy is not a cheat and a mockery, a mere phrase of flattery, invented to gull the people—if it is really true that popular intelligence and virtue are the true source of all political power and the true basis of Government—if these positions are admitted, we can conceive no possible objection to a system of direct taxation which at all counterbalances any of the many important and grave considerations that may be urged in its favour.

For our own part, we profess ourselves to be democrats in the fullest and largest sense of the word. We are for free trade and equal rights. We are for a strictly popular Government. We have none of those fears, which some of our writers, copying the slang of the English aristocrats, profess to entertain of an "unbalanced democracy." We believe when government in this country shall be a true reflection of public sentiment; when its duties shall be strictly confined to its only legitimate ends, the equal protection of the whole community in life, person, and property; when all restrictions on trade shall be abolished, and when the funds necessary for the support of the government and the defence of the country are derived directly from taxation on property—we believe when these objects are brought about, we shall then present to the admiration of the world a nation founded as the hills, free as the air, and prosperous as a fruitful soil, a genial climate, and industry, enterprise, temperance and intelligence can render us.

THE COURSE OF THE EVENING POST

Saturday last was the semi-annual dividend day of this office. It is presumed that a majority of the subscribers of the Evening Post feel sufficient interest in its prosperity to justify our adverting, for a single moment, and in the most general terms, to the private affairs of this office. It is with satisfaction, then,

Evening Post, May 18, 1835. Title added by Sedgwick.

we have it in our power to state, that the business of our establishment, during the past six months, has been flourishing and profitable, and was never more thoroughly and soundly prosperous than at the present moment. The number of subscribers to our journal is larger than at any previous period; the amount received for advertising is undiminished; and the total receipts of the establishment greater than they ever were before.

This result is exceedingly gratifying to us for considerations of a higher kind than those which merely relate to the success of our private business. It furnishes us with an evidence of the public sentiment in relation to those cardinal principles of democratic government which this journal, for a long time past, has laboured zealously to propagate and defend. That evidence is in our favour, and animates us to fresh exertions. We start afresh, then, from this resting-place on our editorial road, invigorated with renewed confidence of ultimately attaining the goal for which we strive, the reward for which we toil, the victory for which we struggle—the establishment of the great principle of Equal Rights as, in all things, the perpetual guide and invariable rule of legislation.

It is now about two years since the Evening Post—having at length seen successfully accomplished one of the great objects for which it had long and perseveringly striven, namely, the principles of free-trade in respect of our foreign commerce—turned its attention to a kindered subject, of equal magnitude, in our domestic policy, and began the struggle which it has ever since maintained in favour of the principles of economic science, as they relate to the internal and local legislation of the country. We had long seen with the deepest regret that the democracy, unmindful of the fundamental axiom of their political faith, had adopted a system of laws, the inevitable tendency of which would be to build up privileged classes and depress the great body of the community. We saw that trade, not left in the slightest respect to the salutary operation of its own laws, had been tied up and hampered in every limb and muscle by arbitrary and unjust statutes; that these restrictions furnished employment for an almost innumerous army of office-holders; and that the phalanx of placemen was yearly augmented by the multiplication of unequal and oppressive restrictions and prohibitions on the body politic. We could not help seeing, also, that this multitude of unnecessary public offices, to be disposed by the Government, was exercising a most vitiating influence on politics, and was constantly degrading, more and more, what should be a conflict of unbiassed opinion, into an angry warfare of heated and selfish partisans, struggling for place.

But besides the various and almost countless restrictions on trade, for the support of a useless army of public stipendiaries, we saw our State Governments vieing with each other in dispensing to favoured knots of citizens trading privileges and immunities which were withheld from the great body of the community. And to such an extent was this partial legislation carried, that in some instances, a State Government, not content with giving to a particular set of men valuable exclusive privileges, to endure for a long term of years, also pledged the property of the whole people, as the security for funds which it raised, to lend again, on easy terms, to the favoured few it had already elevated into a privileged order. These things seemed to us to be so palpable a violation of the plainest principles of equal justice, that we felt imperatively called upon to make them objects of attack.

Of all the privileges which the States were lavishing on sets of men, however, those seemed the most dangerous which conferred banking powers; authorized them to coin a worthless substitute for gold and silver; to circulate it as real money; and thus enter into competition with the General Government of the United States, in one of the highest and most important of its exclusive functions. There was no end to the evils and disorders which this daring violation of the fundamental principle of democratic doctrine was continually occasioning. It was placing the measure of value (the most important of all measures) in the hands of speculators, to be extended or contracted to answer their own selfish views or the suggestions of their folly. It was subjecting the community to continual fluctuations of prices, now raising every article to the extremest height of the scale, and now depressing it to the bottom. It was unsettling the foundations of private right, diversifying the time with seasons of preternatural prosperity and severe distress, shaking public faith, exciting a spirit of wild speculation, and demoralizing and vitiating the whole tone of popular sentiment and character. It was every day adding to the wealth and power of the few by extortions wrung from the hard hands of toil; and every day increasing the numbers and depressing the condition of the labouring poor.

This was the state of things to reform which, after the completion of the tariff compromise, seemed to us an object that demanded our most strenuous efforts. We have consequently sought to draw public attention to the fact that the great principle on which our whole system of government is founded, the principle of Equal Rights, has been grossly departed from. We have sought to show them that all legislative restrictions on trade operate as unjust and unequal taxes on the people, place dangerous powers in the hands of the Government, diminish the efficiency of popular suffrage, and render it more difficult for popular sentiment to work salutary reforms. We have sought to illustrate the radical impropriety of all legislative grants of exclusive or partial privileges, and the peculiar impropriety and various evil consequences of exclusive banking privileges. We have striven to show that all the proper and legitimate ends of Government interference might easily be accomplished by general laws, of equal operation on all. In doing this, we necessarily aroused bitter and powerful hostility. We necessarily assailed the interests of the privileged orders, and endangered the schemes of those who were seeking privileges. We combated long rooted prejudices, and aroused selfish passions. In the midst of the clamour which our opinions provoked, and the misrepresentations with which they have been met, to find that our journal has not merely been sustained, but raised to a higher pitch of prosperity, is certainly a result calculated to afford us the liveliest pleasure, independent altogether of considerations of private gain. We look on it as a manifestation that the great body of the democracy are true to the fundamental principles of their political doctrine; that they are opposed to all legislation which violates the equal rights of the community; that they are enemies of those aristocratic institutions which bestow privileges on one portion of society that are withheld from the others, and tend gradually but surely to change the whole structure of our system of Government.

Animated anew by this gratifying assurance that the people approve the general course of our journal, we shall pursue with ardor the line we have marked out, and trust the day is not distant when the doctrines we maintain will become the governing principles of our party.

CHIEF JUSTICE MARSHALL

We perceive with pleasure that public and spontaneous demonstrations of respect for the character and talents of the late Judge Marshall have taken place in every part of the country where the tidings of his death have been received. These tributes to the memory of departed excellence have a most salutary effect on the living; and few men have existed in our republic who so entirely deserved to be thus distinguished as examples, by a universal expression of sorrow at their death, as he whose loss the nation now laments. Pos-

Evening Post, July 28, 1835. Title added by Sedgwick. Text abridged.

sessed of a vast hereditary fortune, he had none of the foolish ostentation or arrogance which are the usual companions of wealth. Occupying an office too potent—lifted too high above the influence of popular will—there was no man who in his private intercourse and habits, exhibited a more general and equal regard for the people. He was accessible to men of all degrees, and "familiar, but by no means vulgar" in his bearing, he was distinguished as much in the retired walks of life by his unaffected simplicity and kindness, as in public by the exercise of his great talents and acquirements.

The death of such a man, of great wisdom and worth, whose whole life has been passed in the public service, and whose history is interwoven with that of our country in some of its brightest and most interesting passages, furnishes a proper occasion for the expression of general respect and regret. In these sentiments we most fully join; but at the same time we cannot so far lose sight of those great principles of government which we consider essential to the permanent prosperity of man, as to neglect the occasion offered by the death of Judge Marshall to express our satisfaction that the enormous powers of the Supreme tribunal of the country will no longer be exercised by one whose cardinal maxim in politics inculcated distrust of popular intelligence and virtue, and whose constant object, in the decision of all constitutional questions, was to strengthen government at the expense of the people's rights.

. . . .

There is no journalist who entertained a truer respect for the virtues of Judge Marshall than ourselves; there is none who believed more fully in the ardour of his patriotism, or the sincerity of his political faith. But according to our firm opinion, the articles of his creed, if carried into practise, would prove destructive of the great principle of human liberty, and compel the many to yield obedience to the few. The principles of government entertained by Marshall were the same as those professed by Hamilton, and not widely different from those of the elder Adams. That both these illustrious men, as well as Marshall, were sincere lovers of their country, and sought to effect, through the means of government, the greatest practicable amount of human happiness and prosperity, we do not entertain, we never have entertained a doubt. Nor do we doubt that among those who uphold the divine right of kings, and wish to see a titled aristocracy and hierarchy established, there are also very many solely animated by a desire to have a government established adequate to self-preservation and the protection of the people. Yet if one holding a political creed of this kind, and who, in the exercise of high official functions, had done all in his power to change the character of the government from popular to monarchical, should be suddenly cut off by death, would it be unjustifiable in those who deprecated his opinions to allude to them and their tendency, while paying a just tribute to his intellectual and moral worth?

. . . .

Of Judge Marshall's spotless purity of life, of his many estimable qualities of heart, and of the powers of his mind, we record our hearty tribute of admiration. But sincerely believing that the principles of democracy are identical with the principles of human liberty, we cannot but experience joy that the chief place in the supreme tribunal of the Union will no longer be filled by a man whose political doctrines led him always to pronounce such decision of Constitutional questions as was calculated to strengthen government at the expense of the people. We lament the death of a good and exemplary man, but we cannot grieve that the cause of aristocracy has lost one of its chief supports.

PREFATORY REMARKS

. . . .

The title chosen for this publication expresses the character which it is intended it shall maintain. In politics, in literature, and in relation to all subjects which may come under its notice, it is meant that it shall be a PLAINDEALER. But plainness, as it is hoped this journal will illustrate, is not incompatible with strict decorum, and a nice regard for the inviolability of private character. It is not possible, in all cases, to treat questions of public interest in so abstract a manner as to avoid giving offence to individuals; since few men possess the happy art which Sheridan ascribes to his Governor in the Critic, and are able entirely to separate their personal feelings from what relates to their public or official conduct and characters. It is doubtful, too, if it were even practicable so to conduct the investigations, and so to temper the animadversions of the press, as, in every instance, "to find the fault and let the actor go," whether the interests of truth would, by such a course, be best promoted. The journalist who should so manage his disquisitions, would indeed exercise but the "cypher of a function." His censures would be likely to awaken but little attention in the reader, and effect but little reformation in their object. People do not peruse the columns of a newspaper for theoretic essays, and elaborate examinations of abstract questions; but for strictures and discussions, occasional in their nature, and applicable to existing persons and events. There is no reason, however, why the vulgar appetite for abuse and scandal should be gratified, or why, in maintaining the cause of truth, the rules of good breeding should be violated. Plain-dealing requires no such sacrifice. Truth, though it is usual to array it in a garb of repulsive bluntness, has no natural aversion

Plaindealer, December 3, 1836. Text abridged.

to amenity; and the mind distinguished for openness and sincerity may at the same time be characterized by a high degree of urbanity and gentleness. It will be one of the aims of the Plaindealer to prove, by its example, that there is at least nothing utterly contrarious and irreconcilable in these traits.

In politics, the Plaindealer will be thoroughly democratic. It will be democratic not merely to the extent of the political maxim, that the majority have the right to govern; but to the extent of the moral maxim, that it is the duty of the majority so to govern as to preserve inviolate the equal rights of all. In this large sense, democracy includes all the main principles of political economy: that noble science which is silently and surely revolutionizing the world; which is changing the policy of nations from one of strife to one of friendly emulation; and cultivating the arts of peace on the soil hitherto desolated by the ravages of war. Democracy and political economy both assert the true dignity of man. They are both the natural champions of freedom, and the enemies of all restraints on the many for the benefit of the few. They both consider the people the only proper source of government, and their equal protection its only proper end; and both would confine the interference of legislation to the fewest possible objects, compatible with the preservation of social order. They are twin-sisters, pursuing parallel paths, for the accomplishment of cognate objects. They are sometimes found divided, but always in a languishing condition; and they can only truly flourish where they exist in companionship, and, hand in hand, achieve their kindred purposes.

The Plaindealer claims to belong to the great democratic party of this country; but it will never deserve to be considered a party paper in the degrading sense in which that phrase is commonly understood. The prevailing error of political journals is to act as if they deemed it more important to preserve the organization of party, than to promote the principles on which it is founded. They substitute the means for the end, and pay that fealty to men which is due only to the truth. This fatal error it will be a constant aim of the Plaindealer to avoid. It will espouse the cause of the democratic party only to the extent that the democratic party merits its appellation and is faithful to the tenets of its political creed. It will contend on its side while it acts in conformity with its fundamental doctrines, and will be found warring against it whenever it violates those doctrines in any essential respect. Of the importance and even dignity of party combination, no journal can entertain a higher and more respectful sense. They furnish the only certain means of carrying political principles into effect. When men agree in their theory of Government, they must also agree to act in concert, or no practical advantage can result from their accordance. "For my part," says Burke, "I find it impossible to conceive that any one believes in his own politics, or thinks them to be of any weight, who refuses to adopt the means of having them reduced to practice."

From what has been already remarked, it is matter of obvious inference that the Plaindealer will steadily and earnestly oppose all partial and special legislation, and all grants of exclusive or peculiar privileges. It will, in a particular manner, oppose, with its utmost energy, the extension of the pernicious bank system with which this country is cursed; and will zealously contend, in season and out of season, for the repeal of those tyrannous prohibitory laws, which give to the chartered moneychangers their chief power of evil. To the very principle of special incorporation we here, on the threshold of our undertaking, declare interminable hostility. It is a principle utterly at war with the principles of democracy. It is the opposite of that which asserts the equal rights of man, and limits the offices of government to his equal protection. It is, in its nature, an aristocratic principle; and if permitted to exist among us much longer, and to be acted upon by our legislators, will leave us nothing of equal liberty but the name. Thanks to the illustrious man who was called in a happy hour to preside over our country! the attention of the people has been thoroughly awakened to the insidious nature and fatal influences of chartered privileges. The popular voice, already, in various quarters, denounces them. In vain do those who possess, and those who seek to obtain grants of monopolies, endeavour to stifle the rising murmur. It swells louder and louder; it grows more and more distinct; and is spreading far and wide. The days of the chartermongers are numbered. The era of equal privileges is at hand.

There is one other subject on which it is proper to touch in these opening remarks, and on which we desire that there should exist the most perfect understanding with our readers. We claim the right, and shall exercise it too, on all proper occasions, of *absolute freedom of discussion*. We hold that there is no subject whatever interdicted from investigation and comment; and that we are under no obligation, political or otherwise, to refrain from a full and candid expression of opinion as to the manifold evils, and deep disgrace, inflicted on our country by the institution of slavery. Nay more, it will be one of the occasional but earnest objects of this paper to show by statistical calculations and temperate arguments, enforced by every variety of illustration that can properly be employed, the impolicy of slavery, as well as its enormous wickedness: to show its pernicious influence on all the dearest interests of the south; on its moral character, its social relations, and its agricultural, commercial and political prosperity. No man can deny the momentous importance of this subject, nor that it is one of deep interest to every American citizen. It is the duty, then, of a public journalist to discuss it; and from the obligations of duty we trust the Plaindealer will never shrink. We establish this paper, expecting to derive from it a livelihood; and if an honest and industrious exercise of such talents as we have can achieve that object, we shall not fail. But we cannot, for the sake of a livelihood, trim our sails to suit the varying breeze of popular prejudice. We should prefer, with old Andrew Marvell, to scrape a blade bone of cold mutton, to faring more sumptuously on viands obtained by a surrender of principle.* If a paper, which makes the right, not the expedient, its cardinal object, will not yield its conductor a support, there are honest vocations that will; and better the humblest of them, than to be seated at the head of an influential press, if its influence is not exerted to promote the cause of truth.

THE SISTER DOCTRINES

The fanciful parallel which we drew between democracy and political economy, in the first number of this paper has provoked a writer in one of the morning prints to bestow upon us a whole column of animadversions. The points which have particularly excited his indignation, if we may judge from his

* The story to which allusion is here made cannot too often be repeated. We copy it from a life of Marvell, by John Dove. It is as follows: The borough of Hull, in the reign of Charles II. chose ANDREW MARVELL, a young gentleman of little or no fortune, and maintained him in London for the service of the public. His understanding, integrity, and spirit, were dreadful to the then infamous administration. Persuaded that he would be theirs for properly asking, they sent his old schoolfellow, the LORD TREASURER DANBY, to renew acquaintance with him in his garret. At parting, the Lord Treasurer, out of *pure affection*, slipped into his hand an order upon the Treasury for 1,000*l.*, and then went to his chariot. Marvell looking at the paper, calls after the Treasurer "My Lord, I request another moment." They went up again to the garret, and Jack, the servant boy, was called. "Jack, child, what had I for dinner yesterday?" "Don't you remember, sir? you had the little shoulder of mutton that you ordered me to bring from a woman in the market." "Very right, child. What have I for dinner to day?" "Don't you know, sir, that you bid me lay by the *blade-bone to broil?*" " 'Tis so, very right, child, go away. My Lord, do you hear that? Andrew Marvell's dinner is provided; there's your piece of paper. I want it not. I knew the sort of kindness you intended. I live here to serve my constituents; the Ministry may seek men for their purpose; *I am not one.*"

Plaindealer, December 17, 1836.

use of italicks, are, our having spoken of democracy and political economy as twin sisters, pursuing a parallel direction, for the accomplishment of kindred objects; and as both alike considering the people the only proper source of government, and their equal protection its only proper end. We confess the sin of having been rather more figurative in the passage which has given umbrage than is our wont; and shall do penance by using only the soberest expressions in our present article; since it is hardly suitable to mystify so grave a subject with "the sweet smoke of rhetorick," to borrow the phrase of an old English writer.

The critick who querulously assails our positions with regard to the nature and objects of political economy, fortifies himself by citing some sentences from Say, which he unfairly interpolates, however, with parenthetical commentaries of his own, giving them a degree of meaning which, had they been honestly quoted, they would not have expressed. But there is one passage, in the introductory advertisement of the very edition of Say from which he copied his extracts, that he seems wholly to have overlooked. Speaking of the prospects of economick science in America, that writer says, "Where should we expect sound doctrines to be better received, than amongst a nation which supports and illustrates the value of free principles by the most striking examples. The old states of Europe are cankered with prejudices and bad habits: *it is America will teach them the height of prosperity which may be reached, when governments follow the counsels of reason, and do not cost too much.*"

Dugald Stewart, a writer of at least equal authority with Say, in numerous passages expresses his conviction that the same maxims which constitute the fundamental doctrines of political economy, should also be the guiding principles of political government. "*Laissez non faire,*" he says, and "*Pas trop gouverner*" comprise, in a few words, the most important lessons of political wisdom. It will hardly be denied that these sentiments are thoroughly democratick. Adam Smith, also, a writer whose opinions have generally been considered as entitled to some respect, contends, in different places, that the same principles which constitute the foundation on which the whole science of political economy rests, furnish, also, the proper basis of political government. In a passage which is quoted by Stewart in his memoir of the author of the Wealth of Nations, that great writer says, "Man is generally considered by statesmen and projectors as the materials of a sort of political mechanicks. Projectors disturb nature in the course of her operations with human affairs, and it requires no more than to let her alone, and give her fair play in the pursuit of her ends, that she may establish her own designs." And again, "Little else is required to carry a state to the highest degree of opulence, but peace, easy taxes, and a tolerable administration of justice; all the rest being brought about by the natural course of things. All governments which thwart this natural course, which force things into another channel, or which endeavour to arrest the progress of society at a particular point, are unnatural, and to support themselves are obliged to be oppressive and tyrannical."

These sentiments, according to our view, comprise the essence of both democratick and economick theory. The advantages which *modern policy*, says Dugald Stewart, "possesses over the ancient, arise principally from its conformity, in some of the most important articles of political economy to an order of things recommended by nature; and it would not be difficult to show that where it remains imperfect, its errours may be traced to the restraints it imposes on the natural course of human affairs." We might extend this article to a much greater length by similar extracts from various other writers of high repute; but we have adduced sufficient authority for the views we expressed as to the coincidence of democracy and political economy, in their fundamental principles, and in their ultimate ends. They are both for the largest liberty, within the bounds of social order; both are equally opposed to all special privileges and immunities; and both would leave men to manage their own affairs, in their own way, so that they did not invade each others natural rights.

THE TRUE THEORY OF TAXATION

The Evening Post, in one of its recent excellent articles on the protective system, speaking with particular reference to the impost on coal, expresses the opinion that it is the duty of our rulers to lighten the burdens of the people as much as possible, "especially when they fall on articles of first rate necessity; and it is easy," the Evening Post adds, "to distinguish between those that do, and those that do not."

We are very willing to see the protective system attacked, either in gross or in detail. If we find that we cannot procure the immediate reduction of all duties to the exact revenue standard, as graduated on an equal *ad valorem* scale, we must be content to concentrate our forces upon particular articles or classes of articles, and thus attempt to accomplish the overthrow of the tariff, somewhat after the manner that the redoubtable Bobadil proposed to overthrow an army. We are afraid, however, that this mode of operation, in our case, as in his, will fail of effecting any very important result. But while we are willing to join the Evening Post in bringing about a reduction of the tariff, either by piecemeal or wholesale, we cannot quite agree with the sentiment it expresses, as an abstract proposition, that it is the especial duty of rulers to reduce taxes on necessaries, and to discriminate between

Plaindealer, December 24, 1836.

those which are so, and those which are not. It seems to us, on the contrary, that the true theory of taxation, whether direct or indirect, whether levied upon commerce, or assessed, without any intermediary agency or subterfuge, upon the property of the people, is that which falls with equal proportional weight upon every variety of commodity. While we should contend, with the utmost earnestness against the imposition of a tax, the effect of which would be to burden the poor man and let the rich go free; we should oppose as positively, if not as zealously, a contrary system, which tended to place the load, in any undue degree, upon the shoulders of the rich. We are for equal rights; for the rights of the affluent and the needy alike; and we would not admit, in any case, or to any extent whatever, the principle of either laying or repealing duties for the special advantage of the one class or the other. We have had too much already of discriminating duties.

If we must raise the revenues of our federal government from imposts on commerce, the true theory to contend for, in our view of the subject, is an equal *ad valorem* duty, embracing every commodity of traffic. The importer of foreign coal will tell you a pathetic story of the hardships and sufferings of the poor at this inclement season of the year. He will borrow perhaps the eloquent language of the Evening Post, to describe the shivering inmates of garrets and cellars, and the poor lone woman who buys her coal by the peck. He will draw you to her wretched abode, and show her surrounded by her tattered offspring, expanding their defenceless limbs over a few expiring embers that mock them with ineffectual heat. When he has raised your sympathy to the proper pitch, he will then call on you to exert your influence to procure the repeal of a duty which places beyond the reach of thousands of shuddering wretches one of the prime necessaries of life, and leaves them to all the horrors of unmitigated winter, as it visits the unfed sides and looped and windowed raggedness of the poor. The dealer in foreign grain will have a similar tale to relate. He will expatiate on the sufferings of the indigent from the high price of bread, and ask you to exempt breadstuffs from taxation. The importers of books and charts, and of mathematical instruments, will talk of the advantages of a wide diffusion of literature and science, and ask for a repeal of duties on those articles in which their trade consists. Colleges will represent that the cause of education requires their libraries and laboratories should come duty free. Railroad corporations will point out the many political and commercial benefits that must accrue to the country from facilitated intercourse between its distant parts, and ask that their engines and other appliances be released from the burden of taxes. All these applications, and many others of a like kind, have something specious to recommend them to a favourable consideration, and some have been listened to and granted. The prayers of corporate bodies have been affirmatively answered, while a deaf ear has been turned to those of the ill-fed and unprivileged poor. In our sense, however, they ought all to be treated alike, and all to be rejected. The only legitimate purpose of a tariff is that expressed by the Constitution, "to pay the debts and provide for the general welfare;" and the debts should be paid and the general welfare provided for, in strict accordance with the great distinguishing principle of our government—the equal rights of the people. This never can be entirely accomplished while imposts on foreign commerce furnish the means of revenue; but it is the obvious duty of legislators to do nothing to increase the unavoidable inequality of the burden.

The true system of raising revenue, the only democratic system, and the one which we trust the people of this Confederacy will some day insist upon adopting, is that of direct taxation. We hope the day will come, (and we think we see the evidences of its approach) when not a Custom House will exist in the land; when tidewaiters and gaugers, appraisers and inspectors, will be unknown; and when commerce, that most efficient friend of the best interests of man, and brightener of the links of international amity, will be as free to go and come, as the breeze that fills her sails, or the wave that bears her freighted stores. The system from which we now derive the resources of our government is in utter opposition to the maxim on which our government is founded. We build up our institutions professing the utmost confidence in the intelligence and integrity of the people; but our very first act betrays distrust both of their sagacity and virtue. We fear they have neither sense enough to see that the expenses of government must be defrayed, nor honesty enough to pay them if directly applied to for that purpose; and hence we set about, by various modes of indirection, to filch the money from their pockets, that they may neither know how much they contribute, nor the precise purpose to which it is applied. Could a system be devised better calculated to encourage lavish expenditure, and introduce variety of corruption? To preserve the government simple and pure, the people should know what they pay, and for what object. This would excite men to that degree of vigilance which is necessary to the preservation of their rights; it would restrain their political agents from neglecting or exceeding their trusts; and it would prevent government from that otherwise inevitable, however gradual, enlargement of its powers and offices, which, in the end, must prove destructive of the liberties of the people. A system of indirect taxation tends, with steady and constant force, to undermine the basis of popular rights. It is, in its very nature, an aristocratic system, and bears upon its front the evidence of distrust of popular capacity and virtue. A system of direct taxation, on the contrary, is a candid and democratic system. It is built on the presumption that the mass of men have sufficient intelligence to know in what good government consists, and sufficient integrity to pay what is required to maintain their rights. It is, in short, the only true theory of taxation; and the day will be an auspicious one for the great cause of human liberty when it is adopted by the American people.

STRICT CONSTRUCTION

A resolution is before Congress, introduced by Mr. Davis, instructing the Committee on Commerce to inquire into the expediency of making provision for the nautical education of American seamen. It would be well if the first object of their inquiry should be the constitutionality of such a provision. According to our understanding of the federal compact, no such power as that proposed to be exercised is given to the general government. An institution, however, created by the federal authority, for the instruction of seamen, would have precisely the same warrant, as the institution which now exists for the instruction of cadets for the army. Congress might also, by the same latitude of construction, erect colleges for the education of shipwrights, carpenters, riggers, caulkers, blacksmiths, sailmakers, and, in short, for the education of persons for every variety of human occupation. Those who have ever taken the pains to read the Journal of the Convention which framed the Constitution, must be satisfied that the power which Congress has exercised in establishing the Military Academy at West Point was not only never intended to be given, either expressly, or as an incident of express powers, but was in terms, and on three several occasions, plainly denied. The project of Mr. Davis is constitutional, if the Military Academy is a constitutional institution, and not otherwise. A strict construction of the federal charter, which is the only kind of construction consistent with democratick freedom, would prohibit both.

Plaindealer, January 21, 1837.

LEGISLATIVE INDEMNITY FOR LOSSES FROM MOBS

The late disgraceful riot in this city has been followed by its natural consequence: impaired confidence in the security of private right in this community. Persons at a distance, having commercial relations with us, are fearful of trusting their property within the reach of men, who have shown themselves so regardless of the first principles of social order, and so little apprehensive of municipal opposition. The owners of flour and grain, in particular, and of other articles of such universal daily consumption as to be classed among the necessaries of life, hesitate to send them to a city where they may be seized, on their arrival, by an infuriated mob, and scattered to the winds of heaven. The result of this must inevitably be an exacerbation of the misery which the poor now experience. Prices, exorbitant as they are, must rise to a still higher pitch, as the supply, receiving no augmentations from abroad, becomes less and less adequate to the demand. And those miserable creatures, who, in their delusion, thought to overthrow the immutable laws of trade, and effect, by a sudden outbreak of tumultuary violence, what no force of compulsion, however organised and obstinate, could possibly accomplish, will be among the very first to reap the fruit of their folly: for, as they are among the very poorest members of the community, any additional advance in the price of flour must put it wholly beyond their means: Thus even handed justice commends to their own lips the chalice they had drugged for others.

One of the evidences of the consternation which the recent tumult has occasioned in the minds of persons having commercial dealings with this city, particularly in articles of necessary food, is shown in the terms of a memorial which the manufac-

Plaindealer, March 4, 1837. Extract deleted.

turers of flour in Rochester have addressed to the Legislature, praying for the enactment of a law to protect their property in New-York from the destroying fury of mobs.

. . . .

The foregoing memorial is signed by eighteen flour manufacturing firms of Rochester. The trepidation and anxiety which it betrays on the part of all concerned in the flour trade of that city, may serve to show what must be the general feeling throughout the country, and what must be its necessary consequence in withholding from us a further supply of flour, thus inevitably increasing the burden of which we now complain. But while we copy this memorial, for the lesson it furnishes to those who seek to reform legislative abuses, or to relieve themselves from oppressive burdens, by tumultuary violence, we must not suffer it to be inferred that we approve the object of its prayer.

The power which the legislature is asked to exercise seems to us to lie beyond the proper province of government. The legitimate functions of a democratic government are simply to *protect* the citizens in life and property, not to provide *indemnification* for the loss of either. The government is the mere representative or agent of the community, appointed to guard the rights of each individual, by protecting him from the aggressions of others. This duty includes the defending of him from aggression, in the first place, and the punishing of those who commit it, in the second. But it does not extend to the punishment of an entire community for the offences committed by an inconsiderable portion, which is the position assumed by the Rochester petitioners. It is one of the first and most obvious duties of society, in the outset of its political organization, to make provision for the defence of the rights of its members, in whatever form of violence they may be assailed. The legislative agents of each community, in the discharge of this duty, make such provisions, as the general circumstances of the times, and the particular circumstances which lie within their own jurisdiction, may seem to require. Thus, while in thinly inhabited townships a few guardians of the peace, clothed with the simplest powers, are sufficient, in cities an extensive and complicated system of defence is found to be necessary. Guardians of the night, and guardians of the day, an organized force to protect property from conflagration, and an armed force to protect both life and property from riot and insurrection, are necessary in every populous town, requiring to be extended and modified, according to the increase of numbers, or the deterioration of morals. The principle of self-preservation gives rise to these precautionary and defensive measures, in the first place, and the same principle, ever active, demands that they shall be enlarged and improved, from time to time, as new exigencies arise. If anything occurs to show that the municipal authorities of any community are deficient in requisite vigilance, energy, or power, their deficiency is a proper subject of complaint; and all who are aggrieved, whose rights are in any way invaded or jeoparded through such remissness, have unquestionable ground of petition or remonstrance to a higher legislative tribunal. But no tribunal in this country, under the maxims which we acknowledge as the foundation of our political edifice, has the power to inflict the penalties incurred by a few ruffians, concerned in a violation of private right, on those who not only had no share in the offence, but who perhaps exerted themselves to the utmost to prevent it. This would be in dereliction of the plainest principles of natural justice.

Let us suppose a case. A person, residing at the Battery, by some unguarded speech or action, gives offence to a particular class of persons living in his immediate neighbourhood. The cause of umbrage is reported from one to another, with the natural exaggerations of anger. Bad passions are aroused, and some inflammatory demagogue seizes the occasion—perhaps for the gratification of private malice, or perhaps for the opportunity of plunder—to excite the irritated multitude to acts of violence. They rush to the house of the unconscious offender.

Their numbers are rapidly augmented by additions from the crowd of such persons as are ever ready to take part in tumult. Their shouts and cries, echoed from one to another, are as fuel to fire, and increase the fury of their exasperation. They attack the property of him who is the object of their ire, demolish his store-house or dwelling, break its contents into fragments, and scatter them in the streets, or consume them in flames. In the meanwhile the public authorities, informed of the tumult, hasten to the scene. They are joined by numerous bodies of good citizens, desirous to aid them in the suppression of disorder; and, in a little while, but not before the work of destruction is completed, the riot is suppressed, and the chief actors in it apprehended, and committed to safe custody for trial and punishment. But this whole event, from first to last, has occurred, before the tidings can reach other extremes of the metropolis. The citizen at Bloomingdale or Harlem is quietly pursuing his vocation, unconscious of the disorders which disturb the community at another point of the city. Yet the legislation asked for by the petitioners of Rochester would make him responsible for the crimes of others, with which he not only had no participation, but which, could he have known they were meditated, he would have exerted himself with the utmost zeal and diligence to prevent. He would have done so, not only from a sentiment of philanthropy, but from a motive of self-preservation; as one whose individual rights were exposed to similar hazard; as a portion of the body politic, which must always suffer, when it shows itself incompetent to protect its individual members from outrage.

The principle involved in this Rochester memorial might, with equal propriety, be extended to embrace indemnity for losses sustained in consequence of individual outrages. It is no less the duty of a community to protect the property of citizens from the attacks of single ruffians, than from those of ruffians in numbers. If the flour manufacturers of Rochester had visited this city to receive payment from their agent whose store-house was attacked, and if the wretch, who directed the attention of an excited multitude to that store-house, had, instead, chosen to waylay those manufacturers singly, and, assailing them with a bludgeon, forced them to surrender the proceeds of their merchandise, it seems to us that they would have equal ground for a petition to the legislature, asking for a law to compel the city of New-York to indemnify them for the amount of which they had been robbed. The principle of *indemnity* is not included in the principle of *protection*. *Protection* is an obvious duty of humanity, as well as an obvious measure of self-preservation; but the claim for *indemnification* as obviously rests on the unjust and arbitrary principle that the good should be punished for the crimes of the bad, and the weak for the outrages of the strong. Is there any reason, in natural justice, that the lone widow, frugally living, in some obscure corner of this city, on the slender means picked up by perpetual industry, should be burdened with a tax to compensate the flour merchant of Rochester for his losses from an outrage of which she could have had no knowledge, and over which she could exercise no control? Is there any reason why any person in this city, not implicated in the transaction, should be punished in the way proposed, that does not apply as strongly to every inhabitant of the state? If this community, in its corporate capacity did not exercise due vigilance and energy to prevent the riot in question, and protect the property destroyed, it may be that there is good ground for an action for damages; but there is surely none for a law to punish the entire community in all cases, whether the outrage was within or beyond municipal control.

The principles which should guide legislation are always reducible to the simplest elements of natural justice. The code for the government of a community of three hundred thousand persons should stand on the same basis of clear undeniable right, with that which would be instituted for a community of only three. If A, B, and C, enter into a social compact, A is clearly bound to assist B, against any violation of his rights attempted by C. But if before A can render assistance, or in spite of it, C succeeds in rifling the property of B, and escapes with it, or destroys it, any claim which might then be set up by B, for indemnity from A, would be so clearly without foundation in justice, as to shock the natural moral sense of all the rest of the alphabet, supposing them living by themselves, in an entirely distinct community.

The *Journal of Commerce,* we perceive, expresses approbation of the object of the memorial we have copied. It pronounces the plan "a good one," and thinks "it should be made general, applying to all property, and to all the cities and towns in the state." We cannot think the *Journal of Commerce* has given its usual attention to this subject; though this is not the first time it has shown a willingness to strengthen government at the expense of men's equal and inalienable rights.

THE DESPOTISM OF THE MAJORITY

Words undergo variations in their meaning to accommodate them to the varying usages of men. Despotism, though originally confined, according to its derivation, to the government of a single ruler, and considered a term of honour, rather than reproach, is now employed to signify unlimited tyranny, whether exercised by one or legion, whether by a single autocrat, wielding all the power of the state, or by the majority of a community, combined under strict party organization, and ruling the minority with dictatorial and imperious sway. The two most prominent instances which the world now presents

Plaindealer, March 25, 1837.

of these different classes of despotism, is that of a single tyrant in Russia, and that of a multitudinous tyrant in America; and it is a question which some seem to think not easily answered which is the worse, that of an autocracy, or that of a majority.

The intolerance, the bitter, persecuting intolerance, often displayed by a majority in this country, on questions of stirring political interest, towards the rights and feelings of the minority, has come to be a subject of comment by enlightened minds in Europe, that are eagerly watching the results of our great democratic experiment, and drawing arguments in favour of aristocratic government from every imperfection we exhibit. Thus, in the eloquent speech recently delivered by Sir Robert Peel, at Glasgow, there are some allusions to the intolerance of dominant parties in this country, which no candid person can peruse without admitting they contain enough of truth to give great point and sharpness to their sarcasms.

We cannot be suspected of any sympathy with Sir Robert Peel in the purpose with which he made this reference to America. Our love for the democratic principle is too sincere and unbounded, to allow us to have a feeling in common with those who desire to conserve aristocratic institutions. The democratic principle is the only principle which promises equal liberty, and equal prosperity to mankind. We yearn with intense longing for the arrival of that auspicious day in the history of the human race, when it shall everywhere take the place of the aristocratic principle, and knit all the families of mankind together in the bonds of equal brotherhood. Then shall the worn out nations sit down at last in abiding peace, and the old earth, which has so long drunk the blood of encountering millions, grow young again in a millenial holiday.

No American, having sense and soul to feel and appreciate the ineffable blessings of equal liberty, would answer Sir Robert Peel's interrogatory as he supposes. The effeminate popinjays, whom the land, overcloyed with their insipid sweetness, yearly sends abroad to foreign travel, and who prefer the glitter of courtly pomp to the widely diffused and substantial blessings of freedom, might utter such a dissuasion against the adoption of democratic principles. But no honest and manly American, worthy of that name, with intelligence enough to know, and heart enough to feel, that the best and loftiest aim of government is, not to promote excessive and luxurious refinement among a few, but the general good of all—"the greatest good of the greatest number"—would ever lisp a syllable to dissuade England from adopting the glorious democratic principle of equal political rights.

But while we thus differ from Sir Robert Peel in the tenor and purpose of the remarks we have quoted, we are forced to admit that there is but too much truth in the charge of despotism against the majority in our political divisions. The right of the majority to rule, is a maxim which lies at the bottom of democratic government; but a maxim of still higher obligation makes it their duty so to rule, as to preserve inviolate the equal rights of all. This rule of paramount authority is not always obeyed. We have seen numerous and frightful instances of its violation, in those outbreaks of "popular indignation," which men have drawn upon themselves by the fatal temerity of expressing their views on a subject of deep interest to every American, on which their sentiments differed from those of the majority. The wild excesses of riot are not chargeable alone to the madness and brutality of those who take part in them, but to the approval of others, who set on the human bull-dogs to bait the abolitionists, by calling the latter all sorts of opprobrious names; and encouraging the former by bestowing laudatory appellations on their ferocity. They are "true friends of the Constitution," they are men "who appreciate the blessings of liberty," they are "champions of union," they are patriots and heroes; while those against whom their drunken rage is directed are pointed out as fanatics, of the most diabolical temper; as incendiaries, ready to burn to the ground the temple of freedom; as murderers, ready to incite the negro against his master, and incarnadine the whole south with the blood of promiscuous and discriminate slaughter.

But to descend from the terrible instances of despotism, which the conduct of the majority on the slave question displays, we see the consequences of the same tyranny in a thousand matters of less startling moment. Does not our newspaper press show marks of the iron rule of despotism, as exercised by a majority? Whence comes its subserviency? Whence comes it that each journal goes with its party in all things, and to all lengths approving what the party approves, whether men or measures, and condemning what it condemns? Why is it that no journalist dares, in the exercise of true independence, to act with his party in what he deems conformable with its political tenets, and censure its course when it varies from them? Why is it that if, forgetting for a moment that he is not a freeman, he honestly blames some erroneous step, or fails to approve it, his reproach, or his very silence, is made the occasion of persecution, and he finds himself suddenly stripped of support? Whence comes this we ask, but from the despotism of a majority, from that bitter intolerance of the mass, which now supplies an argument to the monarchists and aristocrats of the old world, against the adoption of the principles of popular government?

The book press of our country is not less overcrowed by the despotism of the majority than the newspapers. The very work from which Sir Robert Peel makes his quotation affords us a ready illustration. Thousands are burning to read the production of De Tocqueville, and a hundred publishers are anxious to gratify the desire. But they dare not. The writer has not hesitated to express his opinions of slavery; and such is the despotism of a majority, that it will not suffer men to read nor speak upon that subject; and it would hinder them, if it could, even from the exercise of thought.

There are some bold spirits yet in the land, who are determined to battle against this spirit of despotism, and to assert and defend their rights of equal freedom, let the struggle cost what it may. They will speak with a voice that the roar of tumult cannot drown, and maintain their ground with a firmness that opposition cannot move; and if forced at last to surrender, it will be their lives, not their liberty, they will yield, considering it better to die freemen, than live slaves to the most cruel of all despots—a despotic majority.

MORALS OF LEGISLATION

If Jeremy Bentham were alive now, the doings of our legislature would furnish him with some fine subjects for an additional chapter to his "Principles and Morals of Legislation." There is no subject too high or low for the ken of that sapient and potential body. It undertakes to regulate by statute all sorts of business and all sorts of opinions. A man must neither do anything, nor think anything, except as the law provides. We may eat no meat, burn no fuel, chew no tobacco, nor even visit a theatre, unless such meat, fuel, tobacco, and playhouse, are all stamped with the signet of the law. If you offer a banknote of a certain denomination, you violate a law and incur a penalty. If you receive it from another, you are no less guilty. If a friend desires to borrow money from you, and to accommodate him you withdraw it from a business where it is yielding you twenty percent, you must lend it to him at the rate of seven, or otherwise incur the liability of being sent to prison for your kindness. The good old notion that the world is governed too much, is laughed at as an absurdity by our modern Solons, who act upon the converse of the French merchants' request, to let trade alone, and undertake to regulate it in every particular.

We learn from Albany that Judge Soule's bill of abomi-

Plaindealer, April 15, 1837.

nations is likely to be adopted in the Senate by as large a majority, proportionally, as passed it in the other house. By the way, the orthoepy of this wise lawgiver's name seems to be a matter of dispute, for while some contend that it should be so pronounced as to rhyme with *foul*, others think the word *fool* presents the proper symphony. These last perhaps are governed by an analogy which has respect to something more than sound. But whatever difference of opinion there may be as to the gentleman's name, there is none whatever, in this quarter, as to the true character and effect of his proposed law. It is universally execrated by men acquainted with those laws which should alone regulate financial matters.

The motive which we hear alleged for the concurrence this bill is likely to receive in the Senate is a desire *to force* capital into the old channel of loans on bonds and mortgages. The forcing system is the only system for which our legislature seems to have any fondness. All its business is conducted on the hothouse plan. It first forces credit out of its natural channel, by suddenly acceding to the wishes of dishonest speculators, and multiplying the fatal brood of specially privileged banks. When the floods of paper money which these institutions force upon the community have produced their inevitable consequence, and forced the attention of the community from the regular modes of business to extravagant schemes of speculation, the legislature then undertakes to force things back again to their old positions, heedless of the ruin and distress which these compulsory and contradictory processes may occasion. We trust the day is at hand when the people will exert their moral force, and force the legislature to confine itself to the few and simple objects which alone properly belong to government, leaving men free to make their own bargains, and follow their own pursuits.

We do not believe that any great practical evil will follow immediately from the passing of Judge Soule's usury law. It but compels men to do, what the bad state of things brought about by the opposite forcing system of the legislature was already causing them to do, with an obligation stronger than legal compulsion. The bubble of credit had been inflated to bursting by the prodigal creation of bank monopolies, and astounded by its sudden explosion, the confidence of avarice is too much shaken to allow of his being any longer allured by the bait of three per cent a month. They who have money to lend are now afraid to lend it to men who offer to pay large rates of interest, and capital is on the natural reflux to those borrowers who offer smaller profits and larger securities. The proposed law of Judge Draco, therefore, may do little present harm—it may be, to a great extent, practically inoperative. But it is founded on utterly false principles, and on that account deserves the most earnest opposition. It is not the business of the legislature to make laws for the present hour, framed according to the supposed requirements of instant expediency. It is its business to draw up its code in accordance with the eternal principles of right, so that it may apply with equal justice to-day, to-morrow, and forever. This making a law to force capital one way now, and next winter making a new one to force it another, is the height of legislative folly and injustice. Had the wishes of the people, as emphatically expressed "against all monopolies" four years ago, been respected by their servants; had Andrew Jackson's veto of the charter of the United States Bank been followed, in the principal commercial states, by legislative measures of a kindred spirit; or had this state alone removed the restrictions on trade, and simply instituted a general corporation partnership law instead, leaving the community to pursue what traffick they pleased, to what extent and in what mode they pleased, we should not, at this time, stand amidst such a scene of financial desolation, having nothing but disorder and ruin to contemplate.

We all know and acknowledge the value of political and religious freedom; and we shall yet learn that commercial freedom is the next best blessing that man can enjoy. We shall yet learn, we trust, to practise, as well as to declaim, the noble and just sentiment of Jefferson, that the sum of a good government is to restrain men from injuring one another; to leave them otherwise free to regulate their own pursuits of industry and improvement; and not to take from the mouth of labour the bread it has earned.

THE MORALS OF POLITICS

Public moralists have long noticed with regret, that the political contests of this country are conducted with intemperance wholly unsuited to conflicts of reason, and decided, in a great measure, by the efforts of the worst class of people. We apply this phrase, not to those whom the aristocracy designate as the "lower orders;" but to those only, whether well or ill dressed, and whether rich or poor, who enter into the struggle without regard for the inherent dignity of politics, and without reference to the permanent interests of their country and of mankind; but animated by selfish objects, by personal preferences or prejudices, the desire of office, or the hope of accomplishing private ends through the influence of party. Elections are commonly looked upon as mere game, on which depends the division of party spoils, the distribution of chartered privileges, and the allotment of pecuniary rewards. The antagonist principles of government, which should constitute the sole ground of controversy, are lost sight of in the eagerness of sordid motives; and the struggle, which should be one of pure reason, with no aim but the achievement of political truth, and the promotion of the greatest good of the greatest number, sinks into a mere brawl, in which passion, avarice, and profligacy, are the prominent actors.

Plaindealer, June 3, 1837.

If the questions of government could be submitted to the people in the naked dignity of abstract propositions, men would reason upon them calmly, and frame their opinions according to the preponderance of truth. There is nothing in the intrinsic nature of politics that appeals to the passions of the multitude. It is an important branch of morals, and its principles, like those of private ethics, address themselves to the sober judgment of men. A strange spectacle would be presented, should we see mathematicians kindle into wrath in the discussion of a problem, and call on their hearers, in the angry terms of demagogues, to decide on the relative merits of opposite modes of demonstration.

The same temperance and moderation which characterize the investigation of truth in the exact sciences, belong not less to the inherent nature of politics, when confined within the proper field.

The object of all politicians, in the strict sense of the expression, is happiness—the happiness of a state—the greatest possible sum of happiness of which the social condition admits to those individuals who live together under the same political organization.

It may be asserted, as an undeniable proposition, that it is the duty of every intelligent man to be a politician. This is particularly true of a country, the institutions of which admit every man to the exercise of equal suffrage. All the duties of life are embraced under the three heads of religion, politics, and morals. The aim of religion is to regulate the conduct of man with reference to happiness in a future state of being; of politics, to regulate his conduct with reference to the happiness of communities; and of morals, to regulate his conduct with reference to individual happiness.

Happiness, then, is the end and aim of these three great and comprehensive branches of duty; and no man perfectly discharges the obligations imposed by either, who neglects those which the others enjoin. The right ordering of a state affects, for weal or wo, the interests of multitudes of human beings;

and every individual of those multitudes has a direct interest, therefore, in its being ordered aright.

"I am a man," says Terence, in a phrase as beautiful for the harmony of its language, as the benevolence and universal truth of its sentiment, "and nothing can be indifferent to me which affects humanity."

The sole legitimate object of politics, then, is the happiness of communities. They who call themselves politicians, having other objects, are not politicians, but demagogues. But is it in the nature of things, that the sincere and single desire to promote such a system of government as would most effectually secure the greatest amount of general happiness, can draw into action such violent passions, prompt such fierce declamation, authorize such angry criminations, and occasion such strong appeals to the worst motives of the venal and base, as we constantly see and hear in every conflict of the antagonist parties of our country? Or does not this effect arise from causes improperly mixed with politics, and with which they have no intrinsic affinity? Does it not arise from the fact, that government, instead of seeking to promote the greatest happiness of the community, by confining itself rigidly within its true field of action, has extended itself to embrace a thousand objects which should be left to the regulation of social morals, and unrestrained competition, one man with another, without political assistance or check? Are our elections, in truth, a means of deciding mere questions of government, or does not the decision of numerous questions affecting private interests, schemes of selfishness, rapacity, and cunning, depend upon them, even more than cardinal principles of politics?

It is to this fact, we are persuaded, that the immorality and licentiousness of party contests are to be ascribed. If government were restricted to the few and simple objects contemplated in the democratic creed, the mere protection of person, life, and property; if its functions were limited to the mere guardianship of the equal rights of men, and its action, in all cases, were influenced, not by the paltry suggestions of present expediency, but the eternal principles of justice; we should find reason to congratulate ourselves on the change, in the improved tone of public morals, as well as in the increased prosperity of trade.

The religious man, then, as well as the political and social moralist, should exert his influence to bring about the auspicious reformation. Nothing can be more self-evident than the demoralizing influence of special legislation. It degrades politics into a mere scramble for rewards obtained by a violation of the equal rights of the people; it perverts the holy sentiment of patriotism; induces a feverish avidity for sudden wealth; fosters a spirit of wild and dishonest speculation; withdraws industry from its accustomed channels of useful occupation; confounds the established distinctions between virtue and vice, honour and shame, respectability and degradation; pampers luxury; and leads to intemperance, dissipation, and profligacy, in a thousand forms.

The remedy is easy. It is to confine government within the narrowest limits of necessary duties. It is to disconnect bank and state. It is to give freedom to trade, and leave enterprise, competition, and a just public sense of right to accomplish by their natural energies, what the artificial system of legislative checks and balances has so signally failed in accomplishing. The federal government has nothing to do, but to hold itself entirely aloof from banking, having no more connexion with it, than if banks did not exist. It should receive its revenues in nothing not recognized as money by the Constitution, and pay nothing else to those employed in its service. The state governments should repeal their laws imposing restraints on the free exercise of capital and credit. They should avoid, for the future, all legislation not in the fullest accordance with the letter and spirit of that glorious maxim of democratic doctrine, which acknowledges the equality of man's political rights. These are the easy steps by which we might arrive at the consummation devoutly to be wished.

The steps are easy; but passion, ignorance, and selfishness, are gathered round them, and oppose our ascent. Agrarian, leveller, and visionary, are the epithets, more powerful than arguments, with which they resist us. Shall we yield, discouraged, and submit to be always governed by the worst passions of the worst portions of mankind; or by one bold effort, shall we regenerate our institutions, and make government, indeed, not the dispenser of privileges to a few for their efforts in subverting the rights of the many, but the beneficent promoter of the equal happiness of all? The monopolists are prostrated by the explosion of their overcharged system; they are wrecked by the regurgitation of their own flood of mischief; they are buried beneath the ruins of the baseless fabric they had presumptuously reared to such a towering height.

Now is the time for the friends of freedom to bestir themselves. Let us accept the invitation of this glorious opportunity to establish, on an enduring foundation, the true principles of political and economic freedom.

We may be encountered with clamorous revilings: but they only betray the evil temper which ever distinguishes wilful error and baffled selfishness. We may be denounced with opprobrious epithets; but they only show the want of cogent arguments. The worst of these is only the stale charge of *ultraism,* which is not worthy of our regard. To be ultra is not necessarily to be wrong. Extreme opinions are justly censurable only when they are erroneous; but who can be reprehended for going too far towards the right?

"If the two extremes," says Milton, in answer to the same poor objection, "be vice and virtue, falsehood and truth, the greater extremity of virtue and superlative truth we run into, the more virtuous and the more wise we become; and he that, flying from degenerate corruption, fears to shoot himself too far into the meeting embraces of a divinely warranted reformation, might better not have run at all."

PART TWO

Separation of Bank and State

BANK OF UNITED STATES

In answer to the many objections which are urged with great force of argument against the United States Bank, and against any great national institution of a similar character, there is little put forth in its defence, beyond mere naked allegation. One of the assertions, however, which seems to be most relied upon by the advocates of the Bank, is that it has exercised a most beneficial power in *regulating the currency of the country*. Indeed, the power which it was supposed it would possess to regulate the currency, furnished one of the chief grounds of the support yielded to the original proposition to establish a United States Bank, and the same topic has occupied a prominent place in every subsequent discussion of the Bank question in Congress. It is maintained, in favour of the present institution, that it not merely possesses that power, but that it has exerted it in the most prudent and salutary manner. This is made the theme of many high-wrought panegyrics. It is triumphantly put forth by the journals in the interest of the Bank; it drops from the lips of every Bank declaimer at political meetings, and is asserted and re-asserted by all the orators and editors of the Bank party, with a confidence which should belong only to truth. Many persons, indeed, who are strongly opposed to the United States Bank on moral grounds; who view with dismay its prodigious means of corruption; and shudder with abhorrence at the free and audacious use it has made of those means; yet accede to it the praise of having at least answered one great purpose of its creation—namely, the regulation of the currency of the United States.

It is to be feared that men in general have not very precise notions of what constitutes a regulation of the currency. If the meaning of this phrase is to be limited to the mere sustaining

Evening Post, date uncertain. Sedgwick gives simply "March, 1834." Attempts to locate the original have been unsuccessful.

of the credit of the Bank at such a point, that its notes shall always stand at the par value of silver, then indeed must it be admitted that the United States Bank has, for the greater part of the time performed its functions in that respect. Yet no praise is to be acceded to it on that score; since such an effect must naturally and almost inevitably flow from the self-imposed obligation on the government to receive its notes at their nominal amount, at all places, in payment of debts due to the United States. There is not a bank in the country, accredited and endorsed by the Government to an equal extent, that would not as certainly maintain its paper on a par with the precious metals. Indeed, most of the well-conducted institutions in the Atlantic cities, without the advantage of such countenance from the Government, have preserved their paper in equal credit; or, in other words, have been equally successful in *regulating the currency*, so far as the term implies the affording of a convertible paper substitute for money, which shall pass from hand to hand as the full equivalent of silver coin. The doing of this certainly constitutes an important branch of the regulation of the currency; but there is another and more important branch, and in this the United States Bank has totally and most signally failed.

What is regulating the currency? It is the furnishing of a medium of circulation, either metalic or convertible at par, equal in amount to the real business of the country, as measured by the amount of its exports and the amount of actual capital employed in commercial business. It is the furnishing of that amount of circulation, which is actually absorbed by the commercial transactions of the country—by those transactions which rest on the basis of the exchange continually going on of the commodities of one country for those of another. When bank issues are limited within this circle, the notes of the bank in circulation are founded on the security of the notes of merchants in possession of the bank, and the notes of the merchants rest on the basis of goods actually purchased, which are finally to be paid for with the products of the soil or other articles of export. The maintaining of the circulation at this point would, in the strict and proper sense of the word, be regulating the currency. It would be supplying the channels of business to the degree requisite to facilitate the operations of commerce, without causing those operations to be unduly extended at one time, and unduly contracted at another. It would be causing the stream of credit to glide in an equal and uniform current, never stagnating, and never overflowing its boundaries.

When bank circulation exceeds this measure, an inevitable derangement of the currency takes place. The par of value between the paper representatives of money and money itself may still be maintained; but prices are raised, and raised unequally, and the dollar no longer accurately performs its office as a measure of value. The effects of the expansion of the currency are first seen in the rise of the prices of foreign fabrics. This leads to excessive importation on the part of the competitors anxious to avail themselves of the advance. Goods are purchased from abroad to a much larger amount than the exports of the country will liquidate, and a balance of debt is thus created. The payment of this balance drains the country of specie. The bank, finding its paper return upon it in demand for coin, is obliged suddenly, in self-defence, to curtail its issues. The consequence of this curtailment is a fall of prices. Those who had ordered goods in expectation of deriving the advantage of the high prices, are obliged to sell at a sacrifice, and are fortunate if they can dispose of their commodities at all. Those who had been deluded, by the fatal facility of getting bank favours, into extending themselves beyond the limits of that fair and prudent credit to which their actual capital entitled them, must necessarily be unable to meet the shock of a sudden withdrawal of the quicksand basis on which their business rested, and are thus compelled to become bankrupts. A state of general calamity succeeds—most severe in the commercial cities, and measured in all places by a rule of inverse ratio to the excess of the preceding apparent prosperity. These sudden expansions and contractions of the currency have happened too frequently in this country, and have been followed by effects of too disastrous a nature, for any reader to be ignorant of them.

Has the United States Bank never caused distress of this kind? Has it never caused the amount of circulating medium to fluctuate? Has it never stimulated business into unhealthy activity at one time, and withheld its proper aliment at another? Has it never poured out a sudden flood of paper money, causing the wheels of commerce to revolve with harmful rapidity, and then as suddenly withdrawn the supply, till the channels were empty, and every branch of business languished throughout the land? There are few of our readers who cannot, of their own knowledge, answer these questions in the affirmative.

For the two or three years preceding the extensive and heavy calamities of 1819, the United States Bank, instead of regulating the currency, poured out its issues at such a lavish rate that trade and speculation were excited in a preternatural manner. But the inevitable consequences of over issues did not fail to happen in that case. A large balance of debt was created in Europe, and to pay that debt our metalic medium was sent away from the country. The land was soon nearly exhausted of specie, and still the debt remained unliquidated. The bank, in order to bring business to an equipoise again, exchanged a part of its funded debt for specie in Europe, and purchased a large amount of coin in the West Indies and other places. But it still continued to make loans to a larger degree than the actual business of the country, as measured by the amount of its exports, required, and its purchase was therefore a most ineffectual and childish scheme. It was but dragging a supply of water with much toil and expense, from the lake of the valley to the summit of an eminence, in the vain hope that, discharged there, it would continue on the height and not rush down the declivity, to mix again with the waters of the lake. The specie, purchased at high rates in foreign countries, was no sooner brought to our own, and lodged in the vaults of the bank, than it was immediately drawn thence again, by the necessity of redeeming the notes which poured in upon it in a constant stream in demand for silver. In one year, 1818, upwards of fifteen millions of dollars were exported from the country, and still the debts incurred by the mad spirit of overtrading were not liquidated. The bank itself was now on the very verge of bankruptcy. At the close of its business on the 12th of April, 1819, the whole amount of money in its vaults was only 71,522 dollars, and it at the same time owed to the city banks a clear balance of 196,418 dollars, or an excess over its means of payment of nearly 125,000 dollars. A depreciation of its credit was one of the consequences which had flowed from this state of things, and the notes of the United States Bank—the boasted institution which claims to have regulated the currency of this country—*fell ten per cent. below the par value of silver.*

But the greatest evil was yet behind. The Bank was at length compelled, by the situation in which the rashness of its managers had involved it, to commence a rapid curtailment of discounts. An immediate reduction took place of two millions in Philadelphia, two millions in Baltimore, nearly a million in Richmond, and half a million in Norfolk. This sudden withdrawal of the means of business was, of itself, a heavy calamity to those cities; but the system of curtailment was persevered in, until the foundation of a great part of the commercial transactions of the United States, and of the speculations in land, in internal improvement, and other adventures, which the facility of getting money had induced men to hazard, was withdrawn, and the whole fabric fell to the ground, burying beneath vast numbers of unfortunate persons, and scattering ruin and dismay throughout the Union.

The same scenes, only to a greater extent, and with more deplorable circumstances, were acted over in 1825. There are few inhabitants of this city who can have forgotten the extensive failures, both of individuals and corporate institutions, which marked that period. There are many yet pining in comfortless poverty whose distress was brought upon them by the revulsions of that disastrous year—many who were suddenly cast down from affluence to want—many who saw their all slip from their grasp and melt away, who had thought that they held it by securities as firm as the eternal hills.

But not to dwell upon events the recollection of which time may have begun to efface from many minds, let us but cast a glance at the manner in which the United States Bank *regulated the currency* in 1830, when, in the short period of a twelvemonth it extended its *accommodations* from forty to seventy millions of dollars. This enormous expansion, entirely uncalled for by any peculiar circumstance in the business condition of the country, was followed by the invariable consequences of an inflation of the currency. Goods and stocks rose, speculation was excited, a great number of extensive enterprises were undertaken, canals were laid out, rail-roads projected, and the whole business of the country was stimulated into unnatural and unsalutary activity. The necessary result of the spirit of speculation thus awakened was the purchase of more goods abroad than the commodities of the country would pay for. Hence vast sums of specie soon began to leave the United States; scarcely a packet ship sailed from our wharves that did not carry out to England and France a large sum of money in gold and silver; and it is estimated that in 1831–32 the specie drawn from the country did not fall short of twenty millions of dollars. The Bank of the United States, failing to accomplish the bad design for which it had thus flooded the country with its paper, now began to try the effects of a contrary system, and resorted to coercion. A reduction of its issues must inevitably have taken place in the nature of things, nor could all the means and all the credit of the Bank have removed the evil day to a very distant period. But it had it completely within its power to effect its curtailment by easy degrees, and to bring back business into its proper channels by operations that would have been attended with little general distress. But this was no part of its plan. Its object was to wring from the sufferings of the people their assent to the perpetuation of its existence. Its curtailments were therefore rapid and sudden, and so managed as to throw the greater part of the burden on those commercial places where there was the greatest need of lenity and forbearance. The distress and dismay thus occasioned, were aggravated by the rumours and inventions of hired presses, instructed to increase the panic by all the means in their power. Of the deplorable effects produced by this course, the traces are yet too recent to require that we should enter into any particulars.

The Bank has not yet exhausted its full power of mischief. Since its creation to the present hour, instead of regulating the currency, it has caused a continual fluctuation; but it is capable of doing greater injury than it has yet effected. It is perfectly within its power to cause a variation of prices to the extent of twenty-five per cent. every ninety days, by alternate expansions and contractions of its issues. It is in its power, in the short period that is yet to elapse before its charter expires, so to embarrass the currency, so to limit the amount of circulating medium, so to impair commercial confidence, and shake the entire basis of mercantile credit, as to produce throughout the whole land a scene of the most poignant pecuniary distress—a scene compared with which the dark days of 1819 and 1825, and those through which we have just passed, shall seem bright and prosperous. And there are indications that the Bank will do this. There are signs and portents in the heavens which tell of a coming tempest. There are omens which foreshow that this mighty and wicked corporation means to use to the uttermost its whole machinery of coercion, to wring from the groaning land a hard contest to the renewal of its existence. We trust the People will bear stiffly up under the infliction. We trust they will breast the storm with determined spirits. We trust they will endure the torture, without yielding to a measure which would destroy the best interests of their country, and make them and their children slaves forever.

Regulation of the currency! What a claim to set up for the United States Bank! It has done the very reverse: it has destroyed the equal flow and steady worth of the currency: it has broken up the measure of value: it has kept the circulating medium in a state of continual fluctuation, making the dollar to-day worth a dollar and a half, and to-morrow not worth a half a dollar. Besides the three great periods of sudden excess and rapid curtailment, its whole career has been one series of experiments, more or less general, of inflation and exhaustion of the currency. And this is the institution, which now comes forward, and claims to be re-chartered, on the ground of having well performed the great offices for which it was created. It has failed in *all* its great ends. In its chief purpose, as a fiscal agent and assistant of the Government, one on which it might at all times securely rely, it has wholly failed. We have seen it interfering in the national politics, and endeavouring to rule the suffrages of the people, first by bribery and afterwards by compulsion. We have seen it place itself in open defiance to the Executive, and rank him in its official papers, with counterfeiters and robbers. We have seen it endeavouring to thwart the measures of his administration; collude with foreign creditors of the Government to defeat the avowed objects of the Treasury; refuse to give up the national funds at the commands of the competent authority; and finally turn a committee of congress with contumely from its doors, in violation of its charter, and in violation of every obligation of morality and every principle of public decency. This is the institution which now comes forward for a re-charter. If the people grant it they will deserve to wear its chains!

SMALL NOTE CIRCULATION

Now that *real* money has come into circulation—now that the country is plentifully supplied with gold and silver—we trust the friends of a sound currency will take pains, and adopt all proper measures, to banish small notes from use. We call upon every man who professes to be animated with the principles of the democracy, to assist in accomplishing the great work of redeeming this country from the curse of our bad bank system. We never shall be a truly free and happy people while subject, as we now are, to Bank domination. No system could possibly be devised more certainly fatal to the great principle on which our government rests—the glorious principle of equal rights—than the Banking system, as it exists in this country. It is hostile to every received axiom of political economy, it is hostile to morals, and hostile to freedom. Its direct and inevitable tendency is to create artificial inequalities and distinctions in society; to increase the wealth of the rich, and render more abject and oppressive the poverty of the poor. It fosters a spirit of speculation, destructive of love of country—a spirit which substitutes an idol of gold for that better object which patriotism worships—a spirit which paralyzes all the ardent and generous impulses of our nature, and creates, instead, a sordid and rapacious desire of gain, to minister to the insatiable cravings of which becomes the sole aim of existence.

We do not expect and do not desire to overthrow our pernicious Banking system suddenly. We would not, if we could, do aught to infringe the chartered privileges of Banks already existing. Were they ten times worse in their effects than they are, we would not justify a breach of the public faith to get rid of the evil. But we desire most ardently that it may not be

Evening Post, August 6, 1834. Title added by Sedgwick.

permitted to spread more widely. The legislatures may at least say, "Thus far shalt thou go and no further; here shall thy proud waves be stayed." They may refuse to grant any more charters of incorporation, and may take effectual measures to prohibit the small note issues. These measures constitute the proper first step in the great reformation for which we contend, and these measures the democracy of the country—if we do not strangely misinterpret their sentiments—will demand.

But in the meanwhile, the means are within the reach of the people themselves to do much—very much—towards the accomplishment of the desired object. Let employers provide themselves with gold to pay their hands; and let the hands of those employers who continue in the practice, which has been too extensive, of procuring uncurrent money to pay them, take such measures to remedy the evil as are within their reach, and not inconsistent with prudence. The practice is wholly unjustifiable, and stands, in a moral point of view, on a footing not very different from that of clipping coins. The law, however, which we all know is not always framed in the most perfect accordance with the principles of ethics, makes this important difference, that while to the one species of dishonesty it extends full protection, the other it visits with the most ignominious punishment. But though protected by the law, workmen may do much to rid themselves of the evils of this practise, and at the same time forward the great object of democracy—ultimate emancipation from the shackles of a detestable Bank tyranny. Let them remember, when paid in small uncurrent notes, that the longer they retain possession of those notes the greater is the profit of the Bank that issued them, and therefore let them take the best means within their reach of causing them to be returned to the Bank. Every dollar-note in circulation has displaced an equal amount of gold and silver, and, on the other hand, every dollar of gold and silver you keep in circulation, will displace twice or three times its amount in paper money.

Paper money is fingered by a great many hands, as may be easily perceived from the soiled and worn appearance of many of the bills. A cheap, and, to a certain extent, most effectual method of disseminating the principles of those opposed to incorporated rag-money manufactories, would be for them to write upon the back of every bank-note which should come into their possession, some short sentence expressive of their sentiments. For example—"No Monopolies!" "No Union of Banks and State!" "Jackson and Hard Money!" "Gold before Rags!" and the like. When it should become their duty to *endorse* a bill issued by a Bank, the charter of which was obtained by bribery and collusion, (as many such there be) it would be well to inscribe upon it in a clear and distinct hand, "*Wages of Iniquity!*"

What we have here recommended may seem to be but child's play; but we are satisfied that if the workingmen, upon whom the worst trash of Bank rags are palmed off, would only adopt such a practice, and persist in it for a short time, they would see the good result. The worst class of uncurrent notes would soon be plentifully endorsed, for it is the worst description of money which is generally *bought* to pay away to mechanics, in order that their employers may avoid paying them as large a proportion as possible of their just wages. Let them consider the hints thrown out in this article, and they can hardly fail, we think, to perceive, that if generally acted upon, they would have an important effect in assisting the introduction of gold as a currency, in the place of the small note circulation of which there is so much reason to complain.

THE MONOPOLY BANKING SYSTEM

It is a source of sincere pleasure to us to perceive that the attention of the people is seriously awakened to the subject of the Bank system, as it exists in this country. It seems to us quite evident that the sentiment is daily gaining ground that the whole system is erroneous—wrong in principle and productive of incalculable evils in its practical operation. Those who have been readers of the EVENING POST, for the last six or eight months, have had this subject fully and freely discussed, not only in articles from our own pen, but in numerous excellent communications from able correspondents, and, more especially, in the clear, comprehensive, and unanswerable essays of Mr. Gouge, which, with the author's permission, we copied from his admirable work on American Banking.[1] Those who perused these various productions, with the attention which the important and interesting nature of the subject required, have possessed themselves of sufficient materials for the formation of a correct opinion; and we have the satisfaction of knowing that very many of our readers concur fully with us in the sentiments we entertain with regard to our banking system.

We look upon that system as wrong in two of its leading principles: first, we object to it as founded on a species of monopoly; and secondly, as supplying a circulating medium which rests on a basis liable to all the fluctuations and contingencies of commerce and trade—a basis which may at any time be swept away by a thousand casualties of business, and leave not a wreck behind. There are many other objections

Evening Post, date uncertain. Sedgwick gives simply "December, 1834." Attempts to locate the original have been unsuccessful.

[1] A reference to William M. Gouge, *A Short History of Paper Money and Banking in the United States* (Philadelphia: T. W. Ustick, 1833).—Ed.

incident to these, some of which present themselves in forms which demand the most serious consideration.

Our primary ground of opposition to banks as they at present exist is that they are a species of monopoly. All corporations are liable to the objection that whatever powers or privileges are given to them, are so much taken from the government of the people. Though a state legislature may possess a constitutional right to create bank incorporations, yet it seems very clear to our apprehension that the doing so is an invasion of the grand republican principle of Equal Rights—a principle which lies at the bottom of our constitution, and which, in truth, is the corner-stone both of our national government, and that of each particular state.

Every charter of incorporation, we have said, is, to some extent, either in fact or in practical operation, a monopoly; for these charters invariably invest those upon whom they are bestowed with powers and privileges which are not enjoyed by the great body of the people. This may be done by merely combining larger amounts of capital than unincorporated individuals can bring into competition with the chartered institution; but the end is more frequently effected by the more palpably unjust process of exonerating the chartered few from liabilities to which the rest of the community are subject, or by prohibiting the unprivileged individual from entering into competition with the favoured creature of the law.

When a legislative body restrains the people collectively from exercising their natural right of pursuing a certain branch of business, and gives to particular individuals exclusive permission to carry on that business, they assuredly are guilty of a violation of the republican maxim of Equal Rights, which nothing but the plainest paramount necessity can at all excuse. This violation is the more palpable, when immunities are granted to the few, which would not have been enjoyed by the people, had their natural rights never been restricted by law. In the case of Bank incorporations such is clearly true; since those who are thus privileged are protected by their charters both from the competition of individuals, and from loss to any greater extent than the amount of capital they may risk in the enterprise—a protection which would have been enjoyed by no member of the community, had the law left banking on the same footing with other mercantile pursuits. As a monopoly, then—as a system which grants exclusive privileges—which is at variance with the great fundamental doctrine of democracy—we must oppose Bank incorporations, unless it can be shown that they are productive of good which greatly counterbalances the evil.

A second objection to our banking system is that it is founded on a wrong basis—a basis that does not afford adequate security to the community; since it not only does not protect them from loss by ignorant or fraudulent management, but not even from those constantly recurring commercial revulsions, which, indeed, are one of the evil fruits of this very system. The basis of our banking business is specie capital; yet every body knows that the first thing a bank does, on going into operation, (if we suppose the whole capital to have been honestly paid in, which is very far from being always the case) is to lend out its capital; and the profits of the institution do not commence until, having loaned all its capital, it begins to loan its credit as money. No set of men would desire a bank charter merely to authorize them to lend their money capital at the common rate of interest; for they would have no difficulty in doing that, without a charter, and without incurring the heavy expense incident to banking business. *The object of a bank charter is to enable those holding it to lend their credit at interest,* and to lend their credit too, to twice, and sometimes three times, the amount of their actual capital. In return, then, for its capital, and for the large amount of promissory obligations issued on the credit of that capital, the Bank holds nothing but the liabilities of individual merchants and other dealers. It must be evident then that its capital is liable to all the fluctuations and accidents to which commercial business is exposed. Its integrity depends upon the ability of its dealers punctually to discharge their obligations. Should a series of commercial disasters overwhelm those dealers, the capital of the Bank is lost, and the bill holder, instead of money, finds himself possessed of a mere worthless and broken promise to pay.

Let us trace the progress of a new banking institution. Let us imagine a knot of speculators to have possessed themselves, by certain acts of collusion, bribery, and political management, of a bank charter; and let us suppose them commencing operations under their corporate privileges. They begin by lending their capital. After that, if commercial business is active, and the demand for money urgent, they take care to put as many of their notes in circulation as possible. For awhile this does very well, and the Bank realizes large profits. Every thing seems to flourish; merchants extend their operations; they hire capacious stores, import largely from abroad, sell to country dealers on liberal terms, get the notes of those dealers discounted, and extend themselves still further. Others, in the meanwhile, stimulated by this same appearance of commercial prosperity, borrow money (that is notes) from the Bank, and embark in enterprises of a different nature. They purchase lots, build houses, set railway and canal projects on foot, and every thing goes on swimmingly. The demand for labour is abundant, property of all kinds rises in price, and speculators meet each other in the streets, and exult in their anticipated fortunes.

But by and by things take a different turn. The exports of the country (which furnish the true measure of business) are found to fall greatly short of the amount due abroad for foreign fabrics, and a large balance remains unpaid. The first intimation of this is the rapid advance in the price of foreign exchange. The bank now perceives that it has extended itself too far. Its notes, which, until now, circulated currently enough, begin to return in upon it in demand for specie; while, at the same time, the merchants, whom it has been all along eager to serve, now call for increased accommodations. But the Bank cannot accommodate them any longer. Instead of increasing its loans, it is obliged to require payment of those which it had previously made; for its own notes are flowing in a continual stream to its counter, and real money is demanded instead. But real money it has none, as that was all lent out when it first went into operation. Here then a sudden check is given to the seeming prosperity. The merchants, unable to get the amount of accommodation necessary to sustain their operations, are forced to suspend payment. A rumour of the amount lost by the Bank in consequence of these failures, causes confidence in its solvency to be impaired, and being threatened with a run, it resorts to a still more rapid curtailment. Then follows wider derangement. One commercial house after another becomes bankrupt, and finally the Bank itself, by these repeated losses forced to discontinue its business, closes its doors, and hands over its affairs for the benefit of its creditors, Who are its creditors? Those who hold *its money*, that is, its "*promises to pay.*" On investigation it is discovered, most likely, that the whole capital of the institution has been absorbed by its losses. The enormous profits which it made during the first part of its career, had been regularly withdrawn by the stockholders, and the deluded creditor has nothing but a worthless bit of engraved paper to show for the valuable consideration which he parted with for what he foolishly imagined money.

What we have here stated can hardly be called a suppostititious case—it is a true history, and there are events within the memory of almost every reader of which it is a narrative almost literally correct.

The basis of our banking system, then, if liable to be thus easily dissipated, is certainly wrong. Banks should be established on a foundation which neither panic nor mismanagement, neither ignorance nor fraud, could destroy. The bill-holder should always be secure, whatever might become of the stock-holder. That which is received as money, and which is designed to pass from hand to hand as such, should not be liable to change into worthless paper in the transition.

A very important objection incident to the banking system of this country is the demoralizing effect which it exercises on society. It is a matter of the utmost notoriety that bank charters are in frequent instances obtained by practices of the most outrageous corruption. They are conceived in a wild spirit of speculation; they are brought into existence through the instrumentality of bribery and intrigue; and they exercise over the community the most unsalutary influence, encouraging men of business to transcend the proper limits of credit, and fostering a general and feverish thirst for wealth, prompting the mind to seek it by other than the legitimate means of honest, patient industry, and prudent enterprise. Let any man who has had an opportunity of observing the effect of introducing a banking institution, into a quiet country town, on the moral character of the inhabitants, answer for himself if this is not true. Let any man, whose knowledge enables him to contrast a portion of our country where banks are few, with another where they are numerous, answer if it is not true. Let any man whose memory extends so far back that he can compare the present state of society with what it was in the time of our fathers, answer if it is not true. The time was when fraud in business was as rare—we were about to say—as honesty is now. The time was when a failure was a strange and unfrequent occurrence; when a bankrupt excited the sympathy of the whole community for his misfortunes, or their censure for his rashness, or their scorn for his dishonesty. The banking system has made insolvency a matter of daily occurrence. It has changed the meaning of words, it has altered the sense of things, it has revolutionized our ethical notions. Formerly, if a man ventured far beyond his depth in business—if he borrowed vast sums of money to hazard them in doubtful enterprises—if he deluded the world by a system of false shows and pretences, and extended his credit by every art and device—formerly such a man was called rash and dishonest, but we now speak of him as enterprising and ingenious. The man whose ill-planned speculations miscarry—whose airy castle of credit is suddenly overturned, burying hundreds of industrious mechanics and labourers under its ruins—such a man would once have been execrated; he is now pitied; while our censure and contempt is transferred to those who are the victims of his fraudful schemes.

For its political effect, not less than moral, our bank system deserves to be opposed. It is essentially an aristocratic institution. It bands the wealthy together, holds out to them a common motive, animates them with a common sentiment, and inflates their vanity with notions of superior power and greatness. The bank system is maintained out of the hard earnings of the poor; and its operation is to degrade them in their political rights, as much as they are degraded in a pecuniary respect, by the accident of fortune. Its tendency is to give exclusive political, as well as exclusive money privileges to the rich. It is in direct opposition to the spirit of our constitution and the genius of the people. It is silently, but rapidly, undermining our institutions; it falsifies our grand boast of political equality; it is building up a privileged order, who, at no distant day, unless the whole system be changed, will rise in triumph on the ruins of democracy.

Even now, how completely we are monopoly-governed! how completely we are hemmed in on every side, how we are cabined, cribb'd, confined, by exclusive privileges! Not a road can be opened, not a bridge can be built, not a canal can be dug, but a charter of exclusive privileges must be granted for the purpose. The sum and substance of our whole legislation is the granting of monopolies. The bargaining and trucking away chartered privileges is the whole business of our law makers. The people of this great state fondly imagine that they govern themselves; but they do not! They are led about by the unseen but strong bands of chartered companies. They are fastened down by the minute but effectual fetters of banking institutions. They are governed by bank directors, bank stockholders, and bank minions. They are under the influence of a power whose name is Legion—they are under the influence of bank monopolies, with a host of associate and subordinate agents, the other incorporated companies, depending on bank assistance for their means of operation. These evil influences are scattered throughout our community, in every quarter of the state. They give the tone to our meetings; they name our candidates for the legislature; they secure their election; they control them when elected.

What then is the remedy for the evil? Do away with our bad bank system; repeal our unjust, unsalutary, undemocratic restraining law; and establish, in its stead, some law, the sole object of which shall be to provide the community with security against fraud. We hope, indeed, to see the day when banking, like any other mercantile business will be left to *regulate itself;* when the principles of free trade will be perceived to have as much relation to currency as to commerce; when the maxim of *Let us alone* will be acknowledged to be better, infinitely better, than all this political quackery of ignorant legislators, instigated by the grasping, monopolizing spirit of rapacious capitalists. This country, we hope, we trust, is destined to prove to mankind the truth of the saying, that *the world is governed too much*, and to prove it by her own successful experiment in throwing off the clogs and fetters with which craft and cunning have ever contrived to bind the mass of men.

But to suit the present temper of the times, it would be easy to substitute a scheme of banking which should have all the advantages of the present one, and none of its defects. Let the restraining law be repealed; let a law be substituted, requiring simply that *any person* entering into banking business shall be required to lodge with some officer designated in the law, real estate, or other approved security, to the full amount of the notes which he might desire to issue; and to secure, that this amount should never be exceeded, it might be provided that each particular note should be authenticated by the signature of the comptroller, or other officer entrusted with the business. Another clause might state suitable provisions for having the securities re-appraised, from time to time, so that bill holders might be sure that sufficient unalienable property was always pledged for the redemption of the paper currency founded upon that basis. Banking, established on this foundation, would be liable to none of the evils arising from panic; for each holder of a note would, in point of fact, hold a title-deed of property to the full value of its amount. It would not be liable to the revulsions which follow overtrading, and which every now and then spread such dismay and ruin through commercial communities; for when bankers are left to manage their own business, each for himself, they would watch the course of trade, and limit their discounts accordingly; because if they extended them beyond the measure of the legitimate business of the country, they would be sure that their notes would return upon them in demand for the precious metals, thus forcing them to part with their profits, in order to purchase silver and gold to answer such demand.

But much as we desire to see the wretched, insecure, and, in a political view, dangerous banking system superceded by the more honest and equal plan we have suggested, we would by no means be considered as the advocates of sudden or capricious change. All reformations of the currency—all legislation, the tendency of which is to disturb the relations of value, should be slow, well considered and gradual. In this hasty and unpremeditated article, we have glanced at the system which we desire may ere long take the place of the present one, and have rapidly adverted to some of the reasons which render the change desirable. But as a first step towards the consummation, we should wish the legislature to do nothing more at present than restrain the issue of notes under five dollars, and refuse to charter any more banks. The people demand it, and we do not think that the public sentiment is in favour of any further immediate reformation. As to the prospective legislation which is proposed by some, we think it anti-republican and unwise. We would not take advantage of any present movement of the public mind to fasten a law upon the state, which public sentiment may not afterwards sustain. The same influence of public opinion which, is now about to lead to the long-desired *first step* in Bank reform, will be potent in carrying on the reformation to the desired conclusion. A good maxim, and one which it will be well to be governed by in this matter, is *festina lente.*[2]

UNCURRENT BANK NOTES

We wish some public spirited man who has access to data that would afford a reasonable basis for a conjectural calculation, would furnish us with an estimate of the immense amount of money which is annually lost in this city, by the labouring classes, in the discount upon uncurrent bank notes in circulation. Do the mechanics and the labourers know, that every dollar which is paid in the discounting of uncurrent notes in Wall-street, is filched out of their pockets? That such is the fact is susceptible of the clearest demonstration.

In the first place, the circulation of uncurrent bank notes is chiefly kept up by a direct and infamous fraud upon the working classes. It is a common practise with employers when they pay off their hands on Saturday, to go into Wall-street and purchase of some broker for the purpose, a lot of notes of depreciated value, varying from half to one and a half per cent. below par. These notes they palm off upon their workmen as

[2] "Hurry slowly."—Ed.

Evening Post, March 10, 1835. Title added by Sedgwick.

money. If a master mechanic has a thousand dollars a week to pay to his hands, it is clear that he pockets every week by this operation some ten or fifteen dollars; and it can be shown with equal clearness that those in his employment are defrauded out of this sum. If a man hesitates to take this depreciated paper, he is told that it passes as currently as silver in payment of any thing he may wish to purchase; and so, in truth, it does. Yet he could not exchange it for silver, without paying the broker a discount, and let him not imagine, though he may seem to pass it away to his grocer or his baker at par, that he does not lose this discount all the same. Nay, the mechanic and labouring man whose employers are conscientious enough to pay them their wages in real money, bear their full proportion of the loss on the uncurrent notes in circulation, equally with those to whom the depreciated paper is paid. *The entire sum paid for the discount of depreciated bank paper falls on the mechanics and labourers, and is wrung out of their sweat and toil. Nay more: they not only lose the amount which is actually paid for discount to the money changers, but they also pay a per centage on that amount equal to the average rate of profit which merchants charge on their goods.* We can make this plain to the dullest apprehension.

The labouring man, when he returns home of a Saturday evening, with his week's wages in his pocket, in this depreciated paper, stops at his grocer's, and pays him the amount of his weekly bill. The grocer in the course of a few days pays this money away into the hands of the wholesale merchant from whom he purchases his commodities. The merchant, when a certain amount of this kind of paper has accumulated on his hands, sends it into Wall-street, and sells it to the brokers, and when his clerk returns, an entry is made in his books of the amount paid for discount. The sum total paid in the course of a year for the discount of depreciated paper forms an item of expense which is calculated as one of the elements in the cost of his goods. To pay for his goods he is obliged to buy bills of exchange, or in other words, to remit specie to Europe. Whatever this specie costs him, his goods cost him; and he therefore looks upon the amount he had to pay to turn the uncurrent paper received from his customers into specie as a constituent part of the first cost of his merchandize. Upon the whole sum of the cost, thus ascertained, he puts a certain per centage profit, and fixes his prices accordingly. The retail trader then buying a lot of goods of him, pays him not only a proportional part of the discount which the wholesale merchant actually paid on his uncurrent paper, but a profit thereon. This, however, makes no difference to him, for he has only to put his own profit on above all, and let the loss fall on the labourer, when he comes for his tea and sugar and other little necessaries and comforts for his family. That this is a true, though homely exposition of the case, any body must see who will only give himself the trouble to think about it.

The whole amount of uncurrent notes which pass through the broker's hands annually may be stated at a given sum, and the discount thereupon amounts, on an average to a given per-centage. This sum, whatever it is, (and it must be immense) is a tax on the business of the community, which each individual shuffles off his own shoulders on those of the persons next beneath him, and so it descends by gradation till it reaches the broad backs and hard hands of the mechanics and labourers, who produce all the wealth and bear all the burdens of society.

But the mechanics and labourers have it in their power to rid themselves of this imposition. The task is very easy: it is only to learn the efficacy of the word COMBINATION. There is a magic in that word, when rightly understood and employed, which will force the scrip nobility to do them justice, and yield them, without drawback and without cheatery, the full fruits of their toil. Let them inquire by what means it is that this immense amount of depreciated paper is kept in circulation. They will find it is chiefly through the instrumentality of master-workmen and others having mechanics and labourers in their employment. They will find that this wretched substitute for money is bought, for the express purpose of palming it off upon them as real value, while their task-masters and the brokers share the spoils between them. A mechanic dare not refuse to take the wretched trash; because, if he does, he will be turned away to starve. But what a single mechanic may not be able to compass alone, could be easily effected by *combination*. Will the mechanics and labourers wait for eighteen months, in the hope that the juggling law now before the legislature will by that time go into operation, and rid them of *the paper money curse?* Let them not rest in any such belief. Let them *know their own strength and resolve to be imposed on no longer*. Why are the producers of all the wealth of society the poorest, most despised and most down-trodden class of men? Because they submit to be the dupes of the scrip nobility—because they are ignorant of their own strength. Let them combine together to demand whatever the plain principles of justice warrant, and we shall see what power there is which can deny them.

FANCY CITIES

. . . .

The vast and sudden increase which the paper money circulation of this country has undergone within the last eighteen months is the cause of the feverish thirst of riches which the community now exhibits; and whatever shall check that circulation, and turn it back upon the banks, will arrest the disease, but arrest it with a violence that to many will prove fatal, and give a fearful shock to all. Paper money is, to the people of this

Evening Post, September 14, 1836. Title added by Sedgwick. Text abridged.

country, the insane root that takes the reason prisoner; and they can be restored to sanity only by withholding such stimulating and dangerous aliment. As it now is, their appetite grows by what it feeds on. The demand for money increases with each succeeding day; and every new loan of bank credit but gives rise to new projects of speculation, each wilder and more chimerical than the last.

The effect of this pervading spirit of speculation (or spirit of gambling, as it might with more propriety be called, for it is gambling, and gambling of the most desperate kind) on the morals of the community is dreadful. Its direct and manifest tendency is to blunt men's moral perceptions, and accustom them by degrees to arts and devices of traffic which an honest, unsophisticated mind would shrink from with horror as frauds of the most flagitious dye. It creates a distaste for the ordinary pursuits of industry; it disinclines the mind from gradual accumulation in some regular vocation, and kindles an intense desire, like that expressed in the prayer of Ortogal of Basra, "Let me grow suddenly rich!" To this gambling spirit of the age we may directly trace the most of those prodigious frauds the discovery of which has recently startled the public mind. "Startled the public mind," did we say? The phrase is wrong. The public were not startled. They heard the stories with the most stoical indifference; and if any exclamations were uttered, they conveyed rather a sentiment of commiseration for the criminals, than one of detestation for their stupendous crimes.

But the day of the madness of speculation is drawing to a close. The time must come, nor can it be remote, when some financial or commercial revulsion will throw back the stream of paper circulation to its source, and many a goodly vessel, which had ventured too boldly on the current, will be left by the reflux stranded on its shores. Circumstances may yet defer the evil day for awhile, but it cannot be far off. A failure of the cotton crop, a slight reduction of prices in Europe, or any one of the thousand contingencies to which trade is perpetually liable, will give a shock to the widely expanded currency of the country, which will be felt with ruinous force through every vein and artery of business. Wo unto them in that day who do not now take timely caution. Their cities and towns and villages, which they are now so fertile in planning, as if they thought men might be multiplied as rapidly as paper money, will remain untenanted and desolate memorials of their madness, and the voice of sorrow and mourning, instead of the din of present unreal prosperity, will be heard through the land.

CAUSES OF FINANCIAL DISTRESS

The financial storm long since predicted by this journal has at last commenced in good earnest, and begins now to be severely felt. For a considerable time past a pressure for money has been experienced in this metropolis, and within a few days it has increased to a degree which has made it the subject of general conversation and complaint. Men now perceive that their projects, sustained on the airy basis of too widely extended credit, are in danger of sudden ruin. A sense of general insecurity is awakened, and alarm and consternation are taking the place of that fool-hardy spirit of speculation, which, but a little while ago, kept hurrying on from one mad scheme to another, as if it possessed the fabled art of turning all it touched into gold. A commercial revulsion has commenced, and we fear will not terminate, till it has swept like a tornado over the land, and marked its progress by the wrecks scattered in its path.

Evening Post, October 24, 1836. Title added by Sedgwick. Text abridged.

It is always to be expected in this country, when any thing occurs to create extensive dissatisfaction, that newspaper writers, on one side or the other, will strive to turn it to the uses of party; and we accordingly find, in the present instance, that the opposition journals seize the subject of the financial difficulties as a theme for declamation against the government, and ascribe all our pecuniary embarrassments to the maladministration of public affairs. Some, with singular contempt for the understanding of their readers, deal in mere generalities, and, in all the worn out common places of the political slang vocabulary, denounce the administration as composed of a set of ignorant "tinkers of the currency," or fraudulent speculators, who interfere with the financial arrangements of the country, for the purposes of private gain, perfectly regardless of the wide-spread ruin they may occasion. In the same spirit they call upon the merchants to close their stores and counting-rooms, and go out into the streets as political missionaries, devoting themselves exclusively, for the next twenty days, to the business of electioneering, with a view of putting down a corrupt administration, which is forever trying high-handed experiments with the currency, and obstructing the sources of commercial prosperity. The day has been when the mercantile men of this community suffered themselves to be inflamed by such appeals, and acted in pursuance of such advice. But we trust that day is past, never to return.

Another portion of the opposition papers, with more respect for the intelligence of their readers, endeavour to fortify their charges against the administration by explaining the mode in which they conceive it to be the author of the present difficulties. By some of these, all the embarrassments of the money market are traced to the order of the Treasury Department, requiring payment for public lands to be made in specie. This may do very well as a reason to be urged by those wise journalists who are ever ready to shape their political economy to the exigencies of party; but will hardly satisfy readers of so much intelligence as to demand that the cause shall be adequate to the effect. Any one who will give the slightest attention to the statistics of the land sales, and who will reflect what a vast amount of purchase an inconsiderable sum in specie will pay, in its necessarily constant and rapid circulation from the land office to the neighbouring bank, and from the bank back to the land office, must be perfectly satisfied that the regulation in question cannot have had any perceptible effect in producing the general financial pressure now experienced.

There is a third class of opposition writers who, like the others, imputing all the difficulties to the administration, yet find out an entirely different and much more adequate cause. These impute it entirely to the Treasury orders, issued to various banks in different parts of the Union against the public funds collected on deposite in the banks of this city. By the natural course of trade, New-York is the great money market and storehouse of bullion for the entire confederacy. At this port, four-fifths of the whole revenue of the country are collected, and would here accumulate, affording a substantial basis of credit and reciprocal accommodation to those who pay it, were it not for that "tinkering with the currency" which subverts the natural order of things. To this extent we sincerely go with those who are declaiming against the government. We agree with them that the condition of affairs, as established by the laws of trade, is deranged by government interference, and that the *treasury orders*, which have the effect to cause a sudden dispersion of the public funds accumulated in this city, and to drain the specie from the vaults of our banks, sending it hither and thither, and for a time, entirely destroying its use, as a foundation of commercial credit, are the immediate cause of the prevailing distress. . . .

. . . .

But the first, great, and all important cause of the pecuniary distress lies much deeper than any which the opposition papers assign. It is neither the Treasury order in relation to the public lands, nor the Treasury orders on deposite banks. These last have, at the very worst, but precipitated an evil, which, had no such orders been issued, or no transfers in any way made, could by no possibility have been long averted. It would have come next winter, and with a pressure greatly augmented by the delay. It would have fallen, like an avalanche, at the very season when revulsion is more fatal, because then the largest amounts of payments are to be made. The distribution law takes effect in January, and had not the necessity of complying with the conditions of the supplementary bill given the present harsh, but salutary check to speculation, the amount of credit, now so prodigiously inflated, would have been still further extended, and the shock of a sudden explosion would have been far more fearful and disastrous.

Without the distribution bill, even, a dreadful commercial revulsion could not long have been avoided. We were rushing on madly at a rate which could not long be continued. The first obstacle must have thrown us from our course, and dashed us to pieces. Look at the present state of the country. When did it ever before present such a spectacle of prodigiously distended credit? When did such a fever of speculation madden the brains of whole communities? When did all sorts of commodities bear such enormous prices? And when, at the same time, was there ever such vast consumption—such prodigality, wastefulness, and unthinking profusion? Is the treasury order the cause of this? Alas, it is one of its remote consequences. What filled your treasury to such overflowing, that some cunning politician was prompted by a consideration of the exuberance to devise the scheme of distribution? Speculation. What excited that spirit of speculation? The sudden and enormous increase of bank capital, and the corresponding inflation of bank currency. In the last eighteen months alone *nearly one hundred millions of bank capital* have been added to the previous amount. Examine the following bank statistics, derived from sources believed to be accurate, and see how prodigiously and rapidly our system of bank credit has been swollen:

Aggregate capital of the Banks in the United States.

In the year 1811 the total amount was			$ 52,600,000
	1815		82,200,000
	1816		89,800,000
	1820		102,100,000
	1830		110,200,000
	1835		196,250,000
	1836 (August)		291,250,000
Increase in	*nine years* preceding	1820	$ 49,500,000
Do.	*ten years*	1830	8,100,000
Do.	*six years*	1836	181,050,000

Who can look at this statement, and not feel convinced that the cause of the present financial distress lies deeper than treasury orders, whether in relation to public lands or public deposites? This enormous increase of bank capital in the last six years has been accompanied by a corresponding expansion of bank issues, and by a commensurate extension of private credits. The business of the country has been stimulated into most unwholesome and fatal activity. Circumstances, unlooked for, have occurred to aggravate the epidemic frenzy. The government has obtained the payment of long delayed indemnities from foreign powers; and new formed corporations have contracted large loans abroad. These sums, added to the product of our staples, have been exhausted by the excessive importations. Domestic speculation—speculation in the products of home consumption, in land, in town lots, in houses, in stock enterprises, in every thing, has kept pace, step for step, with the inordinate increase of foreign trade. What is to pay all this vast accumulation of debt? It must come at last out of labour. It must come from the products of industry. We have been borrowing largely of the future, and have at last arrived at the point where we must pause, and wait for the farmer, the mechanic, and patient hewer of wood and drawer of water to relieve us from our difficulties.

Reader, take home to your bosom this truth, and ponder well upon it, it is the bank system of this country, our wretched, unequal, undemocratic system of special privileges, which occasions the difficulty we now begin to feel. It is not pretended that under the free trade system of credit, or under any system, commercial revulsions would not sometimes, and to some extent, take place. They are incident to the nature of man. Prosperity begets confidence; confidence leads to rashness; the example of one is imitated by another; and the delusion spreads until it is suddenly dissipated by some of those rude collisions, which are the unavoidable penalties of a violation of the laws of trade. But such fearful and fatal revulsions as mark the eras of the commercial history of this country, would not, could not, take place under a free trade system of banking.

It is when ignorant legislators pretend to define by law the limits of credit and shaking at one time with unnecessary trepidation refuse to enlarge them to the wants of trade, while at another they extend them far beyond all reasonable scope—it is when such "tamperers with the currency" attempt to control what is in its nature uncontrollable, and should be free as air, that revulsion, panic, and commercial prostration necessarily ensue. While we have restraining laws and specially chartered banks, we shall have periodical distress in the money market, more or less severe, as the period has been hastened or delayed by accidental causes. Party writers may at one time lay every disorder to the removal of the deposites, and at another to a treasury order; but whatever orders the Treasury may issue, the alternate inflations and contractions of the paper currency incident to such a pernicious system as ours will continue to produce their inevitable consequence, unwholesome activity of business, followed by prostration, sudden and disastrous.

. . . .

WHY IS FLOUR SO DEAR?

This question is in every body's mouth, and the following paragraph hints the answer which the writer seems to think will explain the difficulty:

> . . . Is it a scarcity of the article of flour in the market, which raises the price to ten dollars per barrel, at a moment when money is worth two per cent a month? Or have those who had the control of money facilities combined to buy up all the wheat at moderate prices, with the design of speculating by a monopoly of one of the necessaries of life? Mechanicks and others have been indicted for combining to raise the price of labour; and it might be well to inquire whether combinations to raise the price of wood, pork, flour, and other necessaries of life, beyond a fair profit, are not equally offences against society.

The foregoing is from the Albany Argus. The information it conveys in relation to the amount of the wheat crops is valuable. But the measure which it suggests for the purpose of reducing the price of flour is at utter variance with the principles of free trade, and with the natural rights of citizens. If mechanicks combine to raise the price of wages, they but hold forth an invitation to competition from beyond the sphere of combinations, and competition will soon arrange prices according to a just scale of equivalents. If merchants combine to raise the price of flour by purchasing all in the market, they but provoke competitors in foreign ports, whose rivalry will soon set matters right. The *laissez nous faire* maxim applies here as forcibly as in any other concern of trade. The true way is to leave trade to its own laws, as we leave water to the laws of nature; and both will be equally certain to find their proper level.

We already find that, incited by the high prices of bread

Plaindealer, December 3, 1836. Extract abridged.

stuffs here, foreign competitors are sending supplies across the ocean, and underselling our agriculturists at their own doors. Part of the cargo of the Bristol, which was wrecked at Rockaway a fortnight ago, was English wheat; and we notice in the accounts of importations in the newspapers that frequent mention is made of large quantities of foreign grain. Why is this? Why are prices so high in this country that the wheat growers of Europe can incur all the expenses of transportation, freight, insurance, commissions, and storage, and still undersell us in our own markets? Does the Argus really suppose that this result is brought about by a combination among the dealers in flour, "with the design of speculating by a monopoly of one of the necessaries of life?" The cause, let it rest assured, lies deeper than this. The monopoly is one of a worse character, of greater power, of more ruinous operation. Short crops may do something; combination may do something; but the high prices are mainly the result of the *monopoly of banking.* They are the natural and inevitable consequence of the wretched system which places the currency of the country completely under the control of a comparatively few specially privileged chartermongers, who avail themselves of the speculative disposition of the people to flood the country with a paper circulation, till the influx produces its natural effect of causing a vast depreciation of money, or appreciation of money prices, which is the same thing, and attracts competitors from all parts of the world to our market. These competitors do not take in payment, and carry away with them, the spurious currency which the monopoly banks have issued, but demand specie; and then comes the necessity of sudden retrenchment, followed by wide spread commercial distress. Prices then begin to fall; and at this point we are now arrived. Flour must soon go down, despite of all combinations, fancied or real; produce of all kinds must go down; rents must go down, and labour must go down; and all things must gradually adjust themselves to the retrenched state of the currency. When this period of depression is past, and the crops of the next year have paid up the deficit occasioned by over-trading during the present, the banks will begin to be *liberal* again, (munificent institutions!) and, urged on and stimulated by them, the people will act over again the same scenes of mad speculation, till the drama again concludes with a catastrophe of disastrous revulsion.

We should be glad if the Argus would turn its attention to the monopoly which is the true source of our high prices and all our financial difficulties. It will find that our exclusive bank system is the cause of the evil, and the repeal of the restraining law the only effectual remedy.

THOUGHTS ON THE CAUSES OF THE PRESENT DISCONTENTS

The title of this article is borrowed from Burke; and would that we could borrow, also, the power of cogent reasoning and affluence of eloquent expression which distinguished the writings of that strong and original thinker, for the theme we have to treat of is worthy of such qualities. That theme is the present financial difficulties, which press with intolerable weight upon the community, and force a murmur even from the sturdiest of those who have stood unmoved amidst all former revulsions. The pressure now, unlike that of 1834, is not purposely caused by the strategy of a gigantick monied institution, warring with the government of the country, and attempting to set itself up as a second estate, greater than the people. It is not caused by a withdrawal of mutual confidence between man and man, during the temporary influence of a

Plaindealer, December 10, 1837. Text abridged.

panick, created and fomented by the demagogues of a desperate party, for a political end. It is not caused by any failure in the sources of real national wealth; by a sudden falling off in the great staple commodities of the land; nor by any extraordinary or unlooked for vicissitudes in the affairs of the countries with which we carry on reciprocal commerce. What then is the cause of the suffering so keenly felt, and so loudly complained of at the present time? To this we answer, throwing all minor and inadequate circumstances out of view, that *the pernicious bank system of our country is the cause!* That is the fountain from which the stream of mischief issues, swelled, it is true, by unimportant tributaries, but there taking its rise, and thence deriving the chief volume of its waters. That is the source of the modern Phlegethon, whose burning tide sets those who drink it mad, and wastes the land through which it flows, making it a second Tartarus.

Any person who has soberly observed the course of events for the last three years, must have foreseen the very state of things which now exists. Any person who, from the present unhealthy and dangerous elevation to which the business affairs of the community have been pushed, will turn back his eyes in calm retrospection, must perceive that we impute the evil to its true origin. He will see that the banks, ever since the temporary revulsion of 1834, have been striving, with all their might, each emulating the other, to force their issues into circulation, and flood the land with their wretched substitute for money. He will see that they have used every art of cajolery and allurement to entice men to accept their proffered aid; that, in this way, they gradually excited a thirst for speculation, which they sedulously stimulated, until it increased to a delirious fever, and men, in the epidemick frenzy of the hour, wildly rushed upon all sorts of desperate adventures. They dug canals, where no commerce asked for the means of transportation; they opened roads, where no travellers desired to penetrate; and they built cities where there were none to inhabit, which now stand in their newness, like Palmyra in its ruins, untenanted and solitary, amidst a surrounding desert.

. . . .

What has been, what ever must be, the consequence of such a sudden and prodigious inflation of the currency? Business stimulated to the most unhealthy activity; a vast amount of over production in the mechanick arts; a vast amount of speculation in property of every kind and name, at fictitious values; and finally, a vast and terrifick crash, when the treacherous and unsubstantial basis crumbles beneath the stupendous fabrick of credit, and the structure falls to the ground, burying in its ruins thousands who exulted in the fancied security of their elevation. Men, now-a-days, go to bed deeming themselves rich, and wake in the morning to find themselves stripped of even the little they really had. They count, deluded creatures! on the continued liberality of the banks, whose persuasive entreaties seduced them into the slippery paths of speculation. But they have now to learn that the banks cannot help them if they would, and would not if they could. They were free enough to lend their aid when assistance was not needed; but now, when it is indispensable to carry out the projects which would not have been undertaken but for the temptations they held forth, no further resources can be supplied. The banks must take care of themselves. "Charity begins at home." The course of trade is turning against the country. We have purchased more commodities abroad than our products will pay for, and the balance will soon be called for in specie. The banks, which lately vied with one another in effusing their notes, are now as eager competitors in withdrawing them from circulation, and preparing for the anticipated shock. They have no time to listen to the prayers of the deluded men whom their deceitful lures seduced so far upon the treacherous sea of credit. They cast them adrift without remorse and leave them to encounter, unaided and unprepared, the fury of the gathering tempest. Or should, perchance, some tender hearted moneychanger relent, and consent to tow a few victims into harbour, is it unreasonable that he should charge wrecker's fees for the service—half the cargo and twenty per cent commissions on the remainder? The cashiers of some of our banks can tell you that these are but the usual rates.

It suited the purposes of party, a short time since, to lay all the difficulties of the money market to the account of certain orders of the Treasury Department, removing a portion of the government funds from one place of deposit to another. And it equally answered the purpose of another class of politicians to ascribe the evils to the necessary operation of the distribution law. But the election is now past, unduly to influence the result of which both these theories were maintained, and, by common consent, it is now tacitly admitted that neither fully accounts for the effect. Beyond all question, both had some share, and particularly the latter, in swelling the amount of embarrassment; but the great, abiding, all-sufficient causes lay deeper than these: the madness of speculation was the immediate one, the inflation of the currency the remote. A pernicious bank system had stimulated the nation into the wildest overtrading, and we now experience the necessary consequences of reaction. The vehement complaints against the banks, because they do not afford relief, which daily fill the columns of certain newspapers, are utterly absurd. The banks cannot help the community; they have enough to do to take care of themselves. They are fearfully potent in producing the mischief, but utterly impotent to remove it. They have a power of evil, but not of good. They administer the bane, but have no antidote. The same causes which occasion pecuniary distress among the merchants, equally affect the money changers, and in the same way. The banks are overtraders as well as the others, and both have to learn that there is but one relief for an overtrading nation, and it must wait for that to be applied by the slow hand of time. They who borrow from the future, and squander in extravagance what is thus acquired, must drudge slowly on in poverty until they acquit themselves of the debt. It is with a people, as with an individual: when the income of a year is lavished in a month, the costly robes and sumptuous table must be succeeded by such food and apparel as served the prodigal son in his reverse of fortune. An invariable law of mechanicks establishes that what is gained in speed is lost in power; and this is not less true in political economy. We have prematurely exhausted our vigour in too rapid a race, and must now pause to recruit our wasted strength.

It is curious, as well as melancholy, to look round, and note the evidences which everywhere meet the eye of that fever of speculation which, for two years past, has been the moral epidemick of the land. The fields, in many places, lie untilled, because the agricultural population has been drawn off to construct railroads and canals, or lay out sites for cities, and prepare the ground for superb edifices capable of accommodating millions *yet unborn!* Hence we find there are short crops of the main staples of home consumption. Hence we see flour at fifteen dollars a barrel, and hay at forty dollars a ton; and hence foreign agriculturists, the wheat growers of England, and of the very northernmost parts of Europe, are sending their grain to this country—the cultivators on the stormy coast of the Black Sea and the icy shores of the Dnieper send hither their produce, and undersell our farmers on the pleasant banks of the Hudson and the Potomack, at their very doors. During the long wars of Napoleon in Europe, we exported our breadstuffs, and supplied the opposing armies with food. Now we have a standing army at home to support, not of soldiers, but of canal diggers, city builders, and stock gamblers; while the plough stands idle in the unturned furrow, and crows fatten undisturbed in the deserted cornfields. The speculator flaunts by in his carriage, and casts a scrutinizing eye over the neglected farm, not to ascertain the capacities of its soil, but its eligibility as the site for some new scheme of a city, and the probable price it would yield, not by the acre, but by the foot.

The children at the wayside scarcely look up at the shining equipage as it dashes along, for shining equipages have become too common to attract the attention even of rusticks. A coach with footboard and hammercloth is no longer a novelty, when half a nation turn builders of carriages for the other half to ride in. But there is an old saying which foretells the destiny of a beggar on horseback, and we fear that there are many in this community now on the eve of experiencing its truth.

STRICTURES ON THE LATE MESSAGE

The limits into which we were crowded last week by the length of Governour Marcy's message, allowed us to speak of that document only in a brief paragraph, and in the most general terms. But as we felt called upon to speak of it with censure, it is proper that the grounds of our unfavourable opinion should be candidly stated to our readers.

The fault that we find with the message is that it is a timid, indecisive, commonplace document, following, in a cautious and craven spirit, in the path of publick opinion, and afraid to recommend strenuously even those measures which the publick voice has clearly and energetically demanded. The only exception to this remark is the passage concerning the usury laws, which we fancy must have been written while the author's mind was still glowing with indignation from the perusal of some able essay on the subject—Jeremy Bentham's Defence of Usury, perhaps—and sent to the legislature before he

Plaindealer, January 14, 1837. Text abridged and extract deleted.

had time to revise his opinion according to the suggestions of all those busy fears and scruples which commonly seem to exercise the authority of prime ministers in Governour Marcy's cabinet councils.

. . . .

The analogy which the message attempts to trace, between the power claimed and exercised by the General Government of coining money, and the power which it is asserted belongs to the state governments of interdicting the community (all but a favoured few) from issuing their own notes, has no existence, except in the brain of Governour Marcy.

. . . .

The restriction imposed by our federal government on the power of coining money, is much less extensive than is generally supposed; but to whatever extent it exists, it is no infringement of the principle of the equal rights of the citizen, if it is an infringement of the principles of free trade. In the most important view which can be taken of the subject, that of its political character and effect, it is entirely free from the fatal objection which lies against the power claimed for the state governments by Governour Marcy. The provisions of the federal constitution on the subject of coining, and the laws in accordance with them, were instituted for the common protection and convenience of the whole people equally, and give no peculiar facilities and advantages to a few at the expense of the many. In this vital respect the difference is fatal to Governour Marcy's supposed analogy.

But the power claimed by the General Government "to coin money, and regulate the value thereof," does not interdict the citizen from coining money also, but only the state governments. Any person may stamp pieces of metal with their name, weight, and quality, and pass them for what they are worth. Any person may make medals, of any form or device he pleases, and sell them, or barter them away, to the best advantage he can; and this is coining money.[1] He has no power of declaring that pieces of metal bearing a certain stamp shall be received as of a certain value; because this is an attribute of sovereignty which belongs to communities only in their political organization, and can only be exercised by the duly constituted political authorities. It cannot even be exercised by them, however careful in their adjustment of the size and quality of the coins to the general rate of metallick value, without continual arbitrariness and injustice; since silver and gold, to say nothing of copper, are commodities of continually fluctuating values, as much so in fact, though not in degree, as cotton or flour. The discovery of a new mine, or the invention of a labour saving machine, by suddenly increasing the quantity, diminishes the value; precisely in the same way that a favourable season operates on the wheat or cotton crop. A war in South America, or an epidemick disease or insurrection among the slaves employed in mining, by suddenly diminishing the quantity, increases the value; in the same way that a drought, or an exceedingly rainy season, influences the prices of cotton and grain. A government, therefore, which undertakes to say that a given number of grains of pure gold or silver shall always be received at a given value, is necessarily guilty of an arbitrary exercise of power; and we have our doubts, notwithstanding Governour Marcy affirms that this "has never been considered an invasion of a common right," whether it is not so in fact, and whether it would not be better to leave actual money, as well its paper representative, to leave *coining*, as well as *banking*, entirely to the laws of trade. But to consider this subject now would take us too far from our present object.

The reader will see, from what we have already said, that there is not the slightest validity in the pretended analogy which Governour Marcy has brought forward, and that, as he

[1] Leggett may have been aware of the private Bechtler mint in North Carolina, which coined several million dollars worth of Southern Appalachian gold between 1831 and 1850. Congress did not outlaw private coinage until 1864.—Ed.

rests the whole weight of his reasons for the restrictions he recommends on that analogy, they must necessarily fall to the ground. Any individual has a right to stamp his name, and his image too, if he pleases, on a piece of silver or gold, and exchange it for what it is intrinsically worth. In the same way we contend that he has a natural right to give his promise to pay a certain sum on a piece of paper, and, subscribing it with his name, to pass it for what those with whom he deals may be willing to receive it. If he stamps a figure on a piece of gold or silver counterfeiting that made use of on coins authorized or recognized by the government, he is guilty of forgery; and so he would be if he should write a promissory note, and sign it with the name of another person.

But if Governour Marcy's analogy is good for any thing, it is good in a much larger application than he intended. If the issuing of paper promises is, in fact, issuing a substitute for a metallick currency, and therefore forbidden by the restrictions of the Constitution of the United States against coining, the state governments, in authorizing the chartered banks to do this, violate the conditions of the federal compact, and our whole paper currency is destitute of the warrant of constitutional law.

The passage in Governour Marcy's message on the subject of banks betrays a degree of feebleness and indecision for which, we confess, after the almost unanimous expression of publick opinion, through the press and through the resolutions of popular assemblies, we were utterly unprepared. We did think that, thus backed and prompted, even Governour Marcy would have spoken out boldly. Yet all he has ventured to say is to refer the legislature to his equivocal and two-sided remarks in a former message, and to express a hope that they will charter no more banks this session. "If you should do so, however, gentlemen, perhaps it would be well to modify and improve the mode of distributing the stock." How ineffably contemptible! We trust in heaven, if the legislature should pass any more bank charters, that the cupidity and rapaciousness which alone will lead to such legislation may prevent them from making any change in the manner of apportioning stock. A few more such scenes of eager scrambling for the "spoils," and of venality and corruption in distributing them, as was represented when the stock of the State Bank was divided, will do more to promote true principles of legislation, than a thousand such *Bob Acre*[*s*][2] messages as that on which it has been our unpleasant duty to comment. We intended to touch some other points, but we sicken of the subject.

THE VALUE OF MONEY

One of the powers bestowed on the federal government by the Constitution is that of *regulating the value of money*. "Congress shall have power to coin money, *regulate the value thereof*, and of foreign coin," &c. Has any reader a clear conception of the meaning of this phrase? The meaning commonly attached to the word *value*, both by lexicographers and political economists, as well as by men generally, without reference to dictionaries or books of political economy, is the relation which one thing bears to another, as an exchangeable commodity. This is the so commonly received opinion, that it has been reduced to the form of one of those familiar rhymes, into which a large portion of the popular wisdom is condensed.

The worth of a thing
Is what it will bring.

[2] Bob Acres is a shallow-headed comic character in Richard Sheridan's play *The Rivals* (1775).—Ed.

Plaindealer, January 21, 1837.

The worth or value of a dollar, according to this definition, is fixed by the amount of exchangeable commodities which may be procured for it. Thus, if you can buy of a man a day's labour for a dollar, a day's labour is one measure of its value. If you can buy with it eight loaves of bread, those eight loaves of bread are another measure of its value. When the Constitution therefore declares that Congress shall have power to regulate the value of money, is it to be understood that it has the power to say how much labour, or how much bread, shall be given for a coin of silver or gold bearing a certain stamp? We cannot believe that it ever entered into the minds of the people of the United States, or of the framers of the Constitution, to bestow on government such an enormous and terrible power, which could not possibly be exercised, in any case, or to any degree, without the most inconceivable arbitrariness and injustice. Our Restraining Law, and the project of that more infamous law introduced into the Senate of this state by Mr. Maison, were both written with a pencil of light, compared with that clause in the Constitution, if it confers any such absolute and despotick power on Congress. The common sense of every reader will at once reject the idea, as too monstrously at variance with the natural and unalienable rights of man to be entertained for a moment.

What then does the expression, *regulate the value of money,* mean? If we draw our conclusion from what Congress has done on the subject of money, we shall suppose it means the power of regulating the relative exchangeable values of different coins, one with another; a gold coin, bearing a certain stamp, and containing a certain number of grains of pure gold, shall always be deemed to be worth, as a tender in payment of debts, as much as a certain number of silver coins, bearing a given stamp, and containing a given number of grains of pure silver. In other words, ten silver dollars shall at all times be equivalent to one gold eagle, and one gold eagle to ten silver dollars.

But even in this limited sense of the phrase "regulating the value of money," Congress cannot possibly exercise the power without being guilty of injustice, for gold and silver do not, in fact, bear any certain and unchangeable relative value. A grain of gold, considered merely as a merchantable commodity, will at one time purchase a greater quantity of silver than at another. Silver is sometimes relatively dearer than gold, and sometimes relatively cheaper; and Congress, therefore, when it gives to the debtor his option as to which he will make payment in, by any invariable standard of relative value, gives him the power of defrauding his creditor. The errour is the same in principle, though not as extensively injurious to the community as if they should exercise, in its fullest latitude, the power conferred by the terms of the Constitution, and declare how much of every mentionable commodity should be exchangeable for a given number of coined grains of silver or gold. Congress, it seems to us, would best discharge its power "to coin money and fix the value thereof," by simply establishing, for the convenience of traffick, and the deciding of disputes, a unit of value; in other words, by simply declaring that a certain number of grains of pure silver should constitute the dollar; and leave all other divisions and ramifications of currency to adjust themselves by that standard. We threw out a brief hint on this subject in our last number; and have been induced to make these further observations by having our attention drawn to it by a correspondent, whose note we here subjoin:

> MR. PLAINDEALER: I have been an attentive reader of your paper since it first had existence, and I freely confess that I have been much edified in the perusal of your articles on free trade, as applicable to banking, &c. But in your last number, the views you express on coining, strike me as being decidedly bad. What benefit could possibly accrue to the community, were every man to manufacture his own money, after his own capricious ideas? Without some standard to regulate the matter, we would have a currency composed of gold, silver, brass, lead, iron, and, in fact, of every thing under heaven, of the value of which no two people

could be found to agree, and which would give rise to interminable disputes. As well might you recommend that instead of adhering to plain English, in their converse with each other, men should use unintelligible sounds to express their meaning; and certainly to me the one plan appears as feasible as the other.

But, sir, I remain open to conviction, and if you think this worth replying to, I should be pleased to hear your views at length on the subject.

Our correspondent shall hear our views at length on the subject; but not now. Our columns are preoccupied, and besides, this is a topick which does not require instant pressing. It is enough for present purposes to suggest it as theme for reflection; and we shall be mistaken if the result of meditation be not to convince many an intelligent mind that the free trade principle is susceptible of a far more extended application than they had perhaps dreamed before.

The analogous case which our correspondent has furnished us is very appropriate, but he must excuse us if we choose to consider it an analogism sustaining our views rather than his own. The laws of language are not established by Congress or any other body of delegated powers. Words, it is true, are sometimes *coined* by Congress, but they do not pass very current, and are generally soon rejected by common consent. What is it then sustains the language in its purity, fixes the meaning of words, and enables us to give to expression a precise and unchangeable import? Every man is at full liberty to be as unintelligible as he pleases. He may reject alike the authority of Johnson and Webster, and fabricate a new language for himself. What restrains him from doing so? The necessities of social intercourse: the mutual advantage which all men find in promoting the general convenience. The necessities of commercial intercourse, and the mutual advantage which all men would find in promoting the general convenience in matters of traffick, would lead, we think, to as certain and desirable results in regard to money, as in regard to language.

If the laws of trade are adequate to the perfect regulation of the matter, no one, we think, certainly no one animated by the genuine principles of democracy, will hesitate to acknowledge that it were better to deny the right of regulating it to the government. Whatever unnecessarily strengthens government, weakens the people; and whatever tends to narrow the powers of government to the execution of the fewest and simplest functions, increases, in the same degree, the strength and dignity of the people.

THE WAY TO CHEAPEN FLOUR

Our paper contains, under the appropriate head, an account of the daring and causeless outrage which disgraced our city last Monday evening. There never was a riot, in any place, on any previous occasion, for which there existed less pretence. There is no circumstance to extenuate it, in any of the aspects in which it can be viewed. The only alleged excuse is the high price of flour, and a suspicion which it seems was entertained, that the price was in part occasioned by a combination among the dealers. But this suspicion has not only no foundation in fact, but if it were well founded, if it were an established truth too notorious for contradiction, it would afford no sort of justification or shadow of excuse to any portion of the community to commit acts of violence, and much less to that portion which was chiefly concerned in this disgraceful tumult.

The chief actors in the riot of Monday evening were, beyond question, members of some of the numerous associations of artisans and labourers affiliated under the general name of the *Trades Union*. What, let us ask, is the very first and car-

Plaindealer, February 18, 1837. Text abridged.

dinal object of the Trades Union? To enable *labour,* by the means of combination, and of extensive mutual countenance and co-operation, to command its own price. And is not *labour* as much a necessary of life as *flour?* Is it not, in fact, more indispensable? Is it not the chief, the prime, the very first necessary of man, in his social organization? What would this city do for a week, nay, for a single day, if *labour,* in all its varieties of form and application, should wholly and obstinately refuse to perform its offices? It does not require any great fertility of imagination to picture the social anarchy, the chaotic confusion, into which the whole frame of things would be thrown. Yet it is to enable it, on occasion, to do this, or, as the only alternative, to compel *capital* to pay whatever price it chooses to exact, that the combination of different mechanic and operative crafts and callings has been formed. And these very people, thus combining to create, in effect, a monopoly of the chief necessary of life, are so enraged by the mere suspicion that the dealers in flour—a commodity for which there are many substitutes, and not indispensable if there were none—have followed their example that they assault the doors and windows of their storehouses with stones, crowbars, and levers, break down all barriers, scatter their property to the winds, and even tear, into irrevocable fragments, their most valuable books and accounts!

. . . .

With regard to the question of combination we wish to be distinctly understood. If the dealers of flour had combined to monopolize the article, and to fix a high price upon it, we would hold them answerable for their conduct neither to the civil law nor to mob law, but to the inevitable penalties of a violation of the laws of trade. In the same way, when labourers combine to fix the price of labour, we would hold them responsible only to those natural and immutable principles of trade which will infallibly teach them their error, if they do not graduate the price according to the relations of demand and supply. We are for leaving trade free; and the right to combine is an indispensable attribute of its freedom.

That the price of flour is not the result of combination, but of causes which lie much deeper, we fully believe. One of those causes is a deficient crop; but the chief cause of the enhancement in price, not of that article alone, but of every variety of commodity, is the vast inflation which the paper currency has undergone in the last two years. It is not that exchangeable commodities have risen in value, but money, or that substitute for money which the specially privileged banks issue, has depreciated. The fluctuations in the currency must necessarily occasion equal fluctuations in money prices; and these fluctuations must necessarily be exceedingly oppressive to many, since all commodities do not instantly rise and fall in exact relative proportion, but require, some a longer, and some a shorter time, to be adjusted to new standards. The clergyman and the accountant on stated salaries, the tradesman who sells his articles according to a price fixed by ancient custom, and very many others, cannot immediately increase their demands as the price of other things increase; and such are affected most injuriously by the continual augmentation of paper money, resulting from the incorporation, every year, of whole herds of specially privileged bankers.

The true way to make flour cheap, and beef cheap, and all the necessaries of life cheap, is, not to attack the dealers in those articles, and strew their commodities in the streets, but to exercise, through the ballot boxes, the legitimate influence which every citizen possesses to put an end, at once and forever, to a system of moneyed monopolies, which impoverish the poor to enrich the rich; which, building up a class of lordly aristocrats on the one hand, and degrading the mass into wretched serfs on the other; and which has already exercised a vast and most pernicious influence in demoralizing both the educated and the ignorant classes of society—both those who fatten on the spoils of the paper-predatory system, and those from whose very blood the spoils are wrung.

THE MONEY MARKET AND NICHOLAS BIDDLE

The money-market has been in a violent ferment during the past week. Meetings of the merchants, "protracted meetings," and frequent informal conferences have been held. The result of the whole matter has been an application to the Philadelphia Money Autocrat, Nicholas Biddle,[1] for his gracious and merciful interposition. "Drowning men catch at straws," and a mere *man of straw* has the bank potentate proved himself to be on this occasion. His worshippers, however, reverence him as possessing the attributes of potentiality, and their homage is as fervent as that of a race of croakers of old to King Log. . . .[2]

. . . .

Either Nicholas Biddle has the prodigious money power which the merchants ascribe to him, or he has not. If he has in truth the power of relieving the financial distresses of the times, then the ground of the last administration for opposing the renewal of the charter of such a potential institution, which holds the destinies of the Confederacy in the hollow of its hand, and which can create plenty or scarcity, prosperity or ruin, at the volition of a single mind, is shown to have been correct. If he has not this power, what a wretched farce is now played off before the community. But the merchants obviously believe in his potentiality, and thus, so far as they are concerned, acknowledge the validity of General Jackson's

Plaindealer, April 1, 1837. Title added. Text abridged and extract deleted.

[1] President of the Second Bank of the United States, at the date of this editorial operating under a charter from the state of Pennsylvania.—Ed.

[2] An allusion to the fable of the frogs desiring a king, to whom Jupiter sent down a log of wood.—Ed.

original and chief position. Yet they opposed him for assuming it. This, then, shows that their temporary pecuniary interest outweighs with them the eternal political interests of their country. What a commentary on the patriotism of the desk and the ledger!

But are the proposed measures[3] truly measures of relief, or are they only calculated to arrest, for a brief space, the descending blow, to fall at last with accelerated force and augmented weight, not on the heads now justly exposed to the shock, but on the heads of those who, not having been participants in the enormities of mad speculation, have not merited its terrible consequences? The latter clause of this alternative question, it seems to us, must be answered in the affirmative.

What has produced the evil state of things under which the community now groans? A too wide extension of credit, far surpassing the demands of healthy and legitimate business, and diffusing itself to all sorts of chimerical enterprizes. The legitimate business of a country is measured by the amount of its exportation and the domestick consumption of its own products. When it exceeds this limit it becomes unhealthy speculation, certain to terminate, sooner or later, in revulsion and ruin; as the machine, driven beyond the rate of speed fixed by the laws of its mechanism, is sure to be thrown out of repair, if not broken all to pieces. That this is the case with our community is a position too self-evident to require argument. The plan of relief, as it is called, which is now proposed, is a mere plan to put off the day of payment of the immensely over-inflated amount of debt. But the means of procras[tina]tion are of the most expensive kind. Those who are to receive the benefit of the extension of credit, will be obliged, in the nature of things, to pay prodigious rates of interest for the present funds they realize, and the day of ultimate payment will find them less able to meet their obligations than they are now. Those whose imaginary wealth

[3] A reference to Biddle's offer to rediscount bills held by the New York banks—Ed.

consists in houses and lands held at a nominal value far exceeding their intrinsick worth, will not suffer the bubble which they have so long fancied actual substance, to burst into empty air, as long as they can keep up the sparkling nothing by forced loans, procured at any rate of extortion. Neither will they retrench their luxurious style of expenditure, assumed in the confidence of sudden wealth. The shock which is thus deferred will thus fall at last with accumulated force. But in the meanwhile one set of creditors will be substituted for another. The banks, which, if the crisis were now to take place, would sustain their share, or *a* share, of the loss, will, in the interval of prolonged credit, take good care to entrench themselves behind triple securities. The foreign creditors, in extending indulgence, will be equally on the alert to secure ultimate payment; and the blow will finally fall on the mechanick and labourer, on thousands of general creditors, who, if men were now suffered to experience the natural consequences of their rashness and folly of speculation, would come in for an equal portion of indemnity.

It is our s[i]ncere conviction that the proposed measure of procrastination, and any measure of procrastination, can be followed only by an increase of ultimate evil. That evil may be spread over a wider surface, but it will not be diminished in amount. The old saying, that *the hair of the dog is a cure for his bite,* will be found as false in its present, as in its more usual application. It is seldom the same thing possesses utterly opposite qualities. There is a new theory in medicine which administers as a remedy that which caused the disease. The merchants and Mr. Biddle are now for applying this theory to business. An excessive inflation of bank credit caused the evil; and they now propose a still further inflation as the cure. The traveller who warmed his frozen hands with his breath in the cave of the Satyr, and afterwards blew in his porridge for an opposite purpose, excited the admiration of his host. We shall not less admire the miraculous qualities of Nicholas Biddle if the breath of his nostrils can produce such contrary results.

The frog, in the fable, when he was blown up to unnatural dimensions, finding himself in pain, asked to be still further distended; but he was destroyed, not relieved, by the experiment. When the rain for forty days and forty nights covered the earth with a deluge, it was not a continuation of the storm that caused the waters to subside. We doubt if the community can be rescued from the dreadful consequences of a deluge of bank credit, by a further effusion from the fountain of evil.

THE PRESSURE—THE CAUSE OF IT —AND THE REMEDY

These three phrases embrace the only topick which now has interest for the publick mind. Amidst the desolation of the financial tempest raging on every side, men regard nothing but the ruin it is spreading through the land, and think of nothing but staying its progress, or escaping from its wrath. Consternation is painted on every face, and anxiety throbs in every heart. "What shall we do to be saved?" is the question that falters on myriads of lips; while the incoherent and contradictory statements of those who attempt to reply show how feeble are the struggles of reason in minds paralyzed with fear.

It is one of the inevitable consequences of popular institutions, that no subject of general interest can arise, which publick writers will not endeavour to turn to the uses of party. It would be strange, indeed, if wide spread pecuniary embarrassment should constitute an exception to the remark; since, while it obviously furnishes a prolifick theme of criminatory declamation, but few persons, are sufficiently acquainted with

Plaindealer, April 29, 1837. Text abridged and extracts deleted.

the principles of commerce to detect the real cause of derangement, and ascertain what secret spring has interrupted the revolutions of the stupendous machine, and thrown its vast complication of wheels and levers into disorder. While trade is in prosperous operation, it seems governed by laws as fixed and harmonious and to most minds as inscrutable, as those of the universe. Each link in the mighty chain, each part of the prodigious whole, performs its allotted office, and contributes to the grand result—the improvement of the physical and intellectual condition of mankind. But when derangement takes place, when any thing occurs to interrupt the harmonious movement, such are the mutual relation and dependence of the various parts, that the inquirer is bewildered in his attempts to investigate the cause of the confusion, and is ready to listen to any explanation that fixes the blame of the disaster on those whom he had previously regarded with dislike.

That party writers should take advantage of the present commercial embarrassments to impute censure to those of opposite politicks is therefore not surprising; nor need we be surprised that the wildest of their theories are listened to with credulity by some. Those who impute all the disorders of the community to the operation of that order of the General Government which requires that gold and silver only shall be received in payment for publick lands, find themselves followed notwithstanding the monstrous absurdity of their creed, by a numerous class of disciples; while they, on the other hand, who charge the calamity solely to the distribution of the federal revenue, have also their followers who give full faith to the explanation. Our own opinion has been so frequently expressed, both in this journal and elsewhere, and not only since the embarrassments commenced, but long before the activity of commerce received its first check, that it would be idle to repeat it now. Overtrading has been the cause; and the multiplication of specially chartered banks, with the prodigious amount of paper currency issued by them, has been the main cause of the extravagant spirit of traffick and speculation which the whole people have displayed. One branch of this extensive credit business, carried on entirely through the assistance of the false capital of these paper money institutions, is ably exposed in the annexed article from the *Journal of Commerce* of Wednesday morning.[1]

. . . .

There is another branch of enormous overtrading, the data in relation to which are precise and certain. We allude to the speculations in the publick lands—lands yet lying in a state of nature, over many of which the foot of the white man has hardly ever trod, and which, in the ordinary course of events will remain untrodden for years. The speculators have far outrun the tardy operations of nature. If men had the fecundity of fishes, it would yet take a long time for population to increase sufficiently to realize their projects. Their cities, towns, villages and watering places, are yet in the same condition with the cotton on which the New Orleans bank and cotton monopolists have advanced their two hundred millions of paper credit. The seed of the cotton is not yet planted, and the very building materials of those cities and towns are yet to be sought in the quarry, the clay-pit and the forest. But in the meanwhile all engaged in these speculations—in this enormous overtrading—have been living as if their wildest plans had been realized. Bank credit has supplied them with the means of present luxury, and they have not scrupled to use it at the most lavish rate. Much of the real profits of the country have gone to the vintners and lace workers of France. People have worn out in costly clothes, and drank up in costly wines, the products of labour.

But we are tired of contemplating this side of the picture. Let us turn to consider in what manner the evil can be reme-

[1] This extract, and another following it, described speculations in cotton financed by bank credits—Ed.

died. There are those who eagerly avail themselves of the present condition of affairs to demand the reinstitution of a federal bank. But, to say nothing of constitutional objections, and nothing of the political evils to be apprehended from such an institution, has a federal bank ever prevented commercial revulsion? Let the history of 1819, 1825 and 1834 answer the question. As for remedy, there is but one—a steady exercise of industry and frugality. The remedy for a whole community in bankrupt circumstances, is precisely the same as for a single individual. When a man contracts debts to a larger sum than the amount of his earnings, he can pay the balance against him only by increased industry and economy. But the means of avoiding a recurrence of the evils now experienced is as important a subject of consideration, as the means of remedying them. In our judgement, they are exceedingly simple. Perfect freedom of trade presents an effectual safeguard against commercial revulsion, and all the thousand horrours which speculation, stimulated to madness by the intoxicating cup of bank credit, inflicts upon the community. Do you want a banking institution to regulate the currency and exchanges? Freedom of trade will supply you with one. It will supply you with all the facilities of trade which a federal bank could supply, and will be free from all the political objections which rest against such an institution. If the restraints on trade in money and credit which exist in this state alone, were repealed to-day, a voluntary banking association would be formed to-morrow, with an aggregation of capital sufficient for all the mercantile purposes of the community. The liability to boundless competition would lead it to place the most unquestionable security for its issues before the publick. The natural rivalry of trade would cause it to return the notes of other institutions for specie, whenever they accumulated beyond a certain point, and this would prevent overissues. We should have a vast banking institution, in effect monopolizing, to a great extent, the financial business of the country, but without anything odious or oppressive in the character of the monopoly, since it would be hedged round by no special enactments, would be open to universal competition, and would depend for its success, and the continuation of its advantages, on the correctness with which it conducted its affairs. It would partake of the character of a monopoly, simply because of the extent of its real capital; and only in the same way that large capitalists, in all branches of business, monopolize, in proportion to the amount of their means, and the intelligence and activity with which they are employed, the peculiar traffick in which they are engaged. Such an institution, subject to the rivalry of jealous, vigilant, and active competitors, would be the immediate offspring of free trade. We see that all attempts to regulate credit and currency by political intermeddling, both in this country and in Europe, have signally failed. We see that in Scotland, where the business of banking is left as free from legislative interference as the business of boot-making, no revulsions, no panicks, no general bankruptcies, have ever taken place. What obliquity of vision is it then that hinders us from perceiving, that the course which wisdom points out for us is to emancipate commerce and finance from legislative thraldom, and leave them to manage their own affairs, subject only to their own irrevocable and immutable laws?

CONNEXION OF STATE WITH BANKING

A paragraph from a recent number of this paper, under the head of *Political Meddling with Finance*, is copied by the *Richmond Whig*, and commented upon as a concession that the

Plaindealer, May 6, 1837. Text and extract abridged.

"experiment" of the last administration, with regard to the currency, has failed. That journal holds the following language:

"The following article from the *Plaindealer*, the ablest and most honest Van Buren paper with which we are acquainted, makes the important concession that the great '*Experiment*' of the *hero* has failed. . . ."

. . . .

. . . This is not a Van Buren paper. The great purpose of our journal is to advance the cause of political truth. We do not adopt, as our maxim, the stale and deceptive cant of *principia non homines*, which is usually the motto of those whose purposes are utterly selfish and base. We contend for men, as well as principles; but for the former as the means, and the latter as the object. For this reason, we are friendly to Mr. Van Buren, considering him as the instrument chosen by the democracy of the country to carry into effect democratic principles in the administration of the federal government. So far as he is true to that great trust, he shall assuredly have our zealous support; but we shall support him in no deviation, however slight, from the straight and obvious path of democratic duty, and should he, in any instance, stray widely from it, he will assuredly encounter our decided opposition. Of this we have already given an earnest, in our condemnation of the strange and startling avowal with which he commenced his executive career—his precedaneous exercise of the veto power.[1] It is an unwarrantable use of political metonymy, then, to call the *Plaindealer* a Van Buren journal. It is a democratic journal, and is ambitious of no higher name.

With regard to the imputed concession made by this paper, we only ask that our language should not be strained to larger uses than its obvious purport justifies. We do not consider that

[1] See "Commencement of the Administration of Martin Van Buren" below, p. 221.—Ed.

the "*experiment*" has failed, if by that party catchword is meant the measures of the last administration in regard to the United States Bank. We approved then, and approve now, the veto of the bill to recharter that institution. We approved then, and approve now, the removal of the federal revenues from its custody. And we should consider the reinstitution of a bank, in the popular sense of that word, by the federal authority, as one of the very worst evils which could befall our country. What we disapprove now, and what we have always disapproved, is that the government should connect itself, in any way, or to any extent, with the business of banking. When it removed its money from the federal bank, it should not have deposited it with the banks which exist under state authority. It should have stood wholly aloof from such institutions. The only legitimate use which it has for its funds is, in our view, to pay its necessary expenses; and the only legitimate keeper of them in the meanwhile is itself. The treasures of the United States are raised by taxation, in specified modes, for the purpose of paying the debts and providing for the common defence and general welfare of the country. The Constitution recognizes nothing as money but gold and silver coin; and the government should therefore receive its revenues in nothing else. It recognizes, in strictness, nothing as an object to which those revenues are to be applied but the necessary expenses incurred in conducting the general political affairs of the Confederacy. The safe keeping of the money, then, is the only object to be effected, between the collection and the disbursement of it. For this purpose the government is itself fully competent. It has but to establish a place of deposit, under proper guardians, in the commercial focus of the country, and pay the various branches of public service with checks or drafts on that depositary. It has, properly, nothing to do with the exchanges of the country. They are an affair of trade, which should be left to the laws of trade. It has, properly, nothing to do with the currency, which is also an affair of trade, and perfectly within the competency of its own natural laws to govern. Let the government confine itself to its plain and obvious political duties. Let it have nothing to do with a "credit system." Let it connect itself neither with corporations nor individuals. Let it keep its own money, taking care that it is *money*, and not *promises;* and let it leave it to unfettered sagacity and enterprise to devise and carry into effect whatever system of exchange and credit may be found most advantageous to the commercial interests of society.

The first objection which will probably suggest itself to these views is, that they contemplate the keeping of a vast fund of the precious metals hoarded up from use, which might be profitably employed as the basis of commercial credit. But it is not necessary that the fund should be vast, and, on the contrary, it is admitted by politicians both of the democratic and aristocratic sects, the former on general political principle, and the latter from aversion to the dominant party, or distrust of its integrity, that the revenue should be adjusted to the scale of expenditure. The keeping of the surplus safely locked up in the shape of money, would afford an additional motive to both parties to increase their efforts to reduce the revenue to the minimum amount. Again, as to this money being susceptible of being usefully employed as a basis of credit. Credit to whom? The government does not need it; for it has no business to transact on credit. The people collectively do not need it; for it is as much a part of the substantial wealth of the country under the lock and key of the federal treasury, as it would be under that of any bank or individual. And no bank or individual needs it; for the credit of every bank and of every person is sufficiently extended when it covers the basis of their own real wealth. If extended beyond this, on the basis of a loan or deposit from the government, it is obvious such bank or individual would be deriving an advantage by jeoparding the money of the government; that is, of the people; that is, the rights of the many would be endangered for the benefit of the few.

Another objection to our theory may be urged, that if the

government gathered its revenue for safe keeping at any one point, its checks on that fund, in some quarters where payments would be necessary would be below par, and the receiver of them would thus be defrauded of a portion of his dues. This would not be so, in fact, in any part of our country, if the commercial focus of the Confederacy were selected as the place for the federal depositary. Should it happen, however, in relation to any branch of the public service, say, for example, some military outpost, the government would but be under the necessity of transporting the requisite amount of funds to such outposts; and the cost of doing so would be as much the legitimate expense to be defrayed out of the general fund, as any other expense incurred in the conducting of our political affairs. The same remark will hold good of the cost of conveying the revenues from the various points where collected, to the place of general deposit.

These are, in brief, our views as to the duty of the federal government, in regard to the collection and disbursement of its revenues. The great object which we desire to see accomplished, and to the accomplishment of which, we think, the course of things is obviously tending, is the utter and complete divorcement of politics from the business of banking. We desire to see banking divorced not only from federal legislation, but from state legislation. Nothing but evil, either in this country or others, has arisen from their union. The regulation of the currency, and the regulation of credit, are both affairs of trade. Men want no laws on the subject, except for the punishment of frauds. They want no laws except such as are necessary for the protection of their equal rights. If the government deposites its money with a corporation, a voluntary association, or an individual, it does so either on the condition of some return being rendered, or none. If none, an advantage, which is the property of the whole people, is given to one or a few, in manifest violation of the people's equal rights. If it receives a return, that return is either an equivalent or not. But no corporation, association, or individual would render an exact equivalent, since only the profit of the trust would present a motive for assuming it. If the return is not an equivalent, it is still manifest that one or a few are benefited at the expense of the many.

We are no enemy to banking. It is a highly useful branch of trade. It is capable of accomplishing many important results, the advantages of which, without legislative control or impediment, would naturally diffuse themselves over the whole surface of society. Banking is an important wheel in the great machine of commerce; and commerce, not confining the word to merchants, who are mere intermediaries and factors, but using it to express the stupendous aggregate of that vast reciprocal intercourse which embraces alike the products of agriculture and art, science and literature—commerce is the efficient instrument of civilization and promoter of all that improves and elevates mankind. We cannot therefore be an enemy of any essential part in so beneficent a whole. Our hostility is not directed against banking, but against that legislative intermeddling, by which it is withdrawn from the harmonious operation of its own laws, and subjected to laws imposed by ignorance, selfishness, ambition and rapacity.

The "experiment" of the last administration, so far as it was an experiment intended to separate the government from connexion with banks, and to bring about the repudiation of every thing but real money in its dealings with the citizens, has our warmest approbation. The specie circular, for the same reason, is an "experiment" which we wholly approved, and Mr. Van Buren has strengthened our good opinion of him by his firmness in adhering to that measure, against the clamour of which it has been made a prolific theme. Glad should we be, if a law, of a tenor corresponding with that order, were enacted in relation to the payments at the customs. We should be rejoiced if the federal government should set so noble an example to the monopoly-loving legislatures of the states, and teach them that the money of the Constitution is the only money which should be known to the laws. They who ascribe the present embarrassments of trade to the "experiments" of Andrew Jackson are not wholly in the wrong. Much of the present evil, we do not question, might have been avoided, had the United States Bank been quietly re-chartered, without opposition, and without curtailment of its powers. It would then have had no motive for its alternate contractions and expansions, beyond the mere desire of pecuniary gain, unless, indeed, it had chosen to play the part of "king-maker," and dictate to the people whom they should elect to fill their chief political trusts. But not being quietly re-chartered, it undertook to coerce the administration to do what it was not disposed to do of its own free will, and hence was tried, in the first place, the efficacy of a sudden pressure, and afterwards of a sudden expansion. It was this course which gave the original impulse to the spirit of wild speculation, and led to the creation of such a large number of banking institutions by the several states. The result, probably, was not wholly unforeseen by the late President, when he refused his signature to the act renewing the charter of the United States Bank. The path of duty, however, lay plain before him; and to turn aside from it would have been as inexcusable, as would be the conduct of that judge who should pardon an atrocious criminal from the fear that, if executed, his confederates might embrace the occasion to excite a tumult, and throw the community into temporary disorder. The course of justice ought not to be stayed by such a consideration in the one case more than in the other.

If the community desire a banking institution, capable of regulating the currency and the exchanges, and possessed of all the power for good which distinguished the United States Bank, without that enormous power of evil by which it was more distinguished, let them, through the ballot-boxes, insist on the abolition of all restraints on the freedom of trade. Enterprise and competition, if they were free to act, would soon build up a better bank than it is in the power of Congress to create, putting out of sight the constitutional objection; and they would regulate its issues, ensure its solvency, and confine it within the proper field of bank operations, far more effectually than could the most cunningly devised checks and conditions which legislative wisdom ever framed. This is the great "experiment" which has yet to be tried; and it requires no spirit of prophecy to foresee that one of the great dividing questions of politics for some years to come will resolve itself into a demand, on the one hand, for a federal bank, and, on the other, for the total separation of bank and state. We have provided with great care against the union of politics and religion; but in our judgment a hierarchical mixture in our government is not more to be deprecated than an alliance between legislation and banking. *Church and State*, has an evil sound; but *Bank and State* grates more harshly on our ears.

THE CRISIS

"Laissez nous faire."

The community is now experiencing a beautiful illustration of the excellence of the monopoly system. All the banks in this city suspended payment on Wednesday last, and it is to be presumed the example will be followed far and wide. Here, then, is an end of the safety fund bubble, the best system of banks and currency ever devised by human ingenuity, if we may believe the *Albany Argus*, and its followers of the monopoly school, and one of the worst that ever fraud imposed upon credulity, if we will but examine it by the lights of wisdom and experience.

We say here is an end of the safety fund bubble; but this

Plaindealer, May 13, 1837.

position is conditional on the people's asserting their equal rights, and demanding the absolute divorcement of legislation from the business of banking, and from all supervisory connection with trade and credit, further than the mere enforcement of the obligations of contracts, and the punishment of frauds. If the present condition of things does not impel them to do this, they are sunk in a depth of fatuity beyond all hope of redemption. It is as palpable to the mind, as the universal light of day to the senses, that the present anarchical and chaotic condition of financial affairs is the result, the direct and inevitable result, of the unholy alliance between politics and banking. The union of bank and state in this country is crushing the people under the weight of a despotism as grievous as was ever imposed upon mankind by the union of church and state. Better, far better, to be under the dominion of a hierarchy, than under the galling and ignoble rule of legislation money-changers.

What a world of wisdom there is in the brief phrase we have placed as a motto to this article! Society, recovering from the delirium excited by the stimulus of special legislation, begins to see that true wisdom consists, not in regulating trade by a system of artificial checks and balances, perpetually liable to be thrown into disorder, which the very complication of the contrivance then renders almost irremediable, but simply *in letting trade alone.* There are abundant indications around us that we shall not long stand unaided in the views we have frequently expressed of the utter folly and inevitable evil of all legislative intermeddling with the natural laws of trade. Banking is a good thing enough in its intrinsic nature; but government should have no connection with it, and should recognize nothing as money but silver and gold.

We are not an enemy to a paper representative of money, any more than we are to confidence between man and man in any other shape it may naturally assume, for mutual convenience, in the transaction of necessary dealings. We are not an enemy to banking, any more than we are to any other branch of traffic instrumental in carrying on the great commercial intercourse of society. We are an enemy only to a mixture of politics with banking; to the vain attempts to regulate the channels in which trade shall run; to that legislative intermeddling which withdraws credit from the harmonious operation of its own laws, disturbs its equal flow, and leaves the community to be at one time deluged with a cataclysm of paper money, and at another exposed to all the horrors of financial drought.

It would be a happy thing for this country, if the doubtful power under which banks are created had been positively withheld. It would be a happy thing if all right of interference with trade, either by immunities or prohibitions, by restraining laws or special charters, had been solemnly interdicted. More misery, more immorality, more degradation of the many for the undue elevation of the few, than can even be conjectured, have resulted from the vain attempts to regulate the currency. Let commerce, and let the currency, which is but an appendage and accident of commerce, regulate themselves; and let the government confine its attention strictly to the purposes which constitute the sole legitimate ends of political organization, the mere protection of person and property. We should then soon present to the world the spectacle of a people more free, more equally prosperous, and more happy, than has ever yet furnished a subject to the historian. The history of the past is but a Newgate Calender[1] on an extensive scale; the history of the future would be a work of a sublimer-character.

In the midst of the financial desolation which has been brought upon us by the inevitable operation of monopoly legislation—by the wretched charlatanry which seeks to prop up an artificial system of credit with special statutes, and hedge it round with penalties and prohibitions—the community has an ample opportunity to contemplate the con-

[1] A four-volume biographical record of the more notorious criminals confined at London's Newgate Prison, published 1824–28.—Ed.

sequences of that folly which would substitute the laws of man for those of nature, and wholly change the irreversible order of causes and effects. Can any man who has eyes to see, or ears to hear, or understanding to conceive, survey the deplorable wrecks of commerce and credit strewn on every side, the broken columns and arches of the great fabric of trade, or listen to the groans of an agonized community lying prostrate beneath the ruins, without the conviction rushing into his mind, that the melancholy result must be ascribed to those, who, clothed in brief legislative authority, interpose their fantastic expedients in place of that natural system which constitutes the eternal fitness of things. Each fragment of our shattered commerce bears, stamped in characters which he who runs may read, the forceful inscription—"THIS IS THE FRUIT OF MONOPOLY LEGISLATION."

We were forewarned, timely forewarned, and by one whose counsel we had reason to respect, of the embarrassments in which special legislation would involve us. The messages of Andrew Jackson are replete with lessons of admonitory wisdom. But the passion of avarice had seized upon our hearts, and the desire of sudden riches outweighed the suggestions of reason. We behold now the consequences of our infatuation. We are now admonished by that sternest of teachers, experience. But the lesson, though rude, will lead only to good, if we have the sense to pause, and read it aright.

The banks are broken, and, without legislative intervention, will soon forfeit their charters. We have been sorrowfully taught the miserable impotence of legislation; it is the fountain from which the waters of bitterness have flowed; let us not then again unseal it, that it may effuse another desolating flood. What can legislation do? Insult the community, by confirming the special privileges of money changers, after their own acts have declared their utter worthlessness? Enable a band of paper-money depredators to prey more voraciously than before on the vitals of the people? Authorize them to pour out a fresh torrent of their promises, now really of no more value than the paper on which they are writ? Will the community tolerate such an enormous fraud?

Let the Banks perish! Let the monopolists be swept from the board! Let the whole brood of privileged money-changers give place to the hardy offsprings of commercial freedom, who ask for no protection but equal laws, and no exemption from the shocks of boundless competition. We commisserate the innocent who suffer by the downfall of the banks; but we cannot consent that a mitigation of their troubles shall be purchased by the perpetuation of a system fraught with so much evil to the entire community. Now is the time for the complete emancipation of trade from legislative thraldom. If this propitious moment is suffered to pass by unimproved, the fetter, now riven almost asunder, will be rivetted anew, and hold us in slavery forever. The choice is presented to us of freedom or perpetual bondage. Let us demand, then, as with one voice, the reintegration of our natural rights; let us protest against the renovation of that cumbrous fabric of legislative fraud and folly, which has fallen of its own weight, and, if raised again, will again topple before the first commercial revulsion, to bury other myriads in its ruins.

If we knew any form of speech which would arrest the attention of our reader, or any mode of argument which would satisfy his reason, that we have not again and again used, we would employ it now, with all the earnestness of a sincere conviction of the importance of the subject, to persuade him that the only true ground of hope for the enduring prosperity of our commerce, in all its vast and complicated relations, consists in giving freedom to trade. Free banking is the system pursued in Scotland, and that country escapes revulsions, while England and America are exposed to continual paroxysms and collapsions, to expansions that unsettle all the foundations of property, and contractions that reduce whole communities to wretchedness and want. England, with all the monarchical and aristocratic potentiality of its government, has never yet been able to regulate the currency, with its stupendous machinery of finance. But Scotland, without any separate government, and without any legislative machinery of finance, has enjoyed a sta[b]le and uniform currency, because it has wisely been left to the natural laws of trade.

If the wants of the community require a great banking institution, capable of regulating the currency and exchanges, set trade free, and it will supply such an institution of its own accord. We need not go as humble petitioners either to our state or federal government, and beseech it to bestow special privileges on a few, that they may regulate the affairs of the many: we have only to adopt the franker and manlier course of demanding back those natural rights, of which we have been defrauded by dishonest and ignorant legislators. We need seek no immunity, but only claim our own. We need ask for the imposition of no new statute on the overburthened people, but only for the abrogation of laws which now weigh them to the earth. We desire nothing but the common privilege of pursuing our own business, in our own way, without a legislative taskmaster to say how much we shall do, what equivalent we shall have for our toil.

The same enterprise which freights the ocean with our products, which breaks our rivers into a thousand eddies with the revolving wheels of steamboats, which permeates the land with canals, and binds state to state in the iron embrace of railroads, would be abundantly able to perform the humble functions of banker, without the aid of legislative favour, or protection. Enterprise would build up, and competition would regulate, a better system of banks than legislation ever can devise. We have tried, to our cost, the competency of the latter, and we are now tasting the bitter consequences of our credulity.

Let us now test the experiment of freedom. It cannot place us in a worse condition than that to which we have been hurled by the terrible avulsion of the monopoly system.

THE BANKRUPT BANKS

The newspapers, with scarcely an exception, eulogize the banks for suspending payment, and now that they have thus declared themselves bankrupt by their own unanimous act, pronounce them as good and solvent as before, and call upon them to extend their loans. Loans of what? Irredeemable promises! On what possible pretence of justice or common sense, can the banks continue their ordinary business of discount, and charge a difference of six and seven per cent between their dishonoured paper, and the valuable paper of those merchants and traders who have withstood the shock of commercial revulsion, and met all their engagements punctually and to the letter? Will any one be so preposterous as to say that the promises of the banks, which are a lie on their face, are as good as the promises of such individuals? But the banks, it is contended, are perfectly solvent, and have assets sufficient to meet all their engagements. This may be so, or it may not; but, for our own part, we have no confidence in these soulless corporations, managed in secret by a mysterious junto, and shrouded altogether from the wholesome scrutiny of the publick eye. What proof have we that the banks are solvent? Is the testimony of the bank commissioners appealed to? How many days, we would then ask, was it, before the Mechanicks Bank declared itself bankrupt, that the community were solemnly assured by a bank commissioner that that institution had abundance of specie to redeem all its obligations to its bill holders and depositers? We know little of the secrets of the prison house; but we know enough to excite deep distrust of this ready exclamation of a venal press that the banks are all perfectly solvent. We know that at least two of the broken institutions have been lending large sums of money

Plaindealer, May 13, 1837.

without the knowledge of the directors, and one without the knowledge of either president or directors. How many more are in the same category? And to what extent have these unauthorized loans been made? And what is the degree of solvency of those to whom the "accommodations" were extended? Who can answer these questions?

Again, if possibly they are solvent, which is much to be doubted, are they more so, we would ask, than those individuals who are the owners of known and substantial property, and who have not yet suspended payment, but whose promises are scrupulously fulfilled? Who believes that the notes of any of the broken banks are as good as the notes of Mr. Astor? Who would not take, if it were not for the mere facility of passing again, the promise of Mr. Astor, or Mr. Lenox, or Mr. Bronson—nay, who would not take the promise of the humblest mechanick to the extent of his visible means, in preference to the invalidated and faithless promises of those great exclusively privileged bankrupt institutions in Wall street, which now stand as memorials of the egregious folly and dishonesty of special legislation?

Turn a deaf ear then, reader, we entreat you, to all these fraudulent attempts to cajole you into the belief that the banks, though broken, are as good as ever. They may be as good as ever, but they never were good. They were conceived in corruption. They were the spurious offspring of fraud and folly, and their whole career has been illustrative of their parentage. Attempt not, then, to heal the wound inflicted upon their credit by their own suicidal act. Set your face firmly against any legislative resuscitation of the exanimate brood of exclusively privileged money-changers. Now is the accepted time to overthrow forever the ignoble order of rag barons. Now is the auspicious moment when, by an energetick exercise of the popular strength, we may sunder forever the fetters of the paper money feudal system. The utter fatuity of legislative guardianship of the currency is signally illustrated by the present disruption of the links of the most strongly concatenated chain ever fastened by arbitrary power on the limbs of trade; and it is the part of wisdom to see that the broken fragments are not rivetted anew.

Let the banks rise from their ruins, if they can, by the recuperative force of what little vitality is left in them. We would neither render them assistance, nor oppose the slightest hindrance. But let us, in the meanwhile, embrace the lesson taught by their prostration, to insist that our legislative servants should immediately emancipate trade from arbitrary restrictions. If men of capital were at liberty to act, a system of free banking would arise on the ruins of monopoly which would dispense all the good that has ever been performed by the privileged institutions, and would be liable to none of their manifold abuses. The financial facilities which the community requires, in the prosecution of trade, are themselves a branch of trade, and perfectly within the influence of its natural laws. Let us then insist upon the divorcement of legislation from banking. Let us demand commercial freedom. Let us require that politicks shall confine itself to the affairs of government, and leave trade to manage its own concerns.

On the very day when the banks of this city and Brooklyn declared themselves bankrupt, stocks rose in price some fifteen or twenty per cent. This was in the confidence of a new inflation of paper money trash. But will the community consent to this? Will they tamely be imposed upon by a spurious, irresponsible, unredeemable paper currency, not worth so much as the ink wasted in recording the lying promises on its face? Will they witness a fresh series of fluctuating prices; new enterprises of mad speculation; and the prostrate fabrick of monopoly credit, now confessedly without a basis, again reared up to the clouds, to fall again, sooner or later, with more disastrous ruin?

The state of things which now exists we long since foretold; and it does not require a prophetick vision to see that worse difficulties are in reserve, unless we give freedom to trade, separating it from all the corrupt and disordering influences of legislation, and subjecting it to the salutary operation of boundless competition. Leave enterprise and rivalry alone; and the one will build up, and the other regulate, a better system of currency and exchange, than we can ever hope from the wisest legislation, to say nothing of such tampering Solons as govern our political affairs.

WHAT WE MUST DO, AND WHAT WE MUST NOT

. . . .

There are from three to four millions of dollars in specie in circulation in this city at the present moment. That it does not circulate very freely is probable enough; for people may very naturally be supposed not particularly anxious to exchange real value for broken promises. It is nevertheless in circulation, and would circulate actively, if confidence were restored, forming an ample understratum of currency, without the help of small notes. The great object then is to restore confidence, and the question arises, How is this to be done?

The *Journal of Commerce* cannot suppose that legislative authority to bankrupt institutions to continue their business, after they have declared themselves destitute of the means of business, to continue to issue their promises, after they acknowledge they have no means of redeeming them, will restore confidence to the community. Bank notes may, it is true, and perhaps must, be taken as the medium of barter, from those who have no actual money; but it is as certain as any result which depends on figures, that prices will be appre-

Plaindealer, May 13, 1837. Extract deleted.

ciated, and will be constantly fluctuating, while the community has to depend on such a medium, and that there will be a wide difference between the price for money, and the price for the spurious and dishonoured representative of money.

We agree with the *Journal of Commerce* that we require legislative action; but with a difference as to the kind of action we should ask for. That paper would have the legislature tinker and patch up the leaky and battered system of banking; while we would have it remove those impediments which hinder enterprise from supplying the place of the old system, demonstrated to be so utterly inefficient, with a bran[d] new one. Remove all legal restraints from capital, and how long does the *Journal of Commerce* suppose it would be before we should have a voluntary banking association in this city, with fifty millions of actual capital, certified and secured in such a manner as would command the publick confidence, and going into harmonious operation with such celerity as to restore, almost as by magick, financial order out of chaos?

If this is so—and our convictions have not been lightly adopted—it is manifestly the duty of the press to exercise its influence to bring about such a state of things. Let the broken banks take care of their own affairs as well as they can under the conditions of their charters. We are sorry for the losses in which they involve thousands who had no share in their misdoings; but we can see no good reason why these exclusively privileged insolvents should receive aid from the legislature, more than the unprivileged insolvents who have been breaking for months past. The best thing to do, in our judgment, and that which would have the speediest, as well as the most certain efficacy, is to emancipate the trade in money wholly from legal restraint. We have tried the forcing and monopoly system; let us now try the voluntary and free trade system.

"THE FORESIGHT OF INDIVIDUAL ENTERPRISE"

. . . .

Why not leave banking, then, to "the wholesome caution and sagacious foresight which regulate individual enterprise?" Can any one give an intelligible answer why? We have asked this question often, but never met with a response that addressed itself to the judgment of men.

The Board of Trade, of this city, has embraced the occasion of the present crisis in the monetary affairs of the country, to renew its recommendation of the scheme of a federal bank.

. . . .

A National Bank never yet, in this or any other country, afforded an effectual preventive or remedy for revulsion. Unlimited and unrestricted competition would build up the best system. It would give you a bank possessed of all the financial powers which a federal bank could be clothed with, and without the political powers, which, aside from the constitutional difficulty, compose the main ground of objection to such an institution. Let us have no overshadowing monopoly, but as gigantick an institution as you please, so long as its growth is only nourished by the demands of commerce, under the wholesome checks which competition supplies.

We have tried various other experiments; but that last, and best, and most certain experiment, remains yet to be tried. It is an experiment in perfect accordance with the principles of freedom, both political and economical. It violates no man's equal rights. It shuts no man out from the field of enterprise he may deem himself best qualified to cultivate. The time has

Plaindealer, May 13, 1837. Extracts deleted.

arrived when a really energetick demand for the emancipation of the credit system from the fetters of political control would be listened to. Let us not spend our strength, then, in clamouring for a federal bank, which the democracy of the country will never grant. Let us join in the cry for free banking. It cannot at all events, make our condition worse than it has been rendered by the odious system of concatenated state monopolies.

THE SAFETY FUND BUBBLE

——Help me, Cassius, or I sink!
SHAKSPEARE.

The prayer of the insolvent Banks has been granted by our monopoly legislature, and they are permitted, in the teeth of their own confession of inability to perform their contracts, to continue to issue their worthless and lying promises, which the community are virtually obliged to receive as real money. Was there ever a piece of grosser legislative fraud than this? Here have been merchants failing by scores for months past. Many of them show, to the entire satisfaction of their creditors, that their property far overbalances their debts. The difficulty of obtaining ready money has obliged them to suspend their payments; but it is rendered manifest, by a full exposition of their affairs, that not a dollar will ultimately be lost by those having claims upon them. The immediate cause which compelled these persons to suspend their business was

Plaindealer, May 20, 1837. Extract deleted.

the impossibility of obtaining money on any kind of securities. But that impossibility was itself the effect of another cause: and if we trace the connexion of cause and effect to the beginning, we shall find that the whole evil grew out of the monstrous expansion of bank credit, which provoked a most inordinate thirst of speculation, and stimulated men to undertake the wildest enterprises. These enterprises were of a nature to require a continually increasing expansion of bank credit. But there was a limit which the banks did not dare to overpass. When that limit was reached, the demand for money to sustain the mad projects which had been undertaken led to the freely giving of the most exorbitant rates of interest to private money dealers. These rates of interest soon consumed the actual means of speculators, and they were forced to sacrifice their property to meet the further demands upon them. Capitalists, seeing that the financial revulsion had commenced, withdrew from the field in alarm. The banks, fearful of a demand for specie, began to retrench as rapidly as they had expanded; and the merchant, in the meanwhile, who had pursued the even tenor of his way, neither enlarging nor diminishing his business, but keeping within those bounds which all former experience told him were compatible with safety, now began to experience the bitter consequences of folly in which he had had no share. In vain he offered triple and quadruple securities for the sums necessary for the transaction of his business. The extravagance and rapacity of the banks had produced, as their natural fruit, a general prostration of commercial confidence. Individuals were afraid to lend; for in the midst of the fictitious values which speculation had given to every thing, they could not decide whether the proffered security was real or illusory, whether substantial or a mere phantom of property, which would melt to nothing in their grasp. The banks could not lend, for they were involved in the meshes of their own wide-spread net; and to extricate themselves, as the result has shown, was a task beyond their strength. They had been potent instruments in producing the general derangement, but were utterly powerless to remedy it. The consequence was, that many a sound and solvent merchant was arrested by inevitable necessity, in the midst of a prosperous career, and obliged to trust his affairs entirely to the mercy of his creditors, and to the sport of accident.

While these deplorable bankruptcies were taking place, we heard of no proposition of relief from our legislature; but the instant that the banks, those prolific fountains from which the streams of mischief flowed, became insolvent, all other business of the state was laid aside, and the sole question deemed worthy of consideration was what means should be devised for propping up the worthless monopoly institutions. As the result of legislative wisdom, employed on this commendable object, we have the following law.

. . . .

To discuss the particular provisions of the law which we have submitted to our readers would be a waste of their time and our own. It is enough that it is the law. The measure, which the exigency of the times could not but suggest to every mind at all imbued with the true principles of economic freedom, has not been accomplished; but in its stead, a measure has been adopted, by an overwhelming majority, to continue the privileges of an affiliated league of monopolies, after the condition on which those privileges were originally granted has been violated, and the object they were designed to effect has utterly failed. The chartered banks should have been left to their fate. If they are solvent, no loss could occur to any connected with them, nearly or remotely, by such a course; and if they are insolvent, on what principle of justice are they permitted to continue their depredations on the community? The repeal of all the restraints on the trade in money would open the field of banking to universal enterprise and competition; and enterprise and competition, in that branch of business, as in every other, would lead to the happiest results.

It was once feared that religion could not flourish, if separated from the supervision of government; but the success of the voluntary principle in this country has refuted the theories of hierarchists. The success of the voluntary principle in banking would be not less exemplary. The day is coming, we are convinced, when men will universally deprecate all connexion between *Bank and State,* with as much abhorrent earnestness as they now deprecate a connexion between *Church and State.* We have no established religion; why need we have an established bank? One of two things is absolutely certain: either we must utterly dissolve the affairs of politics from those of trade; or we must go back to the system of federal supervision. We must either have no chartered bank, or we must have a national bank. We must either leave trade wholly free, or place it under effectual control. Bad as is the scheme of a federal bank, worse evils are to be dreaded from the fraud and folly of state monopolies. The only true system—the system which has been proved to be good in every thing to which its principles have been applied—the system in entire accordance with the fundamental maxims of liberty—is to confine politics to the affairs of government, and leave trade to its own laws. When our federal Government and our State governments separate themselves entirely from banking and credit, recognizing nothing as money but money, keeping their own revenues in their own custody, and leaving men to form their own system of currency and credit, without intervention, further than to enforce the obligation of contracts, or exact the penalty of violating them—then, and not till then, shall we be a happy and a prosperous people.

SEPARATION OF BANK AND STATE

When a hurricane passes over the land, spreading its surface with wrecks, they who survive its fury, though for a while stupified with terrour, soon recover their faculties, and set about to free the soil of the shivered fragments, and reconstruct their edifices in a mode better able to sustain the violence of future tempests. We are now in this condition. A hurricane has passed over our land, and the traces of its wrath are scattered around us. We have spent a sufficient time in the inactivity of dismay, and it is now proper to bestir ourselves, and make preparations for the future. It is particularly incumbent on those who are imbued with economick principles, and animated by a sincere desire to promote the lasting good of their country, to exert themselves in forming a correct publick opinion as to the course to be pursued. We lay claim to the latter of these qualifications, and obey its promptings to urge upon our readers that plan which we think alone has the recommendation of perfect accordance with the principles of democracy, and which alone promises, as its result, "the greatest good of the greatest number."

Our plan may be stated in a phrase of the utmost brevity; for it consists merely in the absolute separation of government from the banking and credit system. Bank and state have been hitherto joined in an unholy union, and we see the fruits of the connexion. Let us now try if we cannot divorce the ill assorted pair, and by so doing promote the prosperity of both, and of all dependant upon them.

It is to be expected that many projects, differing in their nature, motives, and objects, will be urged upon the people. Every scheme of reformation will find earnest, because inter-

Plaindealer, May 27, 1837.

ested, advocates, and most of them will probably be presented with all the advantages of eloquent exposition and plausible argument. The country constitutes the tribunal which must at last decide the question; and relying, with unbounded confidence, on the foundation which supports the democratick creed, the intelligence and integrity of the great body of the people, we await the final decision with deep interest, but without apprehension.

Among the schemes which will probably be urged, the proposition to reestablish a national bank presents itself most conspicuously. This will assume various modifications. Some will demand the reintegration, in its federal powers, of that gigantick institution which the late administration overthrew, and which now, as a state corporation, lies in wait for a favourable opportunity again to fasten itself upon the American people. Others, rejecting a scheme of resuscitating a bank so justly odious to the great body of the people, will vary their demand, and ask for a federal bank, composed of other corporators, and clothed with more limited powers. A third party, equally anxious for a vast federal engine of finance, will cloak their object under the thin disguise of "a loan office;" while others, having in view the same end essentially, will use a yet more modest appellation, and merely urge the propriety of establishing "a fiscal agent of the government." These propositions will all naturally spring from the professed aristocracy; while another class of schemes will probably be put forward under the name of the democracy. The aim of these will be, either to raise and reconstruct the prostrated system of state banks as depositaries for the federal revenue, or to build up some new monetary agencies under state control.

Against all these plans alike we avow uncompromising hostility. They all rest on principles violative of the equal rights of man. They are all fraught with danger to popular freedom. They are all essentially the same in their intrinsick characters, differing, indeed, in modes and degrees, but all adverse to that great principle of democratick freedom, on which rest the best hopes of political philanthropy for the complete emancipation and happiness of mankind. They alike ask for exclusive privileges to a few, which are to be withheld from the many. They alike ask for powers dangerous in their very nature; powers to regulate the currency and exchanges; powers, in other words, to control every man's business, fix the value of property at their arbitrary will, and take from labour the bread it has earned.

We have twice tried the scheme of a federal bank, and twice found that its fruits are bitter. We have seen it fail in the objects for which it was created; and we have seen it nearly succeed in other objects, fatal to the supremacy of the popular will. As a financial agent, we have proved it impotent for the prevention of fluctuations and revulsions; as a political engine, we have proved it dreadfully potent, and by the use of the most detestable means. We have tried the scheme of state banks, also, and the result which we now behold, and which is but the repetition of former similar results, unanswerably proves its deplorable inefficiency.

This is a plain statement of incontrovertible facts. Shall we, then, have recourse anew to the same system which has so utterly failed us before; or shall we not pause to inquire if there is not another system, more in accordance with natural justice, more effectual for the specifick objects proposed, and more free, besides, from objections which, if incidental and collateral, are yet of the most serious moment? We are no enemy to banking. We are no enemy to credit, in any form it may naturally assume between man and man. We confine our enmity solely to political interference with a subject which belongs to trade, and should be left to be governed by the same principles which harmoniously regulate all the affairs to which they are applied. If competition and enterprise were left in an unbounded field, they could not run to wilder excess, than that which we deplore as the consequence of the monopoly system. If free banking should prove as bad, it could not prove worse than the scheme of exclusively privileged banks, and we should at least escape all the degrading effects of bribery, corruption, and the thousand legislative evils, which are the obvious and inevitable consequences of the present system.

But when we speak of free banking, we deal in general terms, and the reader may desire that our views should be stated somewhat more explicitly. We would have banking, then, placed on the same basis as any other business, and neither protected nor restricted by laws, any more than the commonest traffick in which man engages. This depends upon the action of the states, and the sole legislative measure necessary to accomplish it, is to repeal entirely the act known as the restraining law.[1] We would have the federal government also separate itself wholly from all connexion with banking, recognizing nothing as money but silver and gold, and entrusting its funds to no private individual or association, voluntary or corporate, for safe keeping. The money of the government should be deposited, either in a single depositary at the commercial focus of the country, or at the principal points where collected, and officers appointed charged with the especial duty of guarding it. The various branches of the publick service should be paid with checks or drafts on these depositaries. Banking would thus be reduced to its proper field of action, as a mere auxiliary of commerce. It would not extend itself to a prodigious size, on the borrowed resources of the people, and finally bursting from its own distension, leave the government bankrupt and spread ruin and dismay through all classes of the community.

But under such a system would banks, adequate to the demands of commerce, spring into existence? With the same certainty that the demand brings supply in every other affair of trade. The demands of commerce require an immense number of ships to interchange our commodities with those of every quarter of the globe; but we need no law to say that this

[1] This law prohibited the entry of any bank not expressly chartered by the state legislature.—Ed.

man shall be a shipwright and that a joiner, one a rigger and another a caulker. The supply accommodates itself to the demand under the harmonious operation of the laws of trade. It requires enormous capital to carry on certain branches of commerce, the India trade, for example. But no exclusive legislative privileges are necessary. The mere stimulus of profit, the mere fact of demand, immediately sets capital flowing in that channel.

The same universal principle would supply us with banks adequate to all the legitimate demands of commerce. Competition would regulate them more effectually than law. It would lead to their giving the greatest amount of security, and to their paying the highest rate of interest on deposites, and charging the lowest rate of discount on their loans, compatible with a reasonable profit on the investment of capital.

But would you inundate the country with an irresponsible paper currency? We have already guarded against such a result, by requiring that the government, in all its various branches of receipt and expenditure, should know nothing as money but silver and gold. This would, of necessity, always keep a sufficient amount in circulation for all the purposes of ordinary currency. If the bankers exceeded their proper limits, their notes would immediately depreciate, and thus oblige them to retrench. But in the common affairs of life, in the everyday dealings of men, a paper representative of money would be unknown. Your duties to the Custom House, your purchase of publick lands, your fees in the courts of law, and all payments to the officers and functionaries of the government, of every branch and degree, being absolutely required in *actual money,* the notes of bankers would be restricted to commercial operations, gold and silver would become the common medium of ordinary traffick, and the people would at last realize the prodigious benefits of a Constitutional Currency.

THE REMEDY FOR BROKEN BANKS

Governour Marcy is at present in this city. We understand that more projects for tinkering the currency are on foot. It is said that Governour Marcy has signified his willingness to convene the legislature, if petitioned to do so, for the purpose of recommending it to pass an act authorizing the exclusively privileged broken monopoly banks to issue a spurious small note currency. We should not be at all surprized at such a proceeding from Governour Marcy. We used to look on that man as feeble minded, but honest. Our opinion of him in the former respect has undergone no change, except the change from impression to conviction; but in the latter respect we confess we begin to think we were in errour. There are some points in his conduct which certainly cannot easily be reconciled with the idea of perfect political integrity.

The authorizing of the broken banks to issue a small note currency at this time, we should consider one of the most unwarrantable and knavish exercises of legislative power that ever a free people submitted to. There is, beyond all question, a great want of a circulating medium which would enable persons to make change. But it is equally beyond question that there is an abundance of silver and gold coin in the country to supply this want. There never was, indeed, at any former period of our history, so much specie in the country. The only reason why it does not circulate freely, is because the paper currency is spurious and dishonoured, the banks having refused to redeem it, and the legislature having justified them in that refusal. What then is the proper object of remedial measures? Surely not to increase the amount of spurious paper, by authorizing the banks to issue a new class of un-

Plaindealer, June 3, 1837. Title added.

redeemable notes, which would only put further off the day of ultimate resumption of specie payments; but to give freedom to that spirit of enterprise which even now, in the chaotick state of things to which exclusively privileged bank monopolies have reduced us, stands ready, if only allowed free scope, to rescue the community from the terrible confusion of general bankruptcy. If Governour Marcy wishes to convene the legislature, let it be for the purpose of repealing all the restraints on the trade in credit and money, and not for imposing new burdens on the defrauded people, for the benefit of a few privileged charter mongers.

If an association of individuals, having fifty millions of dollars worth of real property, at a moderate appraisement, should undertake banking business, in the first place, by some publick act, making that property answerable, beyond all peradventure, for the notes they might issue, who can deny that such an institution would command publick confidence? Who can suppose that their notes would not be readily received as equivalent to silver and gold? Such an association would immediately spring into existence if all restraints on banking were removed, and, as a necessary consequence, the money which is now hoarded would again flow in the accustomed channels of circulation. We should thus have an abundance of actual money for the purposes of change, through the assistance of freedom; not a wretched substitute for money obtained by making a further sacrifice of our rights to the insatiate spirit of monopoly.

"BLEST PAPER CREDIT"

The history of paper money is a history of revulsions; of alternate prosperity beyond the natural bounds of health, and adversity as far beyond the ordinary limits of commercial distress. The scenes we are passing through now are but the repetition of scenes that have often been enacted before; and if the ruin occasioned by the present disruption of the paper system is more sweeping and intense than the ruin produced by the same causes on previous occasions, it is only because the business of the country is now conducted on a more extended scale. In 1816 we had but two hundred banks, whereas now we have seven hundred and upwards.

The causes of the terrible revulsion from the effects of which the country is now suffering are the same that produced a similar result in 1816. They may be accurately explained by quoting the very language made use of on that occasion by those who traced the mischief to its proper source. "The evil of the times," said Mr. Randolph,[1] in a memorable speech in Congress, when the proposition for establishing a national bank as a remedy for the financial distress then experienced was before that body, "The evil of the times was a spirit engendered in this republick, fatal to republican principles, fatal to republican virtue; a spirit to live by any means but those of honest industry; a spirit of profusion; in other words, the spirit of Cataline himself, *alieni avidus, sui profusus;*[2] a spirit of *expediency*, not only in publick, but in private life; the system of Diddler in the farce[3]—living any way and well,

Plaindealer, June 10, 1837.

[1] John Randolph of Roanoke, Representative of Virginia, 1800–1824.—Ed.

[2] "Greedy toward others, extravagant toward himself."—Ed.

[3] The character Jeremy Diddler, in James Kenney's farce *Raising the Wind* (1803), continually contrives to borrow money.—Ed.

wearing an expensive coat, and drinking the finest wines, at any body's expense."

Who can deny that it is to this same immoral thirst of sudden affluence, and prodigality of ostentatious luxury, to this *alieni avidus, sui profusus,* to this insane desire of acquisition and display, the present distress is to be ascribed? And who can deny that the bad desire has been provoked now, as it was then, by the effusion of a too copious flood of paper credit, which has borne men far away from a safe footing, and left them at the sport of the most treacherous sea that ever mocked the struggles of drowning wretches in their death-agony?

Our only remedy for the present evils, and our only true means of avoiding a recurrence of them, is to give freedom to trade—to do away with banking as a matter of legislative control, to take from paper the currency which it has received by being recognized as money by the Government, and leave it to find its own level as the mere evidence of private debt. The exclusively privileged paper money system of this country is the greatest curse which we endure. It is a curse in all its relations and influences, political, financial, and moral. It endangers liberty; it destroys the equilibrium of trade; it induces a gambling spirit, in the place of the better spirit of honest industry, and unsettles all the established ethicks of property.

Mr. Randolph, in the same speech from which we have already quoted, well termed the banking system of this country *a monstrous alliance between bank and state.* "We are tied hand and foot," said he, "and bound to conciliate this great mammoth, which is set up to worship in this christian land. Whilst our Government denounces a hierarchy; whilst it will permit no privileged order for conducting the service of the only true God; whilst it denounces a nobility, it has a privileged order of new men, the pressure of whose feet is upon our necks."

Now is the most favourable opportunity we can ever hope to have for crushing this terrible evil. There is no intermediate ground of safety. We must either crush it, or it will crush us.

We must either abolish exclusive privileges, or exclusive privileges will abolish freedom. Let us not be misunderstood, nor misrepresented, as we often are. We neither express nor entertain any desire to abolish banking. We desire merely to separate it from legislation, and to abolish the restraints which shut it up from the salutary influence of enterprise and competition. We desire to take from it every thing of a political character, and restore it to its proper field as a branch of private traffick. When this is done, when banking is left to the laws of trade, and the Government ceases to know anything as money but the money of the Constitution, we shall be a happy and a prosperous people, and not till then.

QUESTIONS AND ANSWERS

A correspondent puts the following questions to us, in relation to the free-trade system of banking:

1. What guarantee can be given to the hard workingman, in need of money, that he will not be obliged to pay private bankers exorbitant rates of interest?

2. Is there bullion enough at command wherewith to supply a constitutional currency?

To the first question we answer, competition between money lenders; to the operation of the same principle which regulates the profits of all other branches of business. The banks, under a free-trade system, would be governed by the same motives, and subject to the same influences, which impel and guide men in other classes of occupation. There is just

Plaindealer, June 17, 1837.

as much need for legislative regulation to restrain the dealers in other kinds of commodities from demanding enormous profits, as there is for restraining the dealers in money or credit. The relations of demand and supply fix the rates of profit in all callings, left free from the impositions of arbitrary enactments.

To the second question we answer yes. There is an ample amount of bullion for all the purposes of a currency. But freedom of trade does not imply the abolition of paper credit. It merely contemplates the separation of government from the credit system, whether in the way of restraint, regulation, or encouragement. There is an ample quantity of bullion in the world for an exclusive metallick currency, but prices would, of course, have to undergo a vast reduction, to adjust them to a hard money scale. But an exclusive metallick currency could only be instituted and maintained by the force of arbitrary government edicts, totally contrary to the first principles of natural justice. Bank-notes, in their intrinsick nature, are nothing more than the promisory notes of one individual to another, they are merely one of the forms which confidence between man and man assumes. So long as the laws do not interfere, and give an adventitious character to these notes, there is no reason, in natural justice or social expediency, why they should be interdicted. If left to themselves, they will not extend beyond the limits of a secure foundation, nor the demands of general convenience.

THE TRUE AND NATURAL SYSTEM

The theory of banking which we are desirous of embracing all opportunities of pressing on the attention of the community, consists simply in giving freedom to that branch of trade, and separating government from all sort of connexion with it. This theory we have maintained for years, and the events of each year have added force to our conviction of its perfect practicability, of the harmony with which it would work, and the diffused prosperity it would occasion. The events of the present year, we think, will do more than a thousand treatises to forward the desired reformation.

In the first place, the utter separation of the federal government from banking would have the inevitable effect of giving the country a hard money currency, as its circulating medium in all the minor and every day dealings of the people. By utter separation of the government from banking, we mean, that it should not only not create any bank by law, whether composed of private corporators, or founded on its own funds or credit, and managed by officers of its own appointment, but also, that it should not recognize the existence of any such institution, whether authorized by state legislation, or founded on the voluntary principle, and should know nothing, as money, in its receipts and expenditures, but the money of the Constitution, namely, gold and silver coin. This absolute disconnexion from banking, includes, as one of its essential features, the duty of keeping the federal revenues, between the time of collection and disbursement, deposited, under its own sole custody, in some place or places of safety, where they could not be used or jeoparded, in any way or degree, as a basis of credit.

Plaindealer, July 8, 1837.

The sole objection to this feature of the plan, is the loss of the profit which might accrue to the government from interest on its funds, if loaned to private associations or individuals, or to bodies politick. But this disadvantage is more than compensated by the single fact of absolute security. If lent out to any class of borrowers, the funds of the government would necessarily be exposed, more or less, to the hazards of trade, and might be totally swept off by an extensive commercial revulsion, the consequence of an extravagant spirit of speculation, fomented, in part, by the very facilities which the loan of the publick treasures afforded. If not so swept off, they would be liable, at any moment, to be withdrawn from use, by sudden political exigences; and this withdrawal would necessarily occasion embarrassments, more or less extensive, according to the amount of the funds, and the nature of the employment of them for which there had arisen unexpected occasion. These embarrassments would naturally cause much clamour against the government and much disaffection, however just its grounds of action, and might thus expose it to serious perplexities in a course of measures absolutely required by the permanent interests of the country, and a comprehensive regard for the publick good.

Another class of evils which would almost inevitably grow out of the lending of the publick money, consists in the facilities thus afforded to those in power to make a corrupt and subsidizing use of it, for the promotion of personal ambition, the enforcing of unwise measures, or maintaining the ascendency of party principles, not in accordance with the unbiased sense of the community. Whether such a use of the publick funds were or were not made in fact, as only a small portion of the applicants for the loan could be successful, those who were disappointed would naturally impute folly and corruption to the government, and thus tend to aggravate factious opposition, unsettle the publick mind, and expose the country to the evils of a fluctuating policy in the management of its political affairs.

It will be perceived that the objections we have here merely hinted at in general terms, might easily be extended into much more particular exposition, and illustrated with references to facts furnished by the present condition and past history of the country. But it is our purpose to be as brief as possible, and we must trust to the intelligence of the reader to carry out the argument to the degree of fulness necessary for a perfect application of it to the objections which may be offered.

For the reasons we have stated, and others that will suggest themselves, we would have the government utterly separate itself from the banking and credit system, collecting its revenues only in gold and silver coin, keeping them, until disbursement, in its own places of secure deposite, and then paying them out to its creditors in the various branches of the publick service. The payments would naturally be made by the officers of the Treasury in drafts on the depositaries. These drafts, on account of their convenience for remittance from place to place, might not be presented for payment immediately upon being issued, but this would in nowise alter the nature of the transaction.

We have said that this plan would inevitably be followed by a hard money currency, abundantly adequate for all the ordinary purposes of a circulating medium. This truth is so obvious that it scarcely requires illustration. The annual expenditures of the federal government are from thirty to forty millions of dollars. The receipts, under any scale of revenue, and any mode of taxation, must, of course, be as much. These revenues are collected chiefly in the principal seaports and at the principal land-offices, but in some measure in every township in the Confederacy. Wherever there is a post-office, there a portion of the federal revenue is collected. The judiciary, the army and navy, those engaged in the dockyards, on fortifications, and lighthouses, in constructing publick roads, in carrying the mails, and in numerous other branches of publick service, are the recipients of the money so collected. These persons are scattered over the entire surface of the country. The silver and gold they would receive in payment from the government, would necessarily flow in a circuitous channel before it emptied itself again into the Treasury in the shape of customs, postages, and the purchase money of publick lands. The action of the federal government alone would thus keep a sum at least equal to thirty or forty millions of dollars in continual circulation—a sum adequate to all the ordinary purposes of currency.

What we have here stated, comprises what we deem to be the duty of the federal government, in reference to the question of banking and credit. The next branch of the subject is the duty of the states. This consists, simply in giving freedom to trade, and leaving men to pursue the business of banking, or any branch of traffick in money and credit, without more restraint upon them, than there is in reference to the commonest vocation of life. The state governments, as well as that of the United States, should also recognize nothing as money but money, and the evidences of publick debt. But this is not absolutely essential to the success of our theory.

This plan, it will be perceived, contemplates no aggression upon existing institutions, no interference with "vested rights," no violent change of established systems. The federal government is now confessedly bankrupt, by reason of the universal disruption of the chartered banks, to the keeping of which its funds were entrusted. All we ask from it is, that for the future it shall collect its revenues only in money, and keep them itself in convenient depositaries situated at the chief commercial points, paying them out again to the different branches of the publick service by drafts on that deposite. All that we ask from the state governments is, that they should repeal those enactments which forbid the free use of capital and credit. Let existing banks be subject to unrestricted competition, and then the banking associations, whether corporate or voluntary, that give the publick the largest securities, and conduct their affairs with the wisest economy, will meet with the greatest success. In the meanwhile the people will have a hard money currency for all the minor purposes of traffick, and banking will naturally confine itself to those operations which constitute its only legitimate field—the mere exchange of bank credit for mercantile credit, to the extent of actual commercial transactions. Bank notes would be used in large commercial dealings, but would not go into the channels of ordinary circulation and become a part of the general currency of the country.

The system which we propose is either a good one or it is not. If not, the particulars wherein it is defective may easily be pointed out. Mere general condemnation of it, as impracticable and visionary, will not satisfy intelligent minds. Yet no stronger objections have ever been urged. It is indeed sometimes asserted that the plan requires the cooperation of twenty-six separate sovereignties, having, in some respects, different interests, and governed by opposite views of economick expediency. But the position is not true. The success of the plan does not depend on the concurrence of so many parties. If the state of New York alone would emancipate the trade in money and credit from legislative control, the result would at once be accomplished. This city is the great commercial mart and the great bullion depot of the entire Confederacy. The rays of trade diverge from this point to all parts of the country. The streams of business all tend to this centre. If the state of New York would dissolve all political connexion with banking, and leave it, as an affair of trade, to manage its own concerns, with no limit or check, other than penalties for frauds, a system of banking would at once arise, at the bidding of associated enterprise, which would answer all the good purposes that banks ever accomplished, with a smaller alloy of evil than banks ever before contained.

There are but two conditions necessary to perfect success—absolute disconnexion of bank and state, and absolute freedom of trade.

THE BUGBEAR OF THE BANK DEMOCRATS

The man in the fable who fought his own shadow got nothing but bruised knuckles as a reward for his valour. It will be well if the monopoly democrats, who are fighting the shadow of an exclusive metallick currency, should come off with as little injury. They lay their blows about them lustily, but the impassive nature of their enemy mocks their sturdiest efforts.

> As easy might they the entranchant air
> With their keen swords impress,

as seek to put down the democracy by attacking the bugbear of an exclusive metallick currency. "There is no such thing." It is an empty phantom conjured up by themselves. The monopoly democrats are the only persons who ever said a word about such a currency. But some of the arguments they use against it are as absurd, as the assertion is false that any party in this country is in favour of an exclusive compulsory circulation of gold and silver money.

In expatiating on the manifold evils of gold and silver, they are fond of drawing highly coloured pictures of the "prodigious ruin and combustion" which a sudden annihilation of the paper credit system would occasion. A farmer or mechanick, they say, has purchased a farm or a workshop under the present system for a given sum of money, half of which perhaps, the earnings of many years of industry and frugality, he has paid, and given a mortgage for the other half. While things are in this posture, they go on to state, you introduce your agrarian notions into legislation, annihilate paper credit, require that gold and silver shall alone circulate as money, and in consequence reduce the prices of all things at least fifty per

Plaindealer, July 22, 1837.

cent; so that the poor farmer or mechanick has to yield up his farm or shop to satisfy the mortgage upon it, and will be lucky indeed if he be not brought into debt for a large remainder.

Statements of this sort, in which "poor farmers" and "poor mechanicks" are made to figure very conspicuously, are every day put forth by the advocates of the bank monopoly. The champions of exclusive privileges display a wonderful degree of sympathy and commisseration for the labouring poor, whenever the principles of the paper money fraud are attacked. The "publick good" is always put prominently forward as the chief, if not the sole motive of the bank philanthropists, in their applications for charters; and no sentiment but solicitude for the "publick good," and more particularly for the good of the agricultural and mechanick classes, animates them in the vehement opposition with which they always resist assaults upon the paper system.

There can be no sort of doubt that a sudden fall of prices, however occasioned, is productive of vast injury to multitudes of men. All fluctuations in the currency, sudden or gradual, are productive of extensive and serious evils, moral and political, as well as financial. Nay, all changes of state policy, of every kind and name, no matter how obviously demanded by the principles of publick justice or expediency, are necessarily injurious, to some extent, greater or less, according to the circumstances. A nation cannot enter into war, however strong the provocation, or however important the interests to be defended, without occasioning vast loss and suffering to a portion of its citizens, whose prosperity depended on the preservation of peace. It cannot make peace, after having entered into war, without causing, by that change of policy, however beneficient in its general and aggregate result, great evils to another portion of inhabitants. It cannot vary its mode of taxation, lay a new impost on commerce, or remove an old one, without disadvantageously affecting the interests of some of those whose equal rights it is bound to respect. Nay, further than this, an improved process in art or agriculture is never discovered, nor a labour-saving machine invented, no matter how much the good of the majority may be promoted by it, that it does not occasion more or less evil and hardship to a portion of society. This is the inevitable consequence of all changes which vary the relations of men.

If we spoke the words which we now address to our readers, they would fall upon the ears of but a few hearers, and would be forgotten almost as soon as uttered. But we address them to thousands of attentive minds, through the aid of that potent and beneficent instrument, the press. There is no one of those thousands who does not entertain a deep conviction of the vast benefits which have resulted to mankind from the assistance of that wonder-working engine. By it, all the accumulated truths of science and art, the lore of sages, the discoveries of genius, the precepts of philosophy, the sallies of wit, and the harmonious numbers of poetry, are diffused over the whole earth, and placed within the reach of the humble, as well as the affluent and lordly. Yet the introduction of the press was a grievous evil to a large class of persons; to the cloistered monks and scholars, who devoted their lives to the painful task of transcription, and some of whose illuminated missals yet remain to attest the wonderful patience and skill they exercised in their art. The invention of the German mechanick deprived this large number of sequestered labourers of their accustomed means of obtaining bread, and many of them, doubtless, underwent severe privations, before they learned to apply themselves with success to other modes of occupation. But survey the vast aggregate of benefits to mankind, and see how gloriously a few cases, comparatively, of individual suffering was atoned for by the inestimable augmentation of general good.

But the reader will perceive that the common argument against an exclusive metallick currency, the evils which must arise from a change of systems, would have applied as strongly against the art of printing. The fact that a sudden change from paper credit to an exclusive metallick currency would occasion great hardship in many particular instances, is not a valid argument against the reformation, if even such a scope were contemplated as is alleged. It ought to be shown that the change is not justified by sound principles of publick economy, and would be productive of a preponderance of evil. Any exposition which falls short of this is wholly destitute of weight to turn the scale in favour of the credit system.

And if a change from high prices to low is an evil to those who have money to pay, is not a change from low prices to high equally an evil to those who have money to receive? Yet this change the advocates of the paper money fraud defend. The introduction of paper originally occasioned a rapid inflation of price, and caused many a poor man who had contracted for wages according to the metallick standard, to be paid in a medium which would not procure him half the same quantity of the necessaries of life. This change has been perpetually progressive, ever since the paper money system was invented. Prices have been forever on the advance, except in as far as counteracted by labour-saving machinery and improved methods of agriculture and the arts; and the continual inflation of the currency has occasioned a continual injustice to one party in all money contracts. The exhaustion of this paper currency, and the return to silver and gold, would but have a retributive effect; yet now, for the first time, the injustice of any fluctuation that changes the relations of value is discovered and made the subject of much intemperate declamation.

It would be well, if those who are so eloquent in illustrating by parables and supposititious instances, the evil effects of a sudden fall of prices, would sometimes turn their attention to the effects which flow from the opposite cause. It must be evident that fluctuations are not more injurious from a decline, than from an appreciation, in the nominal values of things. The farmer, who has to pay for his farm at a time when agricultural products will bring but half as much as when he purchased it, suffers from depreciation. But he who has to receive payment at a time when money will purchase but half the commodities it would have purchased when the debt was contracted is equally injured by the general appreciation. If you look into the particular cases to which this latter statement of the proposition will apply, you will find many of extreme hardship and cruelty. The poor mechanick who, relying on the stability of the currency, contracted to perform a piece of work when materials were low, is involved in irremediable embarrassments by that unexpected rise which the managers of the exclusively privileged monopoly paper money system have it always in their power to occasion by a sudden effusion of their notes—by an exercise of what is commonly considered "bank liberality."

But the defenders of the paper currency have planted their battery on a bed of sand. Their arguments are as destitute of foundation as the system they support, and they are wasting their ammunition in attacking an imaginary foe. No party, no faction, and not a single individual of note, has ever urged nor advised the adoption of an exclusive metallick currency. They war, not against credit, but only against the credit system. They war, not against a paper currency, but only against paper authorized by law, and stamped with an illusory character as money by special and unequal legislation. They war, not against banking, but only against exclusively privileged banks. They ask for no measure by which a sudden change would be made in the relations of value; but a measure which would prevent such sudden and ruinous changes as have marked our history and demoralized our people. They ask, in short, only for freedom; for the complete divorcement of politicks from banking; for the separation of bank and state.

The first inquiry which all intelligent minds should make in regard to the great subject of publick discussion is, what scheme is recommended by abstract truth and justice; for whatever is just and true in theory is not less so in practice. Their next inquiry should be as to the best means of reducing it to practical utility. A large portion of the community have come to the conclusion that the true scheme of government, in the respect in question, is to have no connexion with banking and commercial credit, and to impose no restraints on trade. They have come to the conclusion that the principles of economick and democratick freedom, in regard to currency as in regard to every subject to which they have been applied, will be found to exercise the most beneficent influence, and most effectually promote the general prosperity of mankind. This scheme does not contemplate an exclusive metallick currency. It does not contemplate any measure which need alarm any man not governed by the debasing and aristocratick desire to render the many tributary to the few.

BANK AND STATE

The *Evening Post* a day or two since remarked that, "there never was a more popular catch word than THE SEPARATION OF BANK AND STATE. It is a phrase full of democratick meaning; it is musick to the ears of the people. It is a phrase which will never be laid aside till all that it imports is fully realized. On this feeling in the people the administration may confidently rely, sure that if they trust to it they will be triumphantly sustained." Whatever merit there may be in having originated this phrase, we believe may be justly claimed by this journal. And not the phrase only, but the important measure which it implies, has been urged on the attention of our readers with a frequency which we might fear would weary them, were it not for the vast importance of the subject. The separation of bank and state, and the emancipation of credit

Plaindealer, July 22, 1837. Text abridged and extract deleted.

from legislative fetters are the two great objects for which the real democracy are contending. "DIVORCE OF BANK AND STATE," and "FREEDOM TO TRADE," are phrases which deserve conspicuous and continual insertion in every democratick newspaper. They should constitute our "watchword and reply" in the coming contest.

In the complete separation of government from the bank and credit system consists the chief hope of renovating our prosperity, and restoring to the people those equal rights, which have so long been exposed to the grossest violations. Leave credit to its own laws. It is an affair between man and man, which does not need special government protection and regulation. Leave banking to be conducted on the same footing with any other private business, and leave the banker to be trusted or not, precisely as he shall have means to satisfy those who deal with him of his responsibility and integrity. All this is a matter for men to manage with each other in the transaction of private affairs. But the part which the government shall act in regard to banking and credit is a political matter, to be decided by the voice of communities through the constituted channels of suffrage. There are two principles at war on the subject. One of these is the principle of aristocracy, the other the principle of democracy. The first boasts of the vast benefits of a regulated paper currency, and asks the federal government to institute a national bank "to regulate the currency and exchanges," or, in other words, to regulate the price of the labourer's toil, and enable the rich to grow richer by impoverishing the poor. The principle of democracy, on the other hand, asks only for equal rights. It asks only that the government shall confine itself to the fewest possible objects compatible with publick order, leaving all other things to be regulated by unfettered enterprise and competition. It asks, in short, for free trade, and the divorce of bank and state.

. . . .

THEORY AND PRACTICE

It is a very common thing for the antagonists of the political doctrines maintained by this journal to admit that they are true in theory, but they assert they cannot be reduced to practice. Nothing can be falser than this position. There is no such thing, in morals or politicks (and politicks are, indeed, but a branch of morals) as impracticable truths. Whatever is true in theory it is our duty to reduce to practice; for the great end of human effort is the accomplishment of truth. Whatever is our duty is within the compass of our ability; for it is a condition of our nature that we are endowed with powers for the performance of all the moral obligations under which we are placed. To argue otherwise is to impeach the justice and beneficence, and to deny the order and harmony, displayed throughout the whole system of the universe.

"Nothing," says Say, in his admirable work on Economy,[1]— "Nothing can be more idle than the opposition of theory to practice. What is theory, if it be not a knowledge of the laws which connect effects with their causes, or facts with facts? And who can be better acquainted with facts, than the theorist who surveys them under all their aspects, and comprehends their relation to each other? And what is practice without theory, but the employment of means without knowing how or why they act?" The people of this country have been employing means, in regard to banking, without understanding the theory; without viewing the whole chain of causes and effects, which, in its entire concatenation, constitutes the science of banking. Those who understood the theory, long since fore-

Plaindealer, July 29, 1837.

[1] Jean Baptiste Say, French classical economist, was author of *A Treatise on Political Economy*, the fifth American edition of which was published in 1832, from which this quote is likely taken.—Ed.

told the ruin that would result from the rash and ignorant employment of those means. They explained the principles in accordance with which alone the business of banking can be conducted so as to produce prosperous and equable results. We are told that this is true in the abstract, but utterly impracticable. It is clearly demonstrated, on the other hand, that the system which has been pursued was true neither in theory nor practice. It was founded on false principles. It had its origin in a gross violation of the great maxim of liberty, the equality of man's rights. This is admitted by its champions; but they excuse the deep original sin on account of the good fruit which they alleged would be the consequence of the violation. That fruit is now pressed to our lips, and do we not find that it is bitter?

The exclusively privileged system of banking, then, is proved to be sound neither in the abstract nor concrete, neither in theory nor practice, neither in the inception nor execution. Would it not be the part of wisdom, in this emergency, to make trial of a system which is admitted, on all hands, to have the recommendation of theoretick truth? But we are met on the threshold with an assertion that this system "has been, from time immemorial, demonstrated to be utterly impracticable and visionary for the common affairs of life." Alas! then, for the woful condition of humanity, which is thus forced to reject what it acknowledges to be true, and embrace what it knows to be false, and the progeny of which is ruin.

But when, where, and how, has experience demonstrated our theory to be impracticable? Our theory is, that men have equal rights; that government, which is the guardian of their equal rights, should confine itself within the narrowest circle of necessary duties, the mere protection of that equality, by preventing the encroachment of one man upon the rights of another; and that all beyond this should be left to the influence of publick opinion, and those natural principles of commercial intercourse which are called the laws of trade. This is our theory. This is the theory of a popular government. This is the theory of democracy. We ask again, when, where, and how, has it been demonstrated to be impracticable?

If we look back to ancient times, we shall find that those countries which made the nearest approaches to popular government exhibited a spectacle of the most diffused happiness and prosperity, and that the happiest and most prosperous portion of their history embraced that period when their approach to the popular principle was nearest. We say the period of the greatest happiness and prosperity, not of the greatest splendour. The distinction is a broad one. Autocracies, monarchies, aristocracies, and hierarchies, present spectacles of splendour; democracies the less dazzling, but more pleasing ones of equal and diffused happiness. The contemplation of despotick and kingly governments, from the distant points of historick observation, is like the contemplation of embattled and turreted cities from afar off. Their towers and domes, their palaces and spires, attract the eye, and impress the mind with a sense of grandeur; and it is not led to think of the squat dwellings of wretchedness and toil, and the gloomy dungeons of captivity, which are girt round by the lordly abodes of affluence and power. We survey a democratick government, from a point of distance, as we look on a fertile champaigne country, and find little to attract our attention, which soon tires of the dull uniformity. But on a nearer approach we find, if monotonous, it is at least the monotony of happiness, and that if nothing attracts the eye by the commanding stateliness of its height, nothing repels it by the abject lowness of its degradation. The fancy may be dissatisfied, but the heart acknowledges that the condition of democratick equality is best, since it accomplishes the chief desideratum of philosophy, "the greatest good of the greatest number."

But it is not by a reference to ancient governments alone that we shall discover proofs of the correctness of the theory which shows the superiority of the popular principle of government. Look abroad through Europe at the present day, and tell us what is the result of your observations. Do you not find that each country has increased in general prosperity in the precise ratio that it has made advances towards the democratick principle? Do you not find that the most wretched country is that where the government is most absolute; and the most happy where it is most liberal? What else is it that constitutes the difference between a serf of Russia and a citizen of England? By the plain principles of inductive reasoning, then, as well as abstract and *a priori* speculation, we are led to the conclusion that democracy, in its widest signification, is the most felicitous condition of mankind. America is the happiest country in the world, because it is the most democratick. To be happier, it only needs that the principles of democracy should be more inviolably observed. Every trespass upon the equal rights of men, by conferring exclusively on a few the privileges which belong by nature to all in common, is a breach of those principles. Every breach of principle is sure to be followed by punishment; and under this head we must place the distress we experience from the disruption of our chartered banking system. It will be well if we are effectually admonished by the lesson of experience.

Our theory of banking consists simply in the position, that it is an affair of trade, which ought to be left wholly to the laws of trade. How can it be said that experience has demonstrated this theory to be impracticable, when all experience proves the very opposite to be true? Do not enterprise and competition, in every pursuit in which they are left untrammelled by the laws, produce the most admirable results? The keels of our swift-cleaving vessels seam the ocean with their sparkling wakes; the mighty forest of the west bows and retires before the sturdy salutation of the woodman's axe; and all the vast aggregate of human industry presents a spectacle of order and prosperity, without the intervention of law to regulate its details, designate its field of action, or stimulate or check its operations. Is there anything in the nature of banking which makes it an exception to the universal rule, that enterprise and competition are the best regulators of trade? What is this latent quality, this secret, this mystery, which makes banking so different from every other business, rendering it necessary to have rules of its own, and privileges and immunities; and requiring it to be tenderly cloaked up from the least breath of competition, and screened so that the winds of heaven shall not visit it too rudely? Banking is neither more nor less than an exchange of notes between one individual or association, having such known means as give the publick confidence in the ability to meet their obligations, and another individual, whose means are of a less publick or satisfactory kind, the one paying the other an equivalent for the advantage of the exchange. There is nothing mysterious in this; nothing that withdraws it from the ordinary sphere of trade, or requires special laws and exclusive privileges.

But we are happily not reduced to the necessity of arguing this matter by induction from the nature of banking, and the effect of freedom on other branches of traffick. The success of the principle of unrestrained competition is not a matter of inference only, but of fact. Of all the paper money countries of the world, Scotland is the only one where the banks rest on the basis of individual enterprise, unchartered, unprivileged, and exempt from no penalties or impediments to which other pursuits are subject. Yet Scotland is the only paper money country which escapes commercial revulsion. Bankruptcy has swept through England on more than one memorable occasion, with the desolating fury of a tornado, prostrating the loftiest fabricks, and shattering the firmest institutions. But the storm hurtled over Scotland without injury, for she was ensconced behind the impregnable barriers of free trade. The foresight of individual enterprise had descried, in good season, the gathering of the tempest, and was prepared for its rudest assault.

Let us see what countries will best bide the peltings of the pitiless financial storm which is now raging throughout the commercial world. Our life upon it—the holy cause of free trade and equal rights, dearer to us than life, upon it—that the free banking system of Scotland will stand erect and unshaken amidst the tempest, which will beat all other paper money systems to the earth! Is this demonstrating the impracticability of our theory?

SEPARATION OF BANK AND STATE

We have heretofore more than once invited the attention of our readers to the remarkable sentiment of General Jackson, expressed in the document giving his reasons for the removal of the publick deposites from the Bank of the United States, that it was his desire "that the control of the banks and the currency should, as far as possible, be entirely separated from the political power of the country," and that "the action of the federal government on the subject, ought not to extend beyond the grant in the Constitution which only authorizes Congress to coin money and regulate the value thereof. All else," said General Jackson "belongs to the states and to the people, and should be regulated by publick opinion and the interests of trade."

Here, in the compass of a few words, is given the outline of the only true system for this country to pursue in regard to banking. What alone is needed—what is demanded by both the letter and spirit of our institutions, and by the fundamental principle of liberty, is freedom of trade, and a complete separation of bank and state. We ask that the federal government should not connect itself with any banking association in any way or degree, and that the state governments should likewise wholly separate themselves, in every respect,

Plaindealer, August 5, 1837. Text abridged and extract deleted.

from the banking and credit system. When this is once carried into full effect, and banking is left to be conducted on the same basis with other branches of private traffick, without either peculiar encouragement or peculiar hindrance from the laws, we shall rise to a higher degree of general prosperity than we yet have ever attained.

Under such a free and equitable system, it is true, certain classes of the community, who contribute nothing to the national wealth, the mere buyers and sellers, the mere commercial go-betweens, the mere factors of the farmers, mechanicks, and labourers, (for the merchants are no more) may not be afforded the means of outstripping all others in the fruits of affluence, and enabled to riot in every sort of luxury and extravagance, by incurring enormous debts through the instrumentality of bank-credit, which the hard-working men and women of the country have at last to pay with the earnings of incessant toil. This consequence may not and would not result from a free trade system. And if it can be shown that this consequence is more to be desired than diffused happiness and prosperity; if it can be shown that the encouragement of a mad spirit of commercial enterprize, totally regardless of the good old distinction between *mine* and *thine*, is better than steady industry and gradual accumulation, obtained without violating the principles of morals; if it can be shown, to the conviction of sober reason, that a magnificent city is better than a fruitful and well cultivated country, and a luxurious mercantile class better than a thriving population engaged in all the various branches of productive industry and useful occupation: if these things can be demonstrated, we say, then shall we at once and forever abandon the position we now maintain, and raise our voice, with those of the monopolists, in demanding from the federal government a national bank, and from the states a continuation and extension of their systems of exclusive chartered privileges. But till these points can be clearly proved, we shall continue to do battle on the side of freedom.

It is a very common thing to point to the rapid growth of our commercial marts, our vast enterprises of internal improvement, our canals, railroads, steamboats, spacious hotels, new cities springing up in the midst of deserted cornfields, and untenanted towns all over the country, as evidences of the wonderful effects of the monopoly bank credit system. We admit these are, in a great measure, the effect of that system. But we are of those who consider them, in the quaint phraseology of old Polonius, "effects defective."

> Ill fares the land, to hastening ills a prey,
> Where wealth accumulates, and men decay.

If the great end of the government is to promote the especial good of mercantile speculators, land speculators, and stock speculators, then indeed we shall receive these things as cogent proofs of the excellence of the monopoly bank credit system. But we are of that *agrarian* school of politicks which teaches that the sole duty of government is to extend equal protection to all classes of people, to secure them from mutual aggression, and beyond this to leave them to the influence of their natural desires and affections, to those influences of enterprise and competition which are called the laws of trade. The monopoly bank paper system does a great deal, it is true, for the speculative trader on anticipated means. It enables him to build a princely mansion, fill it with costly furniture, stock his cellar with the choicest wines, and load his board with the most luxurious viands. It enables him, without a dollar of actual property, earned by useful toil, to ride in a splendid equipage, repose on a couch of down, and realize all the advantages of prodigious wealth. But what does it do for the farmer who laboriously cultivates his few acres, and obtains, in return for continual toil, but enough to sustain him in the execution of his task? What does it do for the poor mechanick, whose lap-stone or anvil rings all day long with the click of his incessant hammer? What does it do for the poor labourer, who rises with the sun, and sweats, like a beast of burden, in its burning glare, till evening comes to dismiss him to a few hours of heavy slumber on his straw-filled pallet? Let us hear what praises there are to be bestowed on the monopoly bank credit system as it affects the condition of these people who, if government has privileges to give, are entitled, not less than the mere buyer and seller of silks and laces, or the blowers of stock bubbles, to an equal share.

We are no enemy to credit, as we have said a thousand times. We are no enemy to a free and natural system of credit between man and man, the result of mutual confidence, the exercise of one of the kindliest attributes of our nature, without which the frame of society would fall into dividual fragments, and be utterly destroyed. But we are an enemy to a monopoly credit system, which bestows all its advantages on a few, at the expense of the many; which raises to undue importance the undignified vocations of traffick, and depresses to unnatural lowness, as if they were intrinsically mean, the pursuits of agriculture and the mechanick arts. Your monopoly credit system fosters the city, but it ruins the country; it builds up lordly mansions for the keen-eyed sons of trade, but it leaves to irremediable dilapidation the cabins of the farmer and mechanick; it encourages luxury and profusion among the few, and spreads penury and vice among the many. It is a demoralizing system. It makes the acquisition of sudden wealth the prime object of general effort, and blunts the publick moral sense as to the means of gain. It deranges the whole economy of life, unsettles the natural balance of industry, and leads, with inevitable certainty, at periodical intervals, to such explosions as that which has now scattered ruin over our land.

Give us freedom, and leave credit to adjust itself to the wants of society, without political stimulus or restraint. Give us freedom, that the madness of speculation may not involve the government in all the fluctuations of trade. Give us freedom, that, while we boast of our equal rights, we may not in truth be subjected to a worse tyranny than was ever imposed on man by the feudal oligarchists of the middle ages. We have separated Church from State. It yet remains for us to separate Bank from State, and teach the world, by a new and sublime illustration, the invariable efficacy of THE VOLUNTARY PRINCIPLE.

. . . .

"SPECIE BASIS"

We hear much of the specie "basis" of our paper circulation. The way to ensure an adequate basis to banking institutions, is to give perfect freedom to the trade in money and credit, and leave competition and enterprise to act and react without legislative stimulus or restraint. The inevitable result of wholly emancipating credit from monopoly legislation, from that arbitrary system which affects "to preserve and regulate, but not destroy," would be to build up voluntary associations of great capital, that would immediately enter into banking business, under circumstances that would command the utmost publick confidence. When we say a great capital, we do not mean silver and gold exclusively but a capital of real, substantial, imperishable property, such as lots, farms, houses, ships, and the like. There never was a grosser piece of deception than has been practised upon the world by the financial cant about a specie basis of banking. No bank of discount and circulation ever had a specie basis. The Bank of Amsterdam has a specie basis, or rather a basis of specie, jewels, plate, and other articles of great and unvarying intrinsick value; but this is a mere bank of deposit, deriving its profit

Plaindealer, August 12, 1837.

from the charge it makes for the safe keeping of the treasures entrusted to it, and liable for the redemption of no paper money but the checks drawn against those treasures. But to talk of a specie basis to any of our note issuing banks is preposterous. The basis of a thing is the foundation it rests upon. The foundation of our bank is credit, not money. Few of them have, in the best of times, enough specie in their vaults to redeem a tithe part of their obligations. To speak of that specie, then, as the basis of those institutions, is about as correct as it would be, were a pyramid inverted, to call its cope-stone a basis. If the laws of gravitation were not suspended for its accommodation, the pyramid, tumbling into fragments, would show that its basis was but a poor basis indeed; as our prostrate and shattered banks now show how poor and inadequate was the specie basis on which they pretended to stand.

The true foundation for a bank is actual property to an amount sufficient, under any contingency of trade, for the redemption of its notes. This would be a basis of some solidity, and such a basis competition would lead men to furnish, if our legislative master would throw open this business to the wholesome influences of freedom. The notes of private banking associations would, of course, be redeemable in specie, but this is a very different thing from having, or pretending to have, a *specie basis*. They would be redeemed in silver and gold, and silver and gold may always be procured for that purpose by those who have property. Silver and gold, like iron and lead, are merchandize, and can always be bought for a fair equivalent. A free trade bank, founded on the secure basis of real property, would never had occasion of more silver and gold than could be readily obtained, at a very small sacrifice, from the dealers in those commodities. The greatest drains of specie to which banks are subject, are occasioned by panick—by fear of their insolvency; but a free trade bank, founded on known security of adequate property, would never be liable to the suspicions and apprehensions which the least untoward circumstances in financial affairs are sure to arouse against institutions pretending to rest on a metallick basis, that every man, woman and child in the community know it is not sufficient to redeem a tenth part of their debts.[1]

THE NATURAL SYSTEM

The opposition party and the monopoly democrats are alike the friends of an exclusive banking system, but differ widely, as to the authority on which such a system should rest. The one side advocates the monarchical principle of a great central bank established by federal authority, and the other is equally strenuous in favour of the aristocratic principle of state institutions. They both agree in the most extravagant eulogiums of "the credit system," and consider it the source of all the blessings and advantages which we enjoy. They alike disclaim, with seeming enthusiasm, on the resources of wealth which our country contains, on the activity of its industry, the boldness of its enterprise, and the fertility of its invention, ever on the stretch for new and speedier modes of gain; and they alike demand, with an air of triumph, what has caused these resources of wealth to be explored, what has given energy to industry, confidence, and enterprise, and quickness to the inventive facilities of our countrymen, but the happy influence of "the credit system?" It is this, they tell us which had

[1] In the free banking system of Scotland, which Leggett praises elsewhere, almost all banks operated with unlimited shareholder liability for bank obligations. They experienced no runs for specie, though their specie reserves were a small percentage of their note and deposit liabilities.—Ed.

Plaindealer, August 19, 1837.

dug our canals, constructed our railroads, filled the forest, and caused the wilderness to smile with waving harvests. Every good which has happened to our country they ascribe to the credit system, and every evil which now afflicts it they allege may be effectually remedied by its aid. But they differ widely as to the mode of remedy; a cordon of state monopolies being the object aimed at on the one side, and a great central money power the darling project of the other.

For our own part, we are free to acknowledge that if we were confined to a choice of these evils we should not hesitate to decide in favour of the central bank. We are not alone in this sentiment. There are myriads and tens of myriads of true-hearted democrats in the land who, if the unhappy alternative were alone presented to them of a federal bank or a perpetuation of the system of exclusively privileged state monopolies, would decide promptly and earnestly in favour of the former. Better a single despot, however galling his rule, than more galling tyranny of a contemptible oligarchy. While a federal bank is not more dangerous to the principles of political liberty, its influence would be less extensively pernicious to public morals. They who live in the purlieus of a monarch's court may draw out but a sickly existence; but the moral health of a whole country suffers, when it is under the domination of a league of petty tyrants who fix their residences in every town, and taint the universal atmosphere with the contagion of luxurious example. Bad as is the monarchical principle of a federal bank, the aristocratic principle, which would distribute the same tremendous power among a thousand institutions scattered throughout the confederacy, is worse. Mankind suffered heavier oppression under the rule of the feudal barons, than they had ever before suffered when the political power was centered in the throne. But they arrived not at the rich blessings of freedom, until monarchical and feudal tyranny were both overthrown, and the doctrine of divine right and exclusive privilege gave way before that of universal equality.

He who compares the financial history of Europe with its political, will be surprised to find how perfect is the analogy between them. Her ingenious and philosophical mind would be well employed in running the parallel. It would be found that political revulsions, as well as commercial, are the inevitable result, sooner or later, of conferring exclusively on the few privileges that belong, by nature, in common to all; and that all violations of the holy principle of equal rights, while in politics, they produce tumults, insurrections, and civil war, in economy, exercise a corresponding influence, and are followed by panic, revulsion, and a complete overthrow of all the established commercial relations of society.

The fundamental maxim of democracy and of political economy is the same. They both acknowledge the equal rights of all mankind, and they both contemplate the institution of "a wise and frugal government, which shall restrain men from injuring one another, shall leave them otherwise free to regulate their own pursuits of industry and improvement, and shall not take from the mouth of labour the bread it has earned." The preservation of man's equal rights is the be-all and the end-all of the natural system of government. The great maxim which acknowledges human equality is, in the political world, what gravitation is in the physical—a regulating principle, which, left to itself, harmoniously arranges the various parts of the stupendous whole, equalizes their movements, and reduces all things to the most perfect organization. Monarchy, aristocracy, and all other forms of government, are founded on principles which deny the equal rights of mankind, and they all attempt to substitute an artificial system for that of nature. The effect is sometimes to produce a seeming increase of prosperity for a time; but nature avenges her violated laws sooner or later, and overthrows the unsubstantial fabric of presumption and pride.

The great end which is alone worthy of the efforts of the champions of democratic and economic truth, is to institute the natural system in all matters both of politics and political economy. Let them aim to simplify government, and confine it to the fewest purposes compatible with social order, the mere protection of men from mutual aggression. We need but few laws to accomplish this object. We need particularly few in regard to trade. What is the whole essence and mystery of trade, but an exchange of equivalents to promote the convenience of the parties to the barter? Leave the terms, then, to be settled by men's own notions of mutual convenience and advantage. There is no need of political interference.

Extreme simplicity is usually considered as the condition of barbarism, before man has raised himself by science and art from the degradation of mere animal nature. But the saying that extremes meet is as true in politics as in any of its applications. Simplicity may be the goal, as well as the starting-point, of social effort. Is it not a fact verified by the observation of every man of cultivated mind, that in religion, in literature, in art, and in the conventional manners of a community, simplicity and refinement go hand in hand? As society advances it throws off its cumbrous forms and ceremonies; it follows more and more the simple order of nature, which does nothing in vain, but carries on its stupendous operations by the directest processes, linking cause and effect, without superfluous complication, and adapting its means with the utmost exactness to the end. Compare the nations of the earth, and see if simplicity and refinement are not always found together, in whatever respect the comparison is instituted. In architecture, why are the gorgeous edifices of Constantinople, glittering with "barbaric pomp and gold," deemed inferior to the plainer structures of the cities in western Europe? In literature, why are poems crowded with oriental splendour of imagery, and heaped with elaborate ornaments of diction, thrown aside by the reader of taste for those which breathe the unstudied sweetness of nature? In manners, why do those seem the most refined which seem most truly to flow from the promptings of native amenity and elegance of soul? It is because that is most excellent which comes nearest to the simplicity of nature. Nature does nothing in vain.

Simplicity in government is not less a proper object of those who wish to raise and refine the political condition of mankind. Look at those governments which are the most complex, and you will find that they who live under them are the most wretched. As governments approach simplicity, the people rise in dignity and happiness; and all experience as well as all sound reasoning on the certain data of induction, bears us out in the conclusion, that when they conform most nearly to the simplicity of nature, then will mankind have reached the utmost bound of political prosperity. Then will the cumbrous artificial and arbitrary contrivance of "the credit system," be abandoned, for the harmonious and beneficial operation of natural, spontaneous credit, the free exercise of confidence between man and man.

THE CREDIT SYSTEM AND THE ARISTOCRACY

It is curious to observe what studied and elaborate panegyricks are bestowed by the aristocratick press generally on what they term "the credit system." They seem to be fully impressed with the truth of the sentiment, *"interdum fucata falsitas, in multis est probabilior, sape rationibus vincit nudam veritatem."*[1] It is for this reason they invent sounding names, and use such a profusion of false colours, to deck out a system, which, if called by its proper appellation, and shown in its true, undisguised features, would repel every body by its ugliness. What is their credit system but a system which bestows exclusive privileges on the scheming few, at the expense

Plaindealer, August 26, 1837. Title added.

[1] Roughly, "it stands to reason that painted falsehood, in much it is more likely, occasionally conquers the naked truth."—Ed.

of the industrious and hard handed many? Credit, we admit, in the broadest terms, is a useful and beneficial agent in carrying on the great and various intercourse of society. We avow ourselves the friend of credit—so much its friend, that we are unwilling to see it cramped by arbitrary restrictions. We would have it left to the unbounded freedom of nature. We would have it, like the sunshine and dew of heaven, to dispense its blessings equally upon all. We would have it, like a bounding river, to flow wither it listeth in its natural channels, not dammed up between artificial barriers, and forced to run only in particular directions, fertilizing the lands of a favoured few, and leaving the rest to be parched with drought, or lie in sterile loneliness. We are the friend of credit, for the same reason that we are the friend of any other generous impulse or affection of the human heart, and we would no more regulate its action by law, than we would that of hope, benevolence, friendship or love. If by "the credit system," free spontaneous, natural credit is meant, then we are the friend of the credit system; but if, on the other hand, a system of legislation is meant, by which exclusive privileges of exercising credit, are conferred on a set of men and prohibited to the rest of the community, then are we its determined and unappeasable foe. We are for leaving capital free, and credit free. We are, in all things, for trusting to the glorious principle of freedom—that principle which recognizes the equality of the rights of all mankind, and considers government as having no legitimate functions beyond the mere preservation of those rights. "There is no more reason," says Raymond in his Political Economy,[2] "why a man, or body of men, should be permitted to demand of the publick interest for their reputation of being rich, than there would be in permitting a man to demand interest for the reputation of being wise, learned, or brave. If a man is actually rich, it is enough for him to receive interest for his money, and rent for his land, without receiving interest

[2] A reference to Daniel Raymond, *The Elements of Political Economy,* the second edition of which was published in 1823.—Ed.

for his credit also." We oppose this sentiment not less strenuously than we oppose the opposite system which would annex peculiar privileges to "the reputation of being rich." We would neither confer upon men by law nor deny to them the right of receiving interest on their credit. We see no reason why a man or body of men should not be permitted to demand interest for their credit, as well as for their actual means, provided the rest of men are left equally free to give or refuse that interest as they please. If you go to a wealthy person, and ask him to lend you his promissory note for a given sum, telling him that, by reason of his known wealth, his note will answer all the purposes of money to you, he has a perfect natural right, and we can perceive no good argument in favour of that right being interdicted, to charge you a price for the accommodation he affords by the loan of his credit.—The true credit system is the free trade system. Leave credit free, and the relations of demand and supply will "regulate and preserve," far better than all the quackery and tyranny of special legislation.

But when we pass beyond the ground of mere permission to charge an interest on credit, and come to that of express and exclusive legislative authority to do so, the question assumes a very different shape. With this limitation we wholly agree with the writer. What reason is there, which has not its foundation in palpable injustice, why any particular set of men should be specially privileged by law to issue their promises to pay, their mere acknowledgements of indebtedness, and force the community to pay an interest of seven per cent, not on the money they have, but on that which they have not, on their mere credit? It may be said they do not force the community to do so. They virtually force the community to do so, however, by reason of the false character which their exclusive privileges give to the notes they issue. The law considers those notes as money; the government receives them as such, and becomes, in some measure answerable for their punctual payment on demand; and thus they are necessarily received into general circulation as money. This is a gross and crying injustice.

If the money business of the community were left to take its natural course, does the reader suppose that the principal financial stations would be filled, as many of them now are, by men, not of wealth, not of financial talent nor experience, but mere party electioneerers, mere brawlers at pot houses and ward meetings? Does he suppose, under a system of free trade, that mere fidelity to "party usages," the mere fact of a certain equivocal sort of political influence, the mere having some dozens or some hundreds of voters at one's heels, would constitute such ability to transact banking business, as would be certain to give those possessing such qualifications the confidence of the community? What made Cornelius W. Lawrence, and Gideon Lee, and George D. Strong, and Walter Bowne, presidents of banks? Were they appointed solely in reference to their ability in financial transactions, or was the office given to them as a reward for party services and sacrifices? These are plain questions, but they relate to proceedings of the utmost notoriety, and on such a subject it is needless to mince matters. The time has arrived for plain questions, and plain answers too, and the *argumentum ad hominem* is sometimes a very useful division of logick. We have too long submitted to a system of banking founded on *political capital*, instead of *money capital*, and hedged around with exclusive privileges, instead of being left open to the wholesome influence of the freest competition. If we do not wish to be slaves forever, we must no longer deceive ourselves and others by honeying affairs over with sweet words. "Let the candied tongue lick absurd pomp;" but the honest tongue should speak out boldly, and call things by their right names.

If the political services of Mr. Lawrence, or Mr. Lee, or Mr. Strong, or Mr. Bowne, were of that magnitude and general importance as to entitle them to publick rewards, let them be rewarded openly and liberally, and we shall never utter a word in censure of the act. We give, from the coffers of the federal government, a beggarly annual stipend to the remaining soldiers of the revolution. The only complaint we have ever heard on this account is that the country is so parsimonious in its gratitude. The great body of the people would be willing that a much larger sum should be given to the remnant of the revolutionary veterans, in token of the sense entertained by the country of their heroick services and sacrifices. A similar sentiment would govern them no doubt in relation to Messrs. Lawrence, Lee, Strong and Walter Bowne, if it were distinctly pointed out in what way the signal patriotism of those worthies has been displayed. But they would still ask, and with good reason, that the reward, or token of gratitude, or whatever it might be called, should be bestowed openly and without disguise or indirection. Such a course is due alike to the character of the state, and to that of the patriots for whom the publick purse is opened. The reward, and the illustrious services for which it was rendered, should be inscribed in enduring letters on the muniments of our state, so that all future times might profit by the example of patriotism exhibited by Messrs. Lawrence, Lee, Strong, and Walter Bowne, and by the example of gratitude exhibited by their countrymen. But we protest against the creation of exclusive privileges for the purpose of paying these men for their political services. We protest, in the name of freedom, against such a violation of its fundamental principle. We protest, in the name of the worthies themselves, against fobbing them off with so poor and equivocal an acknowledgement of their claims on legislative munificence.

But gesting apart—for it is a subject which hardly admits of gest—we desire once more to raise our voice against monopoly legislation on the subject of banking. Our state banking system is an odious system of exclusive privileges, dangerous, in their very nature, to the principles of political, as well as gross violations of the plainest fundamental maxims of economick freedom. It is a system of exclusive privileges built up for the especial reward of party services. It is instituted to provide sinecures for a band of gentlemen pensioners. It was conceived in the stews of legislative prostitution, born in corruption, and smells to heaven with the rank odour of hereditary rottenness. How long will freemen—or men claiming to be free—consent to have this bastard offspring of fraud and folly for their master? How long will they consent to be the cringing vassals of a feudal system instituted for the support of such a contemptible baronage as our paper-money lords?

THE DIVORCE OF POLITICKS AND BANKING

Our next number will contain the Message of the President to Congress. We have reason to feel very confident in the expectation that this document will strenuously recommend the complete separation of the federal government from the bank and credit system. This great scheme, we observe, is assailed, in advance, with a good deal of violence by the opposition newspapers; but in their "plentiful lack" of arguments, they for the most part vent their spite only in epithets. Acting upon the sentiment that there is much in a name, they call this proposed separation of bank and state a plan to institute a *Treasury Bank;* and they discourse with a good deal of well affected apprehension of the evils which must flow from placing the sword and purse in the same hands. This cant about the sword and the purse is the merest declamation that ever demagogue employed to gull the minds of a credulous auditory, and never was appellation more misapplied than that of Treasury Bank to the scheme which aims to separate the

Plaindealer, September 2, 1837.

government from all the injustice, favouritism, casualities and fluctuations of the banking system. The effects of the policy would, in all respects, be the very reverse of those which are brought about by our wretched and tyrannous paper money system.

If the government of the United States should absolutely disconnect itself, in every way, from the banking and credit system, receiving and disbursing as money, nothing but the money of the Constitution, one of the necessary consequences would be the continual circulation of an under currency of silver and gold sufficient for all the most ordinary purposes of a circulating medium. Should the principal commercial and agricultural states, then, or even this great state alone, (which is the natural centre of the commercial and monetary concerns of the country) entirely repeal all restraints in the trade in money and credit, banking business, as a natural and inevitable consequence, would immediately be undertaken by private enterprise, and this enterprise would be subject to the regulation of unbounded competition. That competitor, whether an individual or association, who should satisfy the publick of the possession of the largest amount of actual property answerable for his obligations, would naturally enjoy the greatest confidence. It would be the interest, therefore, of all entering into banking business, to give publick evidence of their possessing ample property, liable, in the event of any miscarriage, for the redemption of their issues. Those who did not give such evidence would not enjoy publick confidence. Their notes would not be received by other bankers, nor by individuals generally, except at a discount; for every trader and mechanick would have it perfectly at his option to take nothing but silver and gold, since, by reason of the government recognizing nothing else as money, silver and gold would always freely circulate.

One check on over issues would consist, partly, in the prudence and foresight of those bankers who, having a large aggregation of actual capital, would desire to conduct their business on safe banking principles with the sole purpose of realizing a moderate and steady profit on investment. Whenever other bankers, of a more speculative turn, should show a disposition to extend themselves too far, the prudent ones, both for their own safety, and from the natural rivalry of trade, would be led to discredit the notes of the former, which, in consequence of this repudiation, would immediately fall below par, and thus force those issuing them to retrench.

Another check would be found in the fact, that real money and paper money cannot circulate together. One invariably and inevitably drives the other away. But as there is an absolute necessity, in the state of things supposed, for the circulation of silver and gold to an amount necessary for all the ordinary purposes of daily traffick; so consequently it would be paper that would be expelled. The government would keep an amount, equal to its annual expenditures, say some thirty or forty millions of dollars, in continual and active circulation. It would receive nothing else for lands, customs, postages, or taxes in any shape, and would pay nothing else to the judiciary, the army and navy, publick contractors, workers on the publick roads, fortifications, lighthouses, and, in short, to those engaged in every branch of publick service. These sums would necessarily perform a circuitous circulation between the time of disbursement and of repayment into the publick treasury; and here would be a hard money currency, which, to its extent, would banish paper. This would constitute another check on over issues.

Banking business, under such a free trade system, would naturally confine itself to commercial operations. The sagacity and prudence of individual enterprise, when its own actual means are jeoparded by extravagance, would lead to that result. The notes of bankers would, as a general rule, represent only actual mercantile transactions. They would not be loaned to speculators, as now, to enable them to purchase lands in the moon, or under water "deeper than did ever plummet sound." If they loaned their notes to speculators it would be on real security, and speculation can never produce great publick evil, as long as it does not extend beyond that basis.

That there would be over issues to some extent, and occasional revulsions, under a system of perfect freedom of trade, and perfect disconnexion of bank and state, is highly probable. There are revulsions in nature, and we cannot expect that there should be none in trade. The political circumstances of nations, the instability of seasons, war, pestilence, and famine, are all causes which may jar the great machine of commerce, and throw some of its parts into extreme disorder. But these revulsions would be lighter and less frequent than those which happen under the bad system of exclusively privileged banking, which is wholly artificial, and at utter variance with the natural mechanism of trade. The revulsions of a free trade system would not be political revulsions, they would not provoke to such mad exasperation the bad passions of men, and set a whole people in the deplorable attitude of two opposing parties, surveying each other with the scowl of mutual hatred, instead of the glances of fraternal kindness.

PART THREE

Abolition Insolence

RIOT AT THE CHATHAM-STREET CHAPEL

The morning papers contain accounts of a riot at Chatham-street chapel last evening, between a party of whites and a party of blacks. The story is told in the morning journals in very inflammatory language, and the whole blame is cast upon the negroes; yet it seems to us, from those very statements themselves, that, as usual, there was fault on both sides, and more especially on that of the whites. It seems to us, also, that those who are opposed to the absurd and mad schemes of the immediate abolitionists, use means against that scheme which are neither just nor politic. We have noticed a great many tirades of late, in certain prints, the object of which appeared to be to excite the public mind to strong hostility to the negroes generally, and to the devisers of the immediate emancipation plan, and not merely to the particular measure reprehended. This community is too apt to run into excitements; and those who are now trying to get up an excitement against the negroes will have much to answer for, should their efforts be successful to the extent which some recent circumstances afford ground to apprehend. It is the duty of the press to discriminate; to oppose objectionable measures, but not to arouse popular fury against men; to repress, not to stimulate passion. Reason—calm, temperate reason—may do much to shorten the date of the new form in which fanaticism has recently sprung up among us; but persecution will inevitably have the effect of prolonging its existence and adding to its strength.

. . . .

Evening Post, July 8, 1834. Title added by Sedgwick. Text abridged to omit a recounting of the events leading up to the riot.

. . . That the whole scheme of immediate emancipation, and of promiscuous intermarriage of the two races, is preposterous, and revolting alike to common sense and common decency, we shall be ever ready, on all occasions, to maintain. Still, this furnishes no justification for invading the undoubted rights of the blacks, or violating the public peace; and we think, from the showing of those who mean to establish the direct contrary, that these were both done by the Sacred Music Society [the party of whites].

We are aware that we are taking the unpopular side of this question; but satisfied that it is the just one, we are not to be deterred by any such consideration. Certain prints have laboured very hard to get up an anti-negro excitement, and their efforts have in some degree been successful. It should be borne in mind, however, that fanaticism may be shown on both sides of the controversy; and they will do the most to promote the real interests of their country, and of the black people themselves, who will be guided in the matter by the dictates of reason and strict justice. The plans of the Colonization Society[1] are rational and practicable; those of the enthusiasts who advocate immediate and unconditional emancipation wholly wild and visionary. To influence the minds of the blacks, then, in favour of the first, we must have recourse to temperate argument and authentic facts. Whatever is calculated to inflame their minds, prepares them to listen to the frantic ravings of those who preach the latter notions.

[1] This is a reference to the American Colonization Society, founded 1817 to aid free blacks by resettling them in Africa. The Society founded the colony of Liberia in 1822, and at the time Leggett wrote was at the peak of its influence.—Ed.

GOVERNOR McDUFFIE'S MESSAGE

Governor McDuffie, in his late message to the Legislature of South Carolina, has promulgated various errors in relation to the views and principles of the democracy of the middle and northern states, which might excite astonishment at his ignorance, or regret at his insincerity, did we not know that they are founded on the misrepresentations of the Bank tory organs of this part of the world. Great pains have been taken by these to persuade the people of the south, that all the violent anathemas uttered against the system of slavery, by enthusiasts and fanatics in this quarter, and all their dangerous zeal for immediate emancipation, originate with the democracy. The charge of agrarianism, also, which has with such marvellous propriety been urged against this journal, because it supports the doctrine, not of an equalization of property, which is an impracticable absurdity, but because it maintains the principle of equal political rights, seems to have excited the sensitive apprehensions of the Governor of South Carolina, and prompted him to the utterance of sentiments which we are sorry to see avowed on such a public and grave occasion, as that of addressing the legislature in his official capacity.

We must beg leave to set Governor McDuffie right on these points. In the first place, what is called agrarianism by the Bank tory presses is nothing more than the great principle which has always been maintained with peculiar earnestness by the southern states, and most especially by Virginia and South Carolina. It is simply an opposition to all partial and exclusive legislation, which gives to one profession, one class of industry, one section of the Union, or one portion of the people, privileges and advantages denied to the others, or of

Evening Post, February 10, 1835. Title added by Sedgwick. Text abridged.

which, from the nature of their situation and circumstances, they cannot partake. It is opposition to bounties, protections, incorporations, and perpetuities of all kinds, under whatever mask they may present themselves. It is neither more nor less in short, than a denial of the legislative authority to grant any partial or exclusive privileges under pretence of the "general welfare," the "wants of the community," "sound policy," "sound action," "developing the resources and stimulating the industry of the community," or any other undefinable pretence, resorted to as a subterfuge by avarice and ambition. This is what the whig papers, as they style themselves, hold up to the South as a dangerous doctrine, calculated to unsettle the whole system of social organization, and subject the rights of property to the arbitrary violence of a hungry and rapacious populace!

. . . .

Governor McDuffie is still more misled in his ideas of the part taken by the democracy of this and the eastern states in the mad and violent schemes of the immediate abolitionists, as they are called. He may be assured that the abettors and supporters of Garrison,[1] and other itinerant orators who go about stigmatizing the people of the south as "men stealers," are not the organs or instruments of the democracy of the north, but of the aristocracy—of that party which has always been in favour of encroaching on the rights of the white labourers of this quarter. It is so in Europe, and so is it here. There, the most violent opponents of the rights of the people of England, are the most loud in their exclamations against the wrongs of the people of Africa, as if they sought to quiet their consciences, for oppressing one colour, by becoming the advocates of the freedom of the other. Daniel O'Connell[2] is one of

[1] William Lloyd Garrison, leading advocate of the immediate abolition of slavery.—Ed.

[2] Member of Parliament from Ireland, well known for agitation on behalf of the rights of Roman Catholics and repeal of Ireland's union with England.—Ed.

the few exceptions, and even he, in one of his speeches, with the keenest and most bitter irony, taunted these one-sided philanthropists with perpetuating the long enduring system of oppression in Ireland, while they were affecting the tenderest sympathy for the blacks of the West Indies. Was Rufus King,[3] the great leader on the Missouri question, a representative of the democracy of the north? and were not the interests of the planters of the south sustained by the democracy alone?

Governor McDuffie may make himself perfectly easy on the score of the democracy of the north. They are not agrarians, nor fanatics, nor hypocrites. They make a trade neither of politics, nor philanthropy. They know well that admitting the slaves of the south to an equality of civil and social rights, however deeply it might affect the dignity and interests of the rich planters of that quarter, would operate quite as injuriously, if not more so, on themselves. The civil equality might affect both equally, but the social equality would operate mainly to the prejudice of the labouring classes among the democracy of the north. It is here the emancipated slaves would seek a residence and employment, and aspire to the social equality they could never enjoy among their ancient masters. If they cannot bring themselves up to the standard of the free labouring white men, they might pull the latter down to their own level, and thus lower the condition of the white labourer by association, if not by amalgamation.

Not only this, but the labouring classes of the north, which constitute the great mass of the democracy, are not so short-sighted to consequences, that they cannot see, that the influx of such a vast number of emancipated slaves would go far to throw them out of employment, or at least depreciate the value of labour to an extent that would be fatal to their prosperity. This they know, and this will forever prevent the democracy of the north from advocating or encouraging any of those ill-judged, though possibly well-intended schemes for a

[3] Whig Senator from New York who led anti-slavery opposition to the Missouri Compromise of 1820.—Ed.

general and immediate emancipation, or indeed for any emancipation, that shall not both receive the sanction and preserve the rights of the planters of the south, and, at the same time, secure the democracy of the north against the injurious, if not fatal consequences, of a competition with the labour of millions of manumitted slaves.

If any class of people in this quarter of the Union have an interest in this question, independent of the broad principle of humanity, it is the aristocracy. It is not those who labour and have an interest in keeping up its price, but those who employ labour and have an interest in depressing it. These last would receive all the benefits of a great influx of labourers, which would cause the supply to exceed the demand, and consequently depress the value of labour; while the former would not only experience the degradation of this competition, but become eventually its victims.

. . . .

Again we assure Governor McDuffie, and all those who imagine they see in the democracy of the north, the enemies to their rights of property, and the advocates of principles dangerous to the safety and prosperity of the planters of the south, that they may make themselves perfectly easy on these heads. The danger is not in the democratic, but the aristocratic ascendancy. The whole is a scheme of a few ill-advised men, which certain whig politicians have used to set the republicans of the south against the democracy of the north, and thus, by dividing, conquer them both.

THE ABOLITIONISTS

. . . .

We defy any man to point to a single instance in which fanaticism has been turned from its object by persecution, or in which its ardour has has not been inflamed and its strength increased when opposed by arguments of brute force. On the contrary, history contains many striking cases of fanatical enterprises languishing and being abandoned, when those engaged in them were suffered to take their own course, without any other hinderance than such as was necessary to prevent their overleaping the safeguards of society.

Fanaticism is a species of insanity and requires analogous treatment. In regard to both, the soothing system is proved by its results to be the most effectual. The mind slightly touched with lunacy, may soon be exasperated into frenzy by opposition, or soon restored to perfect sanity by gentle and assuasive means. So, too, the mind, excited to fanaticism on any particular subject, religious, political, or philanthropic, is but heated to more dangerous fervour by violence, when it might easily be reduced to the temperature of health by the lenitives which reason and moderation should apply.

The first great impulse which the abolition cause received in this city was, we are persuaded, the attempt to suppress it by the means of mobs; . . . and we do hope that, in view of the pernicious consequences which have flowed from violent measures hitherto, a course more consistent with the meekness of Christianity, and with the sacred rights of free discussion, will be pursued henceforth.

While we believe most fully that the abolitionists are justly chargeable with fanaticism, we consider it worse than folly to

Evening Post, August 8, 1835. Title added by Sedgwick. Text abridged.

misrepresent their character in other respects. They are not knaves nor fools, but men of wealth, education, respectability and intelligence, misguided on a single subject, but actuated by a sincere desire to promote the welfare of their kind. This, it will hardly be denied, is a true description, of at least a large proportion of those termed abolitionists. Is it not apparent on the face of the matter, that invective, denunciations, burnings in effigy, mob violence, and the like proceedings, do not constitute the proper mode of changing the opinions or conduct of such men? The true way is, either to point out their error by temperate arguments, or better still leave them to discover it themselves. The fire, unsupplied with fuel, soon flickers and goes out, which stirred and fed, will rise to a fearful conflagration, and destroy whatever falls within the reach of its fury.

With regard to the outrage lately committed in Charleston,[1] we do not believe it constitutes any exception to our remarks. The effects of all such proceedings must be to increase the zeal of fanaticism, which always rises in proportion to the violence of the opposition it encounters. . . . Neither the General Post Office, nor the General Government itself, possesses any power to prohibit the transportation by mail of abolition tracts. On the contrary it is the bounden duty of the Government to protect the abolitionists in their constitutional right of free discussion; and opposed, sincerely and zealously as we are, to their doctrines and practise, we should be still more opposed to any infringement of their political or civil rights. If the Government once begins to discriminate as to what is orthodox and what heterodox in opinion, what is safe and what is unsafe in its tendency, farewell, a long farewell to our freedom.

The true course to be pursued, in order to protect the South as far as practicable, and yet not violate the great principle of equal freedom, is to revise the post-office laws, and establish the rates of postage on a more just gradation—on some system

[1] The postmaster of Charleston, South Carolina, had refused to deliver abolitionist tracts.—Ed.

more equal in its operation and more consonant with the doctrines of economic science. The pretext under which a large part of the matters sent by mail are now sent free of postage—either positively or comparatively—is wholly unsound. "To encourage the diffusion of knowledge" is a very good object in itself; but Government has no right to extend this encouragement to one at the expense of another. Newspapers, pamphlets, commercial and religious tracts, and all sorts of printed documents, as well as letters, ought to pay postage, and all ought to pay it according to the graduation of some just and equal rule. If such a system were once established, making the postage in all cases payable in advance, with duplicate postage on those letters and papers which should be returned, not only the flood of abolition pamphlets would be stayed, but the circulation of a vast deal of harmful trash at the public expense would be prevented, creating a vacuum which would naturally be filled with matters of a better stamp.

REWARD FOR ARTHUR TAPPAN

The southern presses teem with evidences that fanaticism of as wild a character as that which they deprecate exists among themselves. How else could such a paper as the Charleston Patriot advert with tacit approval to the statement, that a purse of twenty thousand dollars has been made up in New-Orleans as a reward for the audacious miscreant who should dare to kidnap Arthur Tappan,[1] and deliver him on the Levee in that

Evening Post, August 26, 1835. Title added by Sedgwick.

[1] Tappan was president of the American Anti-Slavery Society, a prominent abolitionist organization.—Ed.

city. Revolting to right reason as such a proposition is, we find it repeated with obvious gust and approbation by prints conducted by enlightened and liberal minds—by minds that ordinarily take just views of subjects, achieve their ends by reasoning and persuasion, and exert all their influence to check the popular tendency to tumult. Is the Charleston Patriot so blinded by the peculiar circumstances in which the south is placed as not to perceive that the proposed abduction of Arthur Tappan, even if consummated by his murder, as doubtless is the object, would necessarily have a widely different effect from that of suppressing the Abolition Association, or in anywise diminishing its zeal and ardour? Does it not perceive, on the contrary, that such an outrage would but inflame the minds of that fraternity to more fanatical fervour, and stimulate them to more strenuous exertions, while it would add vast numbers to their ranks through the influence of those feelings which persecution never fails to arouse.

But independent of the effect of the proposed outrage on the abolitionists themselves, what, let us ask, would be the sentiments it would create in the entire community? Has the violence of the south, its arrogant pretensions and menacing tone so overcrowded our spirits, that we would tamely submit to see our citizens snatched from the sanctuary of their homes, and carried off by midnight ruffians, to be burned at a stake, gibbeted on a tree, or butchered in some public place, without the slightest form of trial, and without even the allegation of crime? Are our laws so inert, are our rights so ill-guarded, that we must bear such outrages without repining or complaint? Is our Governor a wooden image, that he would look on such unheard of audacity and make no effort to avenge the insult? These are questions which it will be well for the south to ponder seriously before it offers rewards to ruffians for kidnapping citizens of New-York. If the south wishes to retain its slaves in bondage, let it not insult the whole population of this great free state by threatening to tear any citizen from the protection of our laws and give him up to the tender mercies of a mob actuated by the most frantic fanaticism. Such a proceeding would make abolitionists of our whole two millions of inhabitants.

THE ANTI-SLAVERY SOCIETY

The annexed address to the public has been sent to us inclosed in a note from an officer of the Anti-Slavery Society, requesting us, in "behalf of the society whose document it is, and in justice to the public who have a right to the information it contains," to publish it in our columns this afternoon. We most cheerfully comply with this request; and furthermore invite the attention of our readers to this address, as not only one which it is incumbent on them in fairness to peruse, but as one, the sentiments of which, with a single exception, deserve, in our judgment, their approval.

It is quite time, since the South seems determined that we shall discuss the question of slavery, whether we will or no, that we remember the maxim which lies at the foundation of justice, *Hear the other side.* We have listened very credulously to the one side. We have with greedy ears devoured up all sorts of passionate invectives against the abolitionists, and received as gospel, without evidence, the most inflammatory and incendiary tirades against them. While appropriating to them exclusively the epithets of incendiaries and insurrectionists, we have ourselves been industriously kindling the flames of domestic discord, and stirring up the wild spirit of tumult. It is high time to pause, and ask ourselves what warrant we have

Evening Post, September 9, 1835. Title added by Sedgwick.

for these proceedings? It is time to balance the account current of inflammatory charges, and see which side preponderates, whether that of the incendiaries of the north or of the south.

We have here, in the subjoined official address, signed with the names of men whom we believe too upright to lie, and who certainly have shown that they are not afraid to speak the truth, an exposition of the creed and practise of the Anti-Slavery Society. We have already said that, in our judgment, the matters contained in this document, with a single exception, deserve cordial approval. This expression we wish taken with a qualification. We do not approve of perseverance in sending pamphlets to the south on the subject of slavery in direct opposition to the unanimous sentiments of the slaveholders; but we do approve of the strenuous assertion of the right of free discussion, and moreover we admire the heroism which cannot be driven from its ground by the maniac and unsparing opposition which the abolitionists have encountered.

The particular portion of the subjoined document which we except from our approval is that wherein it is asserted as the *duty* of Congress to abolish slavery in the District of Columbia. That Congress has the constitutional power so to do, we have not the slightest doubt. But high considerations of expediency, in the largest sense of the word, should be well weighed before an exercise of that power is attempted. A spirit of conciliation and compromise should govern in the matter, as it did in the formation of our sacred *Magna Charta*. Every state in the confederacy should be considered as having an equal interest in the seat of the National Government, and the legislation for it should be of that neutral tint, which results from the mixture of contrary hues of opinion, and is in strong opposition to none. If the free states have a majority in Congress, yet paramount considerations of brotherhood and national amity should prevent them from stirring the question of slavery, by introducing it in any collateral or insidious form. Whenever that question once fully comes into general discussion it is destined to shake our empire to the centre. Let the commotion be then avoided in regard to a spot of ground which is not a pin's point on the map, and in the government of which, more than in almost any other question, the sentiments of the minority ought to be respected.

We are not sure that the Harry Percys[1] of the South, are not by their hot menaces and inconsiderate vaunts precipitating a discussion which must be entered into sooner or later, and may, perhaps, as well be undertaken at once. Be that as it may, their high and boastful language shall never deter this print from expressing its opinion that slavery is an opprobrium and a curse, a monstrous and crying evil, in whatever light it is viewed; and that we shall hail, as the second most auspicious day that ever smiled on our republic, that which shall break the fetters of the bondman, and give his enfranchised spirit leave to roam abroad on the illimitable plain of equal liberty.

We have no right to interfere legislatively with the subject of slavery in our sister states, and never have arrogated any. We have no moral right to stir the question in such a way as to endanger the lives of our fellow human beings, white or black, or expose the citizens of the north, attending to their occasions in the south, to the horrors of Lynch law. Nay, we repeat, what we have often asserted with as sincere earnestness as any loud-mouthed anti-abolitionist, that we deeply deplore all intemperate movements on this momentous subject, in view of the dreadful wrecks which the meeting tides of contrary fanaticism must spread around their borders. But while we truly entertain these sentiments, we know no reason that renders it incumbent on us to conceal how far our views are really opposed to slavery; and while we disclaim any constitutional right to legislate on the subject, we assert, without hesitation, that, if we possessed the right, we should not scruple to exercise it for the speedy and utter annihilation of servitude and chains. The impression made in boyhood by the glorious exclamation of Cato, that

[1] Sir Henry Percy (1366–1403) plotted against the English King Henry IV. The affair is treated in Shakespeare's *Henry IV*.—Ed.

A day, an hour of virtuous liberty,
Is worth a whole eternity of bondage,[2]

has been worn deeper, not effaced, by time; and we eagerly and ardently trust that the day will yet arrive when the clank of the bondman's fetters will form no part of the multitudinous sounds which our country continually sends up to heaven, mingling, as it were, into a song of praise for our national prosperity. We yearn with strong desire for the day when Freedom shall no longer wave

"Her fustian flag in mockery over slaves."[3]

ABOLITIONISTS

There is a class of newspaper writers who seem to think that epithets are more powerful than arguments, and who therefore continually bestow on their opponents odious appellations, instead of counteracting the tendency of their views by temperate expositions of their fallacy. To call names certainly requires less effort of mind than to reason logically, and to persons of certain tastes and powers may therefore be the most congenial mode of disputation. But we are not aware that the highest degree of proficiency in this species of dialectics ever threw much light on the world, or sensibly advanced the cause of truth; and it may be doubted if even the fisherwomen of

[2] From Joseph Addison's play *Cato* (1716), which depicts Cato the Younger's tragic last-ditch defense of the Roman Republic against Julius Caesar.—Ed.

[3] From a poem by Thomas Moore, satirist of the *London Times*. See *The Critic* (January 28, 1829), p. 153, for Leggett's review of Moore.—Ed.

Evening Post, September 7, 1835. Title added by Sedgwick. Text abridged.

Billingsgate,[1] who we believe stand unrivalled in vituperative eloquence, can be considered as ranking among the most edifying controversialists.

There are those, however, who widely differ from us in this opinion, if we may judge by their practise; who deem a harsh epithet more conclusive than a syllogism, and a personal allusion as comprising in itself subject, predicate, and copula. By this class of reasoners it has been our fortune to have many of our views opposed, and it is amusing to see the air of triumph with which they utter their opprobrious terms, as if each one levelled to the earth a whole file of arguments. Thus the fallacy of our views on banking was unanswerably demonstrated by calling us a lunatic; the folly of our opposition to monopolies was made manifest by likening us to Jack Cade;[2] and all reasoning in support of the equal rights of man was summarily overthrown by the tremendous epithet of agrarian. The views which we have felt it our duty to urge on various other subjects were irrevocably scattered by a volley of small shot, among which the phrases "sailor actor editor," and "chanting cherubs of the Post," did the most fatal execution. And now, again, our exertions in support of the sacred right of free discussion, and in defence of the supremacy of the laws, are answered by a single word—by denouncing us as *abolitionists*.

There are persons who might be frightened into silence by the terrors of this formidable epithet; but we have something of the same spirit in us that animates those to whom it more truly applies, and do not choose to be driven back by the mere vulgar exclamations of men who wield no weapon but abuse, and who do not even know the meaning of the words they so liberally employ. The foundation of our political creed is un-

[1] A fish market in London, England, whose fish porters made it synonymous with coarse language.—Ed.

[2] Jack Cade led the Kentish insurrection against Henry the Sixth. See Leggett's defense of him in "Utopia—Sir Thomas More—Jack Cade," in *Political Writings*, vol. I, pp. 125–133.—Ed.

bounded confidence in the intelligence and integrity of the great mass of mankind; and this confidence sustains and emboldens us in our course on every public question which arises. We are led by it, not to inquire into individual prejudices or opinions; not to an anxious examination of the popular pulse on every particular subject; but to an inquiry, simply, into the abstract merits of the question, and an examination of it by the tests of truth and reason, relying on the popular wisdom and honesty to sustain the line of conduct which such scrutiny suggests. It is so in the present case. There is no terror in the term abolitionist for us; for we trust to our readers to discriminate between words and things, and to judge of us by our sentiments, not by the appellations which foul-mouthed opponents bestow. The course we are pursuing is one which we entered upon after mature deliberation, and we are not to be turned from it by a species of opposition, the inefficacy of which we have seen displayed in so many former instances. It is Philip Van Artavelde who says—

> All my life long,
> I have beheld with most respect the man
> Who knew himself, and knew the ways before him,
> And from amongst them chose considerately,
> With a clear foresight, not a blindfold courage;
> And having chosen, with a steadfast mind
> Pursued his purposes.

This is the sort of character we emulate.

If to believe slavery a deplorable evil and a curse, in whatever light it is viewed; if to yearn for the day which shall break the fetters of three millions of human beings, and restore to them their birth-right of equal freedom; if to be willing, in season and out of season, to do all in our power to promote so desirable a result, by all means not inconsistent with higher duty: if these sentiments constitute us abolitionists, then are we such, and glory in the name. But while we mourn over the servitude which fetters a large portion of the American people, and freely proclaim that, did the control of the subject belong to us, we would speedily enfranchise them all, yet we defy the most vigilant opponent of this journal to point his finger to a word or syllable that looks like hostility to the political rights of the south, or conceals any latent desire to violate the federal compact, in letter or spirit.

The obligations of the federal compact, however, are greatly misrepresented by those who contend that it places a ban on all discussion of the question of slavery. It places an interdiction on the discussion of no subject whatever; but on the contrary secures, by an especial guarantee, that no prohibition or limitation of freedom of opinion and speech, in its widest latitude, shall ever be instituted. The federal government cannot directly interfere with the question of slavery, simply because the power of such interference is not included among those conferred upon it; and "all powers not delegated to the United States by the Constitution, nor prohibited by it to the states, are reserved to the states respectively, or to the people." The truth is, the only restraint on the discussion of slavery is that which exists in the good sense and good feeling of the people, in their sentiments of brotherhood, and in the desire which all rational minds must entertain of accomplishing worthy ends by means every way proportioned to the object. Whoever supposes that the question is guarded by any more positive obligation than this, has very imperfectly studied both the Constitution itself, and those documents which illustrate its history, and the sentiments, motives and policy of its founders. The Journal of the Convention which framed the Constitution, and those of the several State Conventions are happily extant. If it is true that the people of the United States are forbidden to speak their sentiments on one of the most momentous subjects which ever engaged their thoughts; if they are so bound in fetters of the mind that they must not allude to the less galling fetters which bind the limbs of the southern slave; let the prohibitory passage, we pray, be quickly pointed out; let us be convinced at once that we are not freemen, as we have heretofore fondly believed; let us know the worst; that we may seek to accommodate our minds and break down our rebellious spirits to the restricted limits in which alone they are permitted to expatiate.

. . . .

SLAVERY NO EVIL

Nothing, in these days of startling doctrines and outrageous conduct, has occurred to occasion us more surprise than the sentiments openly expressed by the southern newspapers, that slavery is not an evil, and that to indulge a hope that the poor bondman may be eventually enfranchised is not less heinous than to desire his immediate emancipation. We could hardly have believed, if we had not seen these sentiments expressed in the southern newspapers, that such opinions are entertained by any class of people in this country. But that they are both entertained and loudly promulgated, the extracts from Charleston papers which our columns contain this afternoon afford abundant and sorrowful proof. These extracts are from journals which speak the feelings and opinions of a whole community; journals conducted with ability, by men who weigh their words before they give them breath, and seldom utter sentiments, particularly on momentous questions, which are not fully responded to by a wide circle of readers. We have made our quotations from the Charleston

Evening Post, September 9, 1835. Title added by Sedgwick.

Courier and Charleston Patriot; but we might greatly extend them, did not our sickened feelings forbid, by similar passages from various other newspapers, published in various parts of the south.

Slavery no evil! Has it come to this, that the foulest stigma on our national escutcheon, which no true-hearted freeman could ever contemplate without sorrow in his heart and a blush upon his cheek, has got to be viewed by the people of the south as no stain on the American character? Have their ears become so accustomed to the clank of the poor bondman's fetters that it no longer grates upon them as a discordant sound? Have his groans ceased to speak the language of misery? Has his servile condition lost any of its degradation? Can the husband be torn from his wife, and the child from its parent, and sold like cattle at the shambles, and yet free, intelligent men, whose own rights are founded on the declaration of the unalienable freedom and equality of all mankind, stand up in the face of heaven and their fellow men, and assert without a blush that there is no evil in servitude? We could not have believed that the madness of the south had reached so dreadful a climax.

Not only are we told that slavery is no evil, but that it is criminal towards the south, and a violation of the spirit of the federal compact, to indulge even a hope that the chains of the captive may some day or other, no matter how remote the time, be broken. Ultimate abolitionists are not less enemies of the south, we are told, than those who seek to accomplish immediate enfranchisement. Nay, the threat is held up to us, that unless we speedily pass laws to prohibit all expression of opinion on the dreadful topic of slavery, the southern states will meet in Convention, separate themselves from the north, and establish a separate empire for themselves. The next claim we shall hear from the arrogant south will be a call upon us to pass edicts forbidding men to think on the subject of slavery, on the ground that even meditation on that topic is interdicted by the spirit of the federal compact.

What a mysterious thing this federal compact must be, which enjoins so much by its spirit that is wholly omitted in its language—nay not only omitted, but which is directly contrary to some of its express provisions! And they who framed that compact, how sadly ignorant they must have been of the import of the instrument they were giving to the world! They did not hesitate to speak of slavery, not only as an evil, but as the direst curse inflicted upon our country. They did not refrain from indulging a hope that the stain might one day or other be wiped out, and the poor bondman restored to the condition of equal freedom for which God and nature designed him. But the sentiments which Jefferson, and Madison, and Patrick Henry freely expressed are treasonable now, according to the new reading of the federal compact. To deplore the doom which binds three millions of human beings in chains, and to hope that by some just and gradual measures of philanthropy, their fetters, one by one, may be unlocked from their galled limbs, till at last, through all our borders, no bondman's groan shall mix with the voices of the free, and form a horrid discord in their rejoicings for national freedom—to entertain such sentiments is treated as opprobrious wrong done to the south, and we are called upon to lock each other's mouths with penal statutes, under the threat that the south will else separate from the confederacy, and resolve itself into a separate empire.

This threat, from iteration, has lost much of its terror. We have not a doubt, that to produce a disrupture of the Union, and join the slave states together in a southern league, has been the darling object, constantly and assiduously pursued for a long time past, of certain bad revolting spirits, who, like the arch-angel ruined, think that "to reign is worth ambition, though in hell." For this purpose all the arts and intrigues of Calhoun and his followers and myrmidons have been zealously and indefatigably exerted. For the achievement of this object various leading prints have long toiled without intermission, seeking to exasperate the southern people by daily efforts of inflammatory eloquence. For the accomplishment of this object they have traduced the north, misrepresented its sentiments, falsified its language, and given a sinister interpretation to every act. For the accomplishment of this object they have stirred up the present excitement on the slave question, and constantly do all in their power to aggravate the feeling of hostility to the north which their hellish arts have engendered. We see the means with which they work, and know the end at which they aim. But we trust their fell designs are not destined to be accomplished.

If, however, the political union of these states is only to be preserved by yielding to the claims set up by the south; if the tie of confederation is of such a kind that the breath of free discussion will inevitably dissolve it; if we can hope to maintain our fraternal connexion with our brothers of the south only by dismissing all hope of ultimate freedom to the slave; let the compact be dissolved, rather than submit to such dishonourable, such inhuman terms for its preservation. Dear as the Union is to us, and fervently as we desire that time, while it crumbles the false foundations of other governments, may add stability to that of our happy confederation, yet rather, far rather would we see it resolve into its original elements tomorrow, than that its duration should be effected by any measures so fatal to the principles of freedom as those insisted upon by the south.

These are the sentiments of at least one northern journal; and these sentiments we shall intermit no occasion of urging with all the earnestness of our nature and all the ability we possess. It is due to ourselves, and it is no less due to the south, that the north should speak out plainly on the questions which the demands of the former present for our decision. On this subject boldness and truth are required. Temporizing, like oil upon the waters, may smooth the billows for a moment, but cannot disperse the storm. Reasonable men and lovers of truth will not be offended with those who speak with boldness what reason and truth conspire to dictate. "As for the drummers and trumpeters of faction," to use the language of Lord

Bolingbroke, "who are hired to drown the voice of truth in one perpetual din of clamour, and would endeavour to drown, in the same manner, even the dying groans of their country, they deserve no answer but the most contemptuous silence."

PROGRESS OF FANATICISM

There are probably a good many readers of this paper who would be startled if we should say to them, in the briefest form of expression, *We are an Abolitionist.* They no doubt agree with us in the sentiment that slavery is a prodigious and alarming evil; that it continually and rapidly grows more and more portentous; and that it exercises a pernicious influence on the dearest interests of the country: on its internal political relations; its commercial and agricultural prosperity; and on the moral character, and social condition of the people. They would agree with us most heartily in wishing that this terrible evil could be remedied, and every vestige of it effaced from the land. They might perhaps go one step further, and acknowledge that the highest obligations of patriotism and philanthropy requre the subject to be discussed, temperately, but thoroughly; and that appeals, strengthened by all the cogency of argument, and animated with all the fervour of eloquence, should be sounded in the ears of the slaveholders, to arouse their humanity, convince their reason, and awaken their fears, and to bring all the agents of their hearts and understandings to cooperate in the great work of human emancipation.

Many persons would perhaps go to this extent with us,

Plaindealer, January 14, 1837. Extracts deleted.

when the propositions are thus broadly and diffusely stated, who would yet shrink back dismayed from a concise and simple declaration of abolitionism. But, reader, if you acknowledge the manifold evils of slavery, in all the aspects in which the subject can be considered; if you desire to see them terminated; and if you are willing, as one of the plainest and most innocent, as well as one of the most effectual modes of accomplishing that object, to discuss the question, *You are an Abolitionist.* That name, at all events, we freely admit belongs to ourselves; nor is there anything in its sound which grates upon our ear, nor in the duties it implies which our mind does not willingly embrace.

There is a class of persons connected with the newspaper press who seem to think that epithets are weapons of more cogency than arguments, and who therefore seek to dispose of every subject, not by an exposition of the correctness of their own opinions, or a refutation of the arguments of their opponents, but by bestowing upon them a shower of odious appellations. To call names certainly requires less exertion of intellect, than to reason soundly; and hence, to persons of certain tastes and capacities, this may be the most natural and congenial method of disputation. But we are not aware that the highest degree of proficiency in this species of dialecticks ever shed much light upon the world. The logick of sweeps and coal heavers, however highly embellished with their peculiar modes of rhetorical illustration, has never afforded any important assistance to the cause of truth; and it may be doubted if even the fishwomen of Billingsgate, who, we believe, stand unrivalled in vituperative and objurgatory eloquence, can be considered as among the most dignified and instructive of controversialists.

But there are those, if we may judge by their practice, who entertain a different opinion; who consider a harsh epithet as more conclusive than a syllogism, and a fierce denunciation as comprehending in itself subject, predicate, and copula. If you meet them with an array of incontrovertible arguments, they answer you with a discharge of opprobrious terms; and a cry of exultation usually succeeds the volley, as if it must necessarily have levelled all your logick to the earth. If you tell them that slavery is an evil, they deride you as a fanatick. If you claim the right to discuss the subject, they denounce you as an incendiary. If you call the poor degraded negro a fellow being, they shout amalgamationist at the top of their lungs, and invoke the mob to pelt you with stones, or to seize you and pour seething tar over your limbs. It is this class of logicians who have given to the term abolitionist its odious import. We are not of those, however, who can be deterred from the assertion of a right, or the performance of a duty, by opprobrium or threats; and we therefore not merely admit that we are an abolitionist, but earnestly lay claim to that appellation, considering it, not an epithet of disgrace, but a title of honour.

There probably is not, in the whole extent of this wide Confederacy, a single man, entitled, on any ground, to the slightest consideration, who would dare to lift up his head, and say, that the abolition of the African slave trade was not a noble and praiseworthy work. Yet reader, if you have ever perused the memoir of that illustrious and indefatigable philanthropist, Clarkson, or if his coadjutors, Roscoe, Wilberforce, and Fox, or even Boswell's biography of Johnson, you must be aware that the same sort of vituperative clamour was exerted to defeat that glorious project, which is now so freely used against the kindred objects of the abolitionists in this country. It is curious, indeed, to notice the positive identity of the phrases of reproach and denunciation made use of in the two cases. Then, as now, fanatick, incendiary, robber, and murderer, were among the terms most frequently employed. But those engaged in the good work persevered to the end, notwithstanding the obstacles they encountered, and by so doing have secured a place in the grateful recollection of all posterity, as among the noblest benefactors of mankind. There is little reason to fear that the glorious example will not be successfully emulated here. The progress of enlightened opinion on the subject of slavery has been wonderfully great in the last two years. The flame is spreading far and wide, and throwing its radiance over the whole land. The very measures taken to extinguish it have caused it to blaze up with greater brilliancy, and extend with a more rapid progress. The people of Charleston, when they broke riotously into the Post Office, and sought to silence discussion by violence, gave a fresh impulse to the spirit which they could not intimidate. The detestable doctrines of Amos Kendall's letter on that occasion,[1] brought myriads of new auxiliaries to the great cause of human freedom; and every succeeding effort of intolerance, every outbreak of violence, every tumultuous attempt to invade the sacred right of speech and of the press, has swelled the number of those who, in the true spirit of the Constitution, assert the equal claim of all mankind to the blessings of liberty.

How poor, how pitiful, to the mind of an enlightened philanthropist, must seem the brief and quibbling paragraph in the recent message of Governour Marcy, which contains all that functionary has thought proper to say on the subject of abolition. To that world-wide theme, which engages the attention of the loftiest minds, and enlists the sympathies of the best hearts in our Confederacy, the governour of this great state, in which the question is most vigourously discussed, can afford to give, in his official communication to the legislature, only the following imperfect notice:

. . . .

Who can read this evasive paragraph without blushing for the cringing spirit it betrays? Who can mark its tenour, without perceiving that it is throughout essentially false? Who can reflect upon its obvious motive and object, without a senti-

[1] Amos Kendall, Postmaster General of the United States, had refused to overrule the postmaster of Charleston's decision not to deliver abolitionist tracts through the mail. Leggett devoted several editorials to denunciation of this postal censorship.—Ed.

ment of contempt for the gubernatorial truckler that penned it? Since politicians first learned the art of misrepresenting truth, there never was a tissue of more disingenuous statements. "Some embarked in the scheme of abolition with good intentions?" Precious admission! Ay, *some* indeed! Take the abolitionists as a body, and there never was a band of men, engaged in any struggle for freedom, whose whole course and conduct evinced more unmixed purity of motive, and truer or loftier devotion to the great cause of human emancipation. Whatever difference of opinion there may be as to the propriety or practicability of their object, or the character of their means, there can be none as to the singleness and holiness of their motive. It is free from all taint of selfishness, from all alloy of personal ambition, and all sordid projects of ultimate gain. They battle for freedom, not for themselves, but for the wretched and degraded negro. To emancipate him, they incur odium, sustain losses, and make vast and continual sacrifices of money and health. They give their days to toil, and their nights to watching. They encounter the derision of the rabble, endure without retaliation the vilest outrages of their persons, see their houses broken into by mobs, their families insulted, their property scattered to the winds, and themselves hunted like beasts of the forest. Nothing but the highest and purest motives could sustain men through such rancour and frenzy of persecution as the abolitionists have endured. Call them fanaticks, if you will; denounce their object as visionary and ruinous, and themselves as actuated by an insane spirit of liberty; but do not—in the face of such proofs of singleness and sincerity as no set of men ever yet transcended—do not impeach the goodness of their intentions. They who sought to turn the question of slavery to party purposes were not abolitionists; they were "scurvy politicians," who denounced the abolitionists, and were anxious to throw the odium of that enterprise on the opposite party, for the base purpose of thereby effecting political results in the slave states. They were men influenced by the same paltry spirit which dictated the paragraph in Governour Marcy's message; a spirit which would conciliate the slaveholders at the expense of freedom and of truth; a spirit as different from that which animates the abolitionists, as the darkest hour of night from the meridian brightness of day. Dr. Channing,[2] in his recent eloquent letter to Mr. Birney, has paid a just tribute to the spirit which guides and sustains those engaged in the great and good cause of the abolition of slavery; and we cannot make a better appropriation of our space, than by here inserting a copious extract from it. We hope Governour Marcy will peruse the passage, and blush at the wretched figure which his own pusillanimous paragraph presents in the contrast.

. . . .

We thank Dr. Channing, from the bottom of our heart do we thank him, for lending the influence of his great name—*clarum et venerabile nomen*—to one of the highest and holiest causes that ever engaged the devoted energies of men. We welcome him to the brotherhood of "abolitionists, fanaticks and incendiaries." We rejoice that he has entered into the companionship of those "despicable and besotted wretches," who place so little value on the blessings of freedom as to desire to emancipate three millions of fellow creatures from galling and abject bondage. It gives us the highest gratification that he has joined himself to a fraternity which Governour Marcy assures us has dwindled into insignificance, and the proof of which is, that where, two years ago, there was one abolitionist, there are a thousand now, and where one press then feebly and timidly espoused the cause of emancipation, a hundred now boldly and energetically discuss the subject, in all its bearings and relations. This assurance of Governour Marcy, coupled with the other, that all cause of disquietude to the south has passed away, comes well upon the heel of those proceedings which it has recently been our duty to state,

[2] William Ellery Channing was a leading Unitarian clergyman and anti-slavery pamphleteer.—Ed.

and some of which are recorded in this very number of our paper. While abolitionists are mobbed in the north, and the chief executive officers of Virginia and South Carolina are calling on the legislatures in this portion of the Confederacy to silence free discussion by penal statutes, under a threat of a dissolution of the Union if they refuse to do so, Governour Marcy gravely announces to the people that all excitement has ceased, and that no cause for disquietude any longer exists. Out upon such official insincerity!

In the closing paragraph of the extract we have given from Dr. Channing's Letter, that great writer has exposed, with peculiar eloquence and force, the emptiness and shadowy nature of the chimera which the political braggarts of the south continually hold up as a bugbear to intimidate the people of the north from the exercise of one of their most sacred rights. If this vain threat were earnest, instead of mere bravado; if the phantasm were corporeal substance, instead of shadow, we would rather, far rather, encounter it, in its most horrid form, than pay the price which we are told will alone purchase security. We cannot give up Freedom for the sake of Union. We cannot give up the principle of vitality, the very soul of political existence, to secure the perishing body from dismemberment. No! rather let it be hewed to pieces, limb by limb, than, by dishonourable compromise, obtain a short renewal of the lease of life, to be dragged out in servitude and chains. Rather let the silken tie, which has so long united this sisterhood of states in a league that has made our country the pride and wonder of the world, be sundered at once, by one fell blow, than exchanged for the iron cord of despotism, and strengthened into a bond fatal to freedom. Dear as the federal compact is, and earnestly as we wish that time, while it is continually crumbling the false foundations of other governments, may add firmness to the cement which holds together that arch of union on which our own is reared, yet rather would we see it broken to-morrow into its original fragments, than that its durability should be accomplished by a measure fatal to the principles of liberty.

AN ARGUMENT AGAINST ABOLITION REFUTED

A calm and temperate writer appeared sometime since in the *American*, under the signature of a *Virginian*, who founded an argument against the abolition of slavery on certain facts derived from a comparison of the tables of mortality of the blacks in a state of servitude and in a state of freedom. The result of his statisticks was to show that the mortality of free blacks is greater than that of slaves, and greater than that of whites also; while the longevity of slaves exceeds even that of their masters. The inference of the writer was that humanity required the slaves to be left in that condition which facts showed to be most favourable to long life. . . .

. . . .

. . . Their superiour longevity may be doubly accounted for; for, on the one hand, while labour and simple diet are favourable to life, on the other, the habits of luxurious indolence which slaveholders fall into have the opposite effect. Such a comparison as the writer to whom the foregoing extract is in answer seeks to institute can be fair only when drawn between blacks in a state of servitude and blacks really free. What would be the effect of absolute and equal freedom on the black race in this country, is an experiment which has not yet been tried, and which, in the nature of things, cannot be tried very soon; for we have not only to do away the legal disabilities now imposed on those negroes whom we term free, but who are free only in a qualified sense, but we have also to do away the disabilities which exist in general and deep rooted prejudices. Opinion is tending in that direction; but its progress is slow, and a long period must elapse before the reformation will be complete. The day will come when the claims of the

Plaindealer, March 4, 1837. Text abridged and extract deleted.

American black race to all the privileges and immunities of equal political freedom will be fully acknowledged, and when the prejudices of society will give way before the steady influence of truth, enlightened reason, and comprehensive philanthropy. But before that time, any argument, founded on a comparison of the different rates of mortality between negroes in a state of slavery and those in a state of bastard freedom, must be wholly defective, even to the extent of proving the opposite influences on life of the two conditions of liberty and bondage. But even after that time, the argument, whatever might be the facts, would not answer the purpose for which it is produced; since longevity is but one of many circumstances which constitute the happiest condition of man. The writer from whom we have borrowed the extract to which we are appending these remarks, has shown that if it were the sole fact to be regarded, the condition of the convicts in our prisons is better than that of the most virtuous portion of society. The savages of our wilderness, before the poison of the distillery was introduced among them, enjoyed longer life, and were more exempt from disease, than the most educated and refined classes of our cities—

> ———But who infers from thence
> That such were happier, shocks all common sense.

COMMENCEMENT OF THE ADMINISTRATION OF MARTIN VAN BUREN

The inauguration of Martin Van Buren, as President of the United States took place at the Capitol, in Washington, on Saturday last, at noon. The day was serene and temperate, and the simple and august ceremonial was performed in the presence of assembled thousands. Mr. Van Buren delivered an Inaugural Address on the occasion, which, probably, most of our readers have already perused, but which, as a portion of the history of the times we insert in our paper. It is longer than the Inaugural Address of his immediate predecessor, but does not contain a tithe part of its pith. It professes to be an avowal of the principles by which the new President intends to be guided in his administration of the government; but with the single exception of the principle of opposition to the abolition of slavery in the District of Columbia, which it expresses with most uncalled for and unbecoming haste and positiveness, he might, with as much propriety, have sung *Yankee Doodle* or *Hail Columbia*, and called it "an avowal of his principles." With the exception of that indecorous announcement of a predetermination to exercise his veto against any measure of abolition which Congress may possibly think proper to adopt during the next four years, the address contains no expression of political principles whatever. . . .

. . . .

But it is not so much for what it has omitted to say, as for what it says, that we feel dissatisfaction with this inaugural address. We dislike exceedingly both the tone and spirit of its remarks on the subject of slavery. On that one topic, there is,

Plaindealer, March 11, 1837. Text abridged.

indeed, no want but a superabundance of "particularity and distinctness." Mr. Van Buren is the first President of the United States who, in assuming that office, has held up his veto power, *in terrorem*, to the world, and announced a fixed predetermination to exercise it on a particular subject, no matter what changes might take place in public opinion, or what events may occur to modify the question on which his imperial will is thus dictatorially announced.

. . . .

. . . Does Mr. Van Buren venture to affirm that such a law as he declares his intention of vetoing would be a violation of any article or clause in the federal compact? No! he believes that such a course will be "in accordance with the spirit which actuated the venerated fathers of the republic," but does not pretend that such a spirit has made itself palpable and unequivocal in any of the written provisions of the instrument which he has sworn to maintain. . . .

When a President announces that the letter of the Constitution shall be his guide of public conduct; when he takes as his rule of action a strict construction of the express provisions of that instrument, we may form some tolerable notion of what will be his course. But when he undertakes to steer by the uncertain light of the spirit, we are tossed about on a sea of vague conjecture, and left to the mercy of winds and waves. Hamilton was guided by the *spirit* in proposing the first federal bank; but Jefferson adhered to the *letter* in his argument against that evil scheme. The high tariff system claims for its paternity the *spirit* of the Constitution; but the advocates of a plan of equal taxation, adjusted to the actual wants of the government, find their warrant in the *letter*. The internal improvement system, the compromise system, the distribution system, and every other unequal and aristocratic system which has been adopted in our country, all claim to spring from the *spirit* of the Constitution; but Andrew Jackson found in the *letter* of that instrument his rule of conduct, and it was fondly hoped that his successor meant to emulate his example. Appearances now authorize a fear of the contrary. The first step is certainly a deviation from the path.

Mr. Van Buren's indecent haste to avow his predeterminations on the subject of slavery has not even the merit of boldness. It is made in a cringing spirit of propitiation to the south, and in the certainty that a majority at the north accord with his views. . . .

There is a single phrase in the anti-abolition portion of Mr. Van Buren's address upon which we shall make one additional comment, and then dismiss the subject. Alluding to the pro-slavery mobs and riots which have taken place in various parts of the country, he says, "a reckless disregard of the consequences of their conduct has exposed individuals to popular indignation." This is an admirable version of the matter. The issuing of a temperate and decorous newspaper, in which a question of great public moment was gravely discussed, showed, beyond all question, a most "reckless disregard of consequences," deserving the harshest rebuke; and the conduct of the mob that broke up the press, demolished the house which contained it, and shockingly maltreated the person of the editor, was merely a natural and justifiable expression of "popular indignation." They who thought the Constitution vouchsafed to them the freedom of speech and of the press, were criminal to act under that singular delusion; while they who dragged these atrocious men from the sanctuaries of God, from their firesides and from the pulpit, pelted them with stones, tore their garments from their limbs, steeped them in seething tar, and heaped all manner of injuries on their defenceless heads—these men were "true friends of the Constitution," and animated by "the spirit which actuated the venerated fathers of the republic." Mr. Van Buren does not say so in express terms; but he alludes to their atrocities in language so soft and sugary, as to sound almost like positive approval.

On the whole, we consider this Inaugual Address as constituting a page of Mr. Van Buren's history which will reflect no credit upon him in after times.

THE QUESTION OF SLAVERY NARROWED TO A POINT

————Farewell remorse!
Evil be thou my good! By thee, at least,
——I more than half, perhaps, will reign.
Milton.

The temperate and well-considered sentiments of Mr. Rives[1] on the subject of slavery, as expressed in the Senate last winter, when certain petitions against slavery in the District of Columbia were under consideration, do not meet with much approval in the southern states. But the violent language of Mr. Calhoun[2] is applauded to the echo. Mr. Rives, it will be remembered, admitted, in the most explicit manner, that "slavery is an evil, moral, social, and political;" while Mr. Calhoun, on the other hand, maintained that "it is a good—a great good."

We have a paragraph lying before us, from the *New-Orleans True American*, in which the sentiments of Mr. Calhoun are responded to with great ardour, and the admission that slavery is an evil is resisted as giving up the whole question in dispute. The writer says:

"If the principle be once acknowledged, that slavery is an evil, the success of the fanatics is certain. We are with Mr. Calhoun on this point. He insists that slavery is a *positive good* in our present social relations—that no power in the Union can touch the construction of southern society, without actual violation of all guaranteed and unalienated rights. This is the threshold of our liberties. If once passed, the tower must fall."

Reader, contemplate the picture presented to you in this

Plaindealer, April 15, 1837.

[1] William C. Rives, senator from Virginia—Ed.

[2] John C. Calhoun, senator from South Carolina.—Ed.

figurative language: the tower of liberty erected on the prostrate bodies of three millions of slaves. Worthy foundation of such an edifice! And appropriately is the journal which displays such anxiety for its stability termed the *True American*.

"Evil, be thou my good," is the exclamation of Mr. Calhoun, and myriads of true Americans join in worship of the divinity thus set up. But truth has always been a great iconoclast, and we think this idol of the slaveholders would fare little better in her hands than the images of pagan idolatry.

If the question of the abolition of slavery is to be narrowed down to the single point whether slavery is an evil or not, it will not take long to dispose of it. Yet it would perhaps not be an easy thing to prove that slavery is an evil, for the same reason that it would not be easy to prove that one and one are two; because the proposition is so elementary and self-evident, that it would itself be taken for a logical axiom as readily as any position by which we might seek to establish it. The great fundamental maxim of democratic faith is the natural equality of rights of all mankind. This is one of those truths which, in our Declaration of Independence, the Bill of Rights of this Confederacy, we claim to be self-evident. Those who maintain that slavery is not an evil must repudiate this maxim. They must be content to denounce the attempts to abolish slavery on the same ground that Gibbon* denounced the petitions to the British Parliament against the slave trade, because there was "a leaven of democratical principles in them, wild ideas of the rights and natural equality of man," and they must join that full-faced aristocrat in execrating "the fatal consequences of democratical principles, which lead by a path of flowers to the abyss of hell." If they admit man's natural equality, they at once admit slavery to be an evil. "In a future day," says Dymond, in his admirable work on morals,[3] "it will

* See his letter to Lord Sheffield, Miscellaneous Works, vol. 1, p. 349.

[3] A reference to Jonathan Dymond's *On the Applicability of the Pacific Principles of the New Testament to the Conduct of States*, the first American edition of which was published in 1832.—Ed.

probably become a subject of wonder how it could have happened that, on such a subject as slavery, men could have inquired and examined and debated, year after year; and that many years could have passed before the minds of a nation were so fully convinced of its enormity, and of their consequent duty to abolish it, as to suppress it to the utmost of their power. This will probably be a subject of wonder, because the question is so simple, that he who simply applies the requisitions of the moral law finds no time for reasoning or for doubt. The question as soon as it is proposed is decided."

But if we shut our eyes upon the moral law, and decide whether slavery is a good or an evil with sole reference to the test of utility; if we consider it merely a question of political economy, and one in which the interests of humanity and the rights of nature, as they affect the slave, are not to be taken into account, but the mere advantage of the masters alone regarded, we shall still come to the same conclusion. The relative condition of any two states of this Confederacy, taking one where slavery exists, and one where it does not, illustrates the truth of this remark. But it would not be difficult to prove, by a process of statistical arguments, that slave labour is far more costly than free, wretchedly as the wants and comforts of the slaves are provided for in most of the southern states. So that, limiting the inquiry to the mere question of pecuniary profit, it could be demonstrated that slavery is an evil. But this is a view of the subject infinitely less important than its malign influence in social and political respects, still regarding the prosperity of the whites as alone deserving consideration. When the social and political effects on three millions of black men are superadded as proper subjects of inquiry, the evil becomes greatly increased.

But to enter seriously into an argument to prove that slavery is an evil would be a great waste of time. They who assert the contrary do so under the influence of such feelings as are evinced by the ruined archangel, in the words from Milton which we have quoted at the head of these remarks. They do so in a tone of malignant defiance, and their own hearts, as they make the declaration, throb with a degrading consciousness of its falsehood.

The position that no power in the Union can touch the construction of southern society without violating guaranteed rights, will no more bear the test of examination, than the assertion that slavery is not an evil. There is no power, we concede, in the federal government to abolish slavery in any state, and none in any state to abolish it except within its own limits. But in as far as a free and full discussion of slavery, in all its characteristics and tendencies, may be considered as touching the construction of southern society, the right belongs to every citizen; and it is by this mode of touching it that it is hoped eventually to do away entirely with the deplorable evil. It cannot always exist against the constant attrition of public opinion.

The right to discuss slavery exists in various forms. It is claimed, in the first place, that Congress has absolute authority over that subject, so far as it relates to the District of Columbia. Every state, also, has authority over it within its own limits. And the people of the United States have absolute authority over it, so far as it presents a question to be considered in reference to any proposed amendment of the federal constitution. Suppose, for example, it should be desired by any portion of the people, to change the basis of southern representation in Congress, on the ground that slaves, being allowed to have no political rights, but being considered mere property, ought not to be enumerated in the political census, any more than the cattle and sheep of northern graziers and woolgrowers. The Constitution is amenable in this, as in every other respect, with the single exception of the equal representation of every state in the federal Senate; and it is consequently a legitimate subject of discussion. Yet the discussion of this subject involves, naturally and necessarily, a consideration of slavery in all its relations and influences. Suppose, again, any portion of the citizens of a state where negroes are not held to bondage, but are not admitted to equal suffrage, as in this state, should desire those distinctive limitations to be removed. This is a legitimate question to be discussed, and the discussion of this brings up the whole subject of slavery. Or suppose, thirdly, that any persons in a free state should desire to re-instate negro slavery. The south would scarcely quarrel with them for seeking to carry their wishes into effect; yet they could only hope to do so through the means of a discussion which would legitimately embrace every topic connected with slavery, nearly or remotely.

It is by discussion alone that those who are opposed to slavery seek to effect a reconstruction of southern society; and the means, we think, if there is any virtue in truth, will yet be found adequate to the end. If slavery is really no evil, the more it is discussed, the greater will be the number of its advocates; but if it is "an evil, moral, social and political," as Mr. Rives has had the manliness to admit, in the very teeth of Mr. Calhoun's bravado, it will gradually give way before the force of sound opinion.

"ABOLITION INSOLENCE"

. . . .

. . . The oppression which our fathers suffered from Great Britain was nothing in comparison with that which the negroes experience at the hands of the slaveholders. It may be "abolition insolence" to say these things; but as they are truths which justice and humanity authorize us to speak, we shall not

Plaindealer, July 29, 1837. Text abridged and extract deleted.

be too dainty to repeat them whenever a fitting occasion is presented. Every American who, in any way, authorizes or countenances slavery, is derelict to his duty as a christian, a patriot, and a man. Every one does countenance and authorize it, who suffers any opportunity of expressing his deep abhorrence of its manifold abominations to pass by unimproved. If the freemen of the north and west would but speak out on this subject in such terms as their consciences prompt, we should soon have to rejoice in the complete enfranchisement of our negro brethren of the south.

If an extensive and well-arranged insurrection of the blacks should occur in any of the slave states, we should probably see the freemen of this quarter of the country rallying around that "glorious emblem"[1] which is so magniloquently spoken of in the foregoing extract, and marching beneath its folds to take sides with the slaveholders, and reduce the poor negroes, struggling for liberty, to heavier bondage than they endured before. It may be "abolition insolence" to call this "glorious emblem" the standard of oppression, but, at all events, it is unanswerable truth. For our part, we call it so in a spirit, not of insolence, not of pride speaking in terms of petulant contempt, but of deep humility and abasement. We confess, with the keenest mortification and chagrin, that the banner of our country is the emblem, not of justice and freedom, but of oppression; that it is the symbol of a compact which recognizes, in palpable and outrageous contradiction of the great principle of liberty, the right of one man to hold another as property; and that we are liable at any moment to be required, under all our obligations of citizenship, to array ourselves beneath it, and wage a war, of extermination if necessary, against the slave, for no crime but asserting his right of equal humanity—the self-evident truth that all men are created equal, and have an unalienable right of life, liberty, and the pursuit of happiness. Would we comply with such a requisi-

[1] Namely, the American flag.—Ed.

tion? No! rather would we see our right arm lopped from our body, and the mutilated trunk itself gored with mortal wounds, than raise a finger in opposition to men struggling in the holy cause of freedom. The obligations of citizenship are strong, but those of justice, humanity and religion stronger. We earnestly trust that the great contest of opinion which is now going on in this country may terminate in the enfranchisement of the slaves, without recourse to the strife of blood; but should the oppressed bondmen, impatient of the tardy progress of truth urged only in discussion, attempt to burst their chains by a more violent and shorter process, they should never encounter our arm, nor hear our voice, in the ranks of their opponents. We should stand a sad spectator of the conflict; and whatever commiseration we might feel for the discomfiture of the oppressors, we should pray that the battle might end in giving freedom to the oppressed.

PART FOUR

The Division of Political Classes

DESPOTISM OF ANDREW JACKSON

I

Hitherto despotism has assuredly been considered as the concentration of all power in one man, or in a few privileged persons, and its appropriate exercise the oppression of the great majority of the people. But the Presidential Bank candidates in the Senate of the United States, and the bribed tools of the Bank who preside over the Bank presses, have lately discovered, or rather invented, an entire new species of despotism. They have found out that pure republican despotism consists in administering the Constitution and laws with an express reference to, and entirely for, the benefit of the people at large.

If we examine the whole course of that extraordinary despot, the President of the United States, it will be found that the very essence of his usurpation consists in interpreting the Constitution, and administering the laws, for the benefit of the many instead of the few. This is the true character of his despotism, and for this is he denounced by those who wish to free the people from this original and extraordinary tyranny, by reversing the picture, and placing the rights and interest of the many at the mercy of the few. In order more clearly to exemplify the character of General Jackson's despotism, we will pass in brief review the prominent acts of his administration.

If we comprehend the nature and principles of a free government, it consists in the guaranty of EQUAL RIGHTS to all

Evening Post, May 22 and 23, 1834. Title added by Sedgwick; Roman numerals added.

free citizens. We know of no other definition of liberty than this. Liberty is, in short, nothing more than the total absence of all MONOPOLIES of all kinds, whether of rank, wealth, or privilege. When General Jackson was elected by a large majority of the people of the United States to the first office in their gift, he found in successful operation a system calculated, if not intended, to sap the whole fabric of equal rights, because it consisted of little else than monopolies, either open and palpable, or in some flimsy disguise or other calculated to cheat the people into a quiet acquiescence.

The first was an oppressive tariff, a system of bounties in disguise, under the operation of which the consumers of domestic manufactures were obliged to pay from twenty-five to two hundred per cent. more for certain indispensable articles of consumption than he would have paid had things been suffered to take their natural course. The consumers of an article always constitute a much greater number of the people than the manufacturers, simply because one man can supply the wants of many. Hence this bounty was a device to tax the many for the benefit of the few. It operated exclusively in favour of the smaller class, and exclusively against the most numerous. It was, therefore, not only destructive of the principle of EQUAL RIGHTS, but it was a sacrifice of the rights of a great majority in behalf of a small minority.

The first act of General Jackson was to set his face against this anti-republican principle of protecting one class of labour at the expense of the others. He made use of his personal and political influence to bring down the rate of duties on importations to their proper standard, namely, the wants of the government, in which all were equally concerned; and that influence, aided by the good sense of the people, was on the point of being successful, when, by a juggle between Messrs. Clay and Calhoun, the measure was transferred to the Senate. That body passed a bill similar to one on the eve of passing the House of Representatives, which was sent to the latter as an amendment to their own bill, and adopted with wonderful docility. The object of this most excellent legerdemain was to give to Messrs. Clay and Calhoun the credit of an adjustment of the tariff, which but for General Jackson would have remained a subject of heart burning and contention, in all probability to this day. By this notorious assumption Mr. Clay sought to gain credit for his disinterestedly sacrificing his friends on the altar of Union, while Mr. Calhoun was delighted with so capital an excuse for postponing his plan of nullification to a more favourable opportunity. It was a cunning manoeuvre; but, cunning is not wisdom, any more than paper money is gold. Notwithstanding the absurd pretensions of these two gentlemen to the honour of adjusting the tariff, there is probably not a rational man in the United States who is not satisfied that the real pacificator was General Jackson, and that Mr. Clay only assented to what he could not prevent. He found the current going strongly against him, and was nothing more than honest King Log, floating with the tide.

This was General Jackson's first act of despotism. He interfered to relieve the many from those burthens which had been imposed on them for the benefit of the few; he restored, in this instance, the EQUAL RIGHTS of all, and for this he is denounced a despot and usurper.

When General Jackson came into office he found another system in operation, calculated not only to undermine and destroy the principles and independence of the people, but to trench upon the sacred republican doctrine of EQUAL RIGHTS. We allude to Mr. Clay's other grand lever by the aid of which he hoped to raise his heavy momentum to the height of his lofty ambition—his system of national internal improvement. Besides the constitutional difficulty arising from the necessary interference with state jurisdictions, there were other powerful objections to this system. It placed the whole revenues of the people of the United States at the disposal of Congress, for purposes of political influence. It enabled ambitious politicians to buy up a township with a new bridge; a district with a road, and a state with a canal. It gave to the

General Government an irresistible power over the elections of the states, and constituted the very basis of consolidation. In addition to all this, it was a direct and palpable encroachment on the equal rights of the citizens. It was taxing one state for the exclusive benefit of another; nay, it was diverting money contributed by one state to purposes injurious to the interests of that state. It was appropriating the funds contributed by New-York for the general benefit, to the Ohio and Chesapeake Canal, the successful completion of which it was boasted would be highly injurious to her own internal navigation. In short, it was a system of favouritism entirely destructive to EQUAL RIGHTS, inasmuch as it was entirely impossible that all should partake equally in its benefits, while all were taxed equally for its expenditures.

To test the firmness of the old patriot, the great champion of EQUAL RIGHTS, a bill was concocted by the combined ingenuity of the advocates of internal improvement, combining such powerful temptations, and appealing to so many sectional interests, that it was hoped General Jackson either would not dare to interpose his constitutional prerogative to arrest its passage, or that if he did, the consequences would be fatal to his popularity. But the old patriot was not to be frightened from his duty, and besides has a generous confidence in the intelligence and integrity of his fellow-citizens. He knows by glorious experience that the true way to the affections and confidence of a free and enlightened people, is to stand forth in defence of the EQUAL RIGHTS of all. He vetoed this great bribery bill and the people honoured his firmness, and sustained him in the great effort he had made in their behalf. This is the second great usurpation of General Jackson, and the second great example of his despotism. He interposed to protect the people from a system which afforded a pretext for applying the means of the many to the purposes of the few, and furnished almost unbounded resources for corrupting the people with their own money.

We shall continue the history of the despotism of Andrew Jackson in our paper of to-morrow.

II

The next text on which the Bank coalition have rung the changes of "tyranny," "despot," and "usurper," is the veto on Mr. Clay's bill for distributing the public lands among the respective states. The people should understand that these lands are their exclusive property. They contribute a general source of revenue common and equal to all. But the bill of Mr. Clay, no doubt for the purpose of raising the popularity of that permanent candidate for national honours in the west, established a distinction in favour of certain states, of either twelve or fifteen per cent.—we cannot just now be certain which—on the plea that a large portion of these lands were within their limits, although they were the property of the people of the United States.

General Jackson justly considered this preference of certain states over others as not only unconstitutional, but unjust, and for these and other cogent reasons, to which the coalition has never been able to fabricate an answer, declined to sanction the bill. Here, as in every other act of his administration, he stood forward the champion of the EQUAL RIGHTS of the people, in opposing an unequal distribution of their common property. Yet for this, among other acts equally in defence or vindication of these rights it has been thundered forth to the people that he is a tyrant and usurper.

But it is in relation to his course with regard to the Bank of the United States, that he appears most emphatically as the champion of the Constitution and the EQUAL RIGHTS of the people. Fully aware of the great truth, that monopolies, whether of rank or privilege, whether possessed by virtue of hereditary descent or conferred by legislative folly or legislative corruption, were the most sly and dangerous enemies to equal rights ever devised by the cunning of avarice or the wiles of ambition, he saw in the vast accumulation of power in that institution, and its evident disposition to exercise, as well as perpetuate it, the elements of destruction to the freedom of the people and the independence of their government. He, therefore, with the spirit and firmness becoming his character and station as the ruler of a free people, determined to exercise his constitutional prerogative in arresting its usurpations, and preventing their being perpetuated.

The child, the champion, and the representative of the great democracy of the United States, he felt himself identified with their interests and feelings. He was one of themselves, and as such had long seen and felt the oppressions which a great concentrated money power, extending its influence, nay, its control, over the currency, and consequently the prosperity of the country throughout every nook and corner of the land, had inflicted or might inflict upon the people. He saw in the nature, and in the acts, of this enormous monopoly, an evident tendency, as well as intention, to subjugate the states and their government to its will; and like himself, and in conformity with the whole tenor of his life, he resolved to risk his place, his popularity, his repose, in behalf of the EQUAL RIGHTS of the people.

He saw, moreover, as every true democrat must see, who interprets the Constitution upon its true principles, that the creation of a Bank with the privilege of establishing its branches in every state, without their consent, was not delegated by the states to the general government; and he saw that by one of the first declaratory amendments of the Constitution, that *"The powers not delegated to the United States by the Constitution, nor prohibited to it by the states, are reserved to the states respectively, or to the people."*

But there is, unfortunately, a clause in the Constitution, which is somewhat of the consistency of India rubber, and by proper application can be stretched so as to unite the opposite extremes of irreconcileable contradictions. It is somewhat like the old gentleman's will in the Tale of a Tub, about which Lord Peter, Martin and Jack disputed so learnedly, and which at one time was a loaf of brown bread, at another a shoulder of mutton. It admits of a wonderful latitude of construction, and an ingenious man can find no great difficulty in interpreting it to suit his own particular interests. We allude to the following, which will be found among the enumeration of the powers of Congress:

"To make all laws which shall be *necessary and proper* for carrying into execution the foregoing powers, and all other powers vested in the government of the United States, or in any department or officer thereof."

The sticklers for state rights in the Convention which adopted the Constitution, and in the State Conventions to which it was referred for acceptance or rejection, did not much relish this saving clause. They imagined they saw in it a sort of Pandora's box, which, if once fairly opened, would cast forth a legion of constructive powers and constructive usurpations. They thought they perceived in these two little words "NECESSARY AND PROPER," a degree of elasticity which might be expanded so as to comprehend almost any thing that a majority of Congress might choose to ascribe to them. They were, in our opinion, not much mistaken in their anticipations, although probably they scarcely dreamed that the constructive ingenuity of the times would find *that* to be indispensably "necessary" which the country was enabled for many years to dispense with, during which time it enjoyed a degree of prosperity which excited the envy and admiration of the world!

However this may be, the people of the United States will do well to bear in mind, when they hear General Jackson denounced as a tyrant and usurper for the course he has pursued in relation to the Bank, that this institution has no other legs in the Constitution to stand upon than those two little words "necessary and proper." If it is necessary and proper, then it *may* be re-chartered under the Constitution; but it has no right to demand a re-charter. If it is not necessary and proper, then it ought never to have been chartered, and ought not to be continued one moment longer than the faith of the nation is pledged.

As this is one of those points which rests on the nice interpretation of words, it naturally depends for its decision on the general bias of the two parties in the controversy. The party attached by habit, education, interests, or prejudice, to a consolidated or strong government, will interpret "necessary and proper" one way, and the party opposed to any accumulation of constructive powers in the federal government, will interpret them the other way. General Hamilton, for example, considered a Bank of the United States "necessary and proper," while Mr. Jefferson believed, and has repeatedly denounced it, to be the most dangerous infraction of the constitution ever attempted under the cloak of constructive power. Such has always been the opinion of the great leaders of the democracy of the United States, although some of them have yielded to the voice of a majority of Congress, mistaking it for that of the people.

We have premised thus much in order to show that the course pursued by General Jackson, in regard to the Bank of the United States, is in perfect consonance with the known principles of the democracy, the people of the United States. When the Democratic Party had the ascendency, they took the first opportunity that offered to put an end to the first Bank of the United States, and now they avail themselves of a similar occasion to give a like demonstration of their settled principles and policy. General Jackson would not have been re-elected by that party, against all the corruptions of the Bank, combined with the whole force of all the disjointed, incongruous elements of opposition, *after* he had placed his *Veto* on its re-charter, had he not acted in this instance in strict conformity with the sentiments of a great majority of the democracy of the United States. Here as in every other act of his administration, they saw in him the great opponent of monopolies, the stern, inflexible champion of EQUAL RIGHTS.

With regard to the other alleged acts of despotism charged upon this true unwavering patriot, such as the removal of Mr. Duane from office,[1] and the appointment of one of the very ablest and purest men of this country in his stead; the subsequent removal of the deposites from the Bank of the United States, and the protest against the *ex-parte* condemnation of the "Independent Aristocratic Body," more has already been said in his defence than such charges merited. We do not believe the Senators making them believed one word they themselves uttered on the subject, because, though tainted to the core by personal antipathies and personal ambition, they are men of too clear intellect, seriously to cherish such ideas of the constitution as they have lately put forth to the people. These speeches and denunciations, like those on the subject of universal distress and bankruptcy, were merely made for effect. They certainly could not believe that what the constitution expressly delegates was intended to be withheld; that what was expressly conceded by the charter of the Bank of the United States was intended to be denied; or that the exercise of a privilege inherent in human nature, to wit, that of self-defence, was an outrage on the privileges of the Senate. Real honest error may sometimes be combated successfully by argument; but we know of no way of convincing a man who only affects to be in the wrong in order to deceive others, and shall therefore spare ourselves and our readers any further discussion with opponents who are not in earnest, but who have so high an opinion of the sagacity of the people, that they think they can make them believe what they do not believe themselves.

It will be perceived from this brief analysis of the leading measures of General Jackson's administration, that all his

[1] William John Duane, secretary of the treasury from June to October of 1833, was removed after refusing to obey Jackson's directive to transfer federal government deposits from the Bank of the United States to state banks.—Ed.

"tyranny" has consisted in successfully interposing the Constitution of the United States in defence of the EQUAL RIGHTS of the people; and that all his "usurpations" have been confined to checking those of the advocates of consolidation, disunion, monopolies, and lastly a great consolidated moneyed aristocracy, equally dangerous to liberty from the power it legally possesses, and those it has usurped. Yet this is the man whom the usurpers themselves denounce as a usurper. This is the man against whom the concentrated venom of disappointed ambition and baffled avarice is vainly striving to contend in the heads and hearts of the American people, and to bury under a mass of wilful calumnies. This is the very man whose whole soul is wound up to the great and glorious task of restoring the EQUAL RIGHTS of his fellow-citizens, as they are guarantied by the letter and spirit of the constitution. May Providence send us a succession of such USURPERS as Andrew Jackson, and spare the people from such champions of liberty as Henry Clay, John C. Calhoun, Daniel Webster, George Poindexter, and Nicholas Biddle!

THE DIVISION OF PARTIES

Since the organization of the Government of the United States the people of this country have been divided into two great parties. One of these parties has undergone various changes of name; the other has continued steadfast alike to its appellation and to its principles, and is now, as it was at first, the DEMOCRACY. Both parties have ever contended for the same

Evening Post, November 4, 1834. Title added by Sedgwick.

opposite ends which originally caused the division—whatever may have been, at different times, the particular means which furnished the immediate subject of dispute. The great object of the struggles of the Democracy has been to confine the action of the General Government within the limits marked out in the Constitution: the great object of the party opposed to the Democracy has ever been to overleap those boundaries, and give to the General Government greater powers and a wider field for their exercise. The doctrine of the one party is that all power not expressly and clearly delegated to the General Government, remains with the States and with the People: the doctrine of the other party is that the vigour and efficacy of the General Government should be strengthened by a free construction of its powers. The one party sees danger from the encroachments of the General Government; the other affects to see danger from the encroachments of the States.

This original line of separation between the two great political parties of the republic, though it existed under the old Confederation, and was distinctly marked in the controversy which preceded the formation and adoption of the present Constitution, was greatly widened and strengthened by the project of a National Bank, brought forward in 1791. This was the first great question which occurred under the new Constitution to test whether the provisions of that instrument were to be interpreted according to their strict and literal meaning; or whether they might be stretched to include objects and powers which had never been delegated to the General Government, and which consequently still resided with the states as separate sovereignties.

The proposition of the Bank was recommended by the Secretary of the Treasury on the ground that such an institution would be "of primary importance to the prosperous administration of the finances, and of the greatest utility in the operations connected with the support of public credit." This scheme, then, as now, was opposed on various grounds; but the constitutional objection constituted then, as it does at the present day, the main reason of the uncompromising and invincible hostility of the democracy to the measure. They considered it as the exercise of a very important power which had never been given by the states or the people to the General Government, and which the General Government could not therefore exercise without being guilty of usurpation. Those who contended that the Government possessed the power, effected their immediate object; but the controversy still exists. And it is of no consequence to tell the democracy that it is now established by various precedents, and by decisions of the Supreme Court, that this power is fairly incidental to certain other powers expressly granted; for this is only telling them that the advocates of free construction have, at times, had the ascendancy in the Executive and Legislative, and, at all times, in the Judiciary department of the Government. The Bank question stands now on precisely the same footing that it originally did; it is now, as it was at first, a matter of controversy between the two great parties of this country—between parties as opposite as day and night—between parties which contend, one for the consolidation and enlargement of the powers of the General Government, and the other for strictly limiting that Government to the objects for which it was instituted, and to the exercise of the means with which it was entrusted. The one party is for a popular Government; the other for an aristocracy. The one party is composed, in a great measure, of the farmers, mechanics, labourers, and other producers of the middling and lower classes, (according to the common gradation by the scale of wealth,) and the other of the consumers, the rich, the proud, the privileged—of those who, if our Government were converted into an aristocracy, would become our dukes, lords, marquises and baronets. The question is still disputed between these two parties—it is ever a new question—and whether the democracy or the aristocracy shall succeed in the present struggle, the fight will be renewed, whenever the defeated party shall be again able to muster strength enough to take the field. The privilege of self-government is one which the people will never be permitted to enjoy unmolested. Power and wealth are continually stealing from the many to the few. There is a class continually gaining ground in the community, who desire to monopolize the advantages of the Government, to hedge themselves round with exclusive privileges, and elevate themselves at the expense of the great body of the people. These, in our society, are emphatically the aristocracy; and these, with all such as their means of persuasion, or corruption, or intimidation, can move to act with them, constitute the party which are now struggling against the democracy, for the perpetuation of an odious and dangerous moneyed institution.

Putting out of view, for the present, all other objections to the United States Bank,—that it is a monopoly, that it possesses enormous and overshadowing power, that it has been most corruptly managed, and that it is identified with political leaders to whom the people of the United States must ever be strongly opposed—the constitutional objection alone is an insurmountable objection to it.

The Government of the United States is a limited sovereignty. The powers which it may exercise are expressly enumerated in the Constitution. None not thus stated, or that are not "necessary and proper" to carry those which are stated into effect, can be allowed to be exercised by it. The power to establish a bank is not expressly given; neither is incidental; since it cannot be shown to be "necessary" to carry the powers which are given, or any of them, into effect. That power cannot therefore be exercised without transcending the Constitutional limits.

This is the democratic argument stated in its briefest form. The aristocratic argument in favour of the power is founded on the dangerous heresy that the Constitution says one thing, and means another. That *necessary* does not mean *necessary*, but simply *convenient*. By a mode of reasoning not looser than this it would be easy to prove that our Government ought to be changed into a Monarchy, Henry Clay crowned King, and the opposition members of the Senate made peers of the realm; and power, place and perquisites given to them and their heirs forever.

RICH AND POOR

The rich perceive, acknowledge, and act upon a common interest, and why not the poor? Yet the moment the latter are called upon to combine for the preservation of their rights, forsooth the community is in danger! Property is no longer secure, and life in jeopardy. This cant has descended to us from those times when the poor and labouring classes had no stake in the community, and no rights except such as they could acquire by force. But the times have changed, though the cant remains the same. The scrip nobility of this Republic have adopted towards the free people of this Republic the same language which the Feudal Barons and the despot who contested with them the power of oppressing the people, used towards their serfs and villains, as they were opprobiously called.

These would-be lordlings of the Paper Dynasty, cannot or will not perceive, that there is some difference in the situation and feelings of the people of the United States, and those of the despotic governments of Europe. They forget that at this moment our people, we mean emphatically the class which labours with its own hands, is in possession of a greater portion of the property and intelligence of this country, ay, ten times

Evening Post, November 4, 1834. Misdated by Sedgwick.

over, than all the creatures of the paper credit system put together. This property is indeed more widely and equally distributed among the people than among the phantoms of the paper system, and so much the better. And as to their intelligence, let any man talk with them, and if he does not learn something it is his own fault. They are as well acquainted with the rights of person and property, and have as just a regard for them, as the most illustrious lordling of the scrip nobility. And why should they not? Who and what are the great majority of the wealthy people of this city—we may say of this country? Are they not (we say it not in disparagement, but in high commendation) are they not men who began the world comparatively poor with ordinary education and ordinary means? And what should make them so much wiser than their neighbours? Is it because they live in better style, ride in carriages, and have more money—or at least more credit than their poorer neighbours? Does a man become wiser, stronger, or more virtuous and patriotic, because he has a fine house over his head? Does he love his country the better because he has a French cook, and a box at the opera? Or does he grow more learned, logical and profound by intense study of the daybook, ledger, bills of exchange, bank promises, and notes of hand?

Of all the countries on the face of the earth, or that ever existed on the face of the earth, this is the one where the claims of wealth and aristocracy are the most unfounded, absurd and ridiculous. With no claim to hereditary distinctions; with no exclusive rights except what they derive from monopolies, and no power of perpetuating their estates in their posterity, the assumption of aristocratic airs and claims is supremely ridiculous. To-morrow they themselves may be beggars for aught they know, or at all events their children may become so. Their posterity in the second generation will have to begin the world again, and work for a living as did their forefathers. And yet the moment a man becomes rich among us, he sets up for wisdom—he despises the poor and ignorant —he sets up for patriotism: he is your only man who has a stake in the community, and therefore the only one who ought to have a voice in the state. What folly is this? And how contemptible his presumption? He is not a whit wiser, better or more patriotic than when he commenced the world, a waggon driver. Nay not half so patriotic, for he would see his country disgraced a thousand times, rather than see one fall of the stocks, unless perhaps he had been speculating on such a contingency. To him a victory is only of consequence, as it raises, and a defeat only to be lamented, as it depresses a loan. His soul is wrapped up in a certificate of scrip, or a Bank note. Witness the conduct of these pure patriots, during the late war, when they, at least a large proportion of them, not only withheld all their support from the Government, but used all their influence to prevent others from giving their assistance. Yet these are the people who alone have a stake in the community, and of course exclusively monopolize patriotism.

But let us ask what and where is the danger of a combination of the labouring classes in vindication of their political principles, or in defence of their menaced rights? Have they not the right to act in concert, when their opponents act in concert? Nay, is it not their bounden duty to combine against the only enemy they have to fear as yet in this free country, monopoly and a great paper system that grinds them to the dust? Truly this is strange republican doctrine, and this is a strange republican country, where men cannot unite in one common effort, in one common cause, without rousing the cry of danger to the rights of person and property. Is not this a government of the people, founded on the rights of the people, and instituted for the express object of guarding them against the encroachments and usurpations of power? And if they are not permitted the possession of common interest; the exercise of a common feeling; if they cannot combine to resist by constitutional means, these encroachments; to what purpose were they declared free to exercise the right of suffrage in the choice of rulers, and the making of laws?

And what we ask is the power against which the people, not

only of this country, but of almost all Europe, are called upon to array themselves, and the encroachment on their rights, they are summoned to resist? Is it not emphatically, the power of monopoly, and the encroachments of corporate privileges of every kind, which the cupidity of the rich engenders to the injury of the poor?

It was to guard against the encroachments of power, the insatiate ambition of wealth that this government was instituted, by the people themselves. But the objects which call for the peculiar jealousy and watchfulness of the people, are not now what they once were. The cautions of the early writers in favour of the liberties of mankind, have in some measure become obsolete and inapplicable. We are menaced by our old enemies, avarice and ambition, under a new name and form. The tyrant is changed from a steel-clad feudal baron, or a minor despot, at the head of thousands of ruffian followers, to a mighty civil gentleman, who comes mincing and bowing to the people with a quill behind his ear, at the head of countless millions of magnificent *promises.* He promises to make every body rich; he promises to pave cities with gold; and he promises to pay. In short he is made up of promises. He will do wonders, such as never were seen or heard of, provided the people will only allow him to make his promises, equal to silver and gold, and human labour, and grant him the exclusive benefits of all the great blessings he intends to confer on them. He is the sly, selfish, grasping and insatiable tyrant, the people are now to guard against. A CONCENTRATED MONEY POWER; a usurper in the disguise of a benefactor; an agent exercising privileges which his principal never possessed; an impostor who, while he affects to wear chains, is placed above those who are free; a chartered libertine, that pretends to be manacled only that he may the more safely pick our pockets, and lord it over our rights. This is the enemy we are now to encounter and overcome, before we can expect to enjoy the substantial realities of freedom.

THE STREET OF THE PALACES

There is, in the city of Genoa, a very elegant street, commonly called, *The Street of the Palaces.* It is broad and regular, and is flanked, on each side, with rows of spacious and superb palaces, whose marble fronts, of the most costly and imposing architecture, give an air of exceeding grandeur to the place. Here reside the principal aristocracy of Genoa; the families of Balbi, Doria, and many others of those who possess patents of nobility and exclusive privileges. The lower orders of the people, when they pass before these proud edifices, and cast their eyes over the striking evidences which the lordly exteriors exhibit of the vast wealth and power of the titled possessors, may naturally be supposed to think of their own humble dwellings and slender possessions, and to curse in their hearts those institutions of their country which divide society into such extremes of condition, forcing the many to toil and sweat for the pampered and privileged few. Wretched indeed are the serfs and vassals of those misgoverned lands, where a handful of men compose the privileged orders, monopolising political power, diverting to their peculiar advantage the sources of pecuniary emolument, and feasting, in luxurious idleness, on the fruits of the hard earnings of the poor.

But is this condition of things confined to Genoa, or to European countries? Is there no parallel for it in our own? Have we not, in this very city, our "*Street of the Palaces,*" adorned with structures as superb as those of Genoa in exterior magnificence, and containing within them vaster treasures of wealth? Have we not, too, our *privileged orders?* our scrip nobility? aristocrats, clothed with special immunities, who control, indirectly, but certainly, the political power of the state,

Plaindealer, December 10, 1836.

monopolise the most copious sources of pecuniary profit, and wring the very crust from the hard hand of toil? Have we not, in short, like the wretched serfs of Europe, our lordly masters,

> "Who make us slaves, and tell us 'tis *their charter*?"

If any man doubts how these questions should be answered, let him walk through Wall-street. He will there see a street of palaces, whose stately marble walls rival those of Balbi and Doria. If he inquires to whom those costly fabrics belong, he will be told to the *exclusively privileged of this land of equal laws!* If he asks concerning the political power of the owners, he will ascertain that three-fourths of the legislators of the state are of their own order, and deeply interested in preserving and extending the privileges they enjoy. If he investigates the sources of their prodigious wealth, he will discover that it is extorted, under various delusive names, and by a deceptive process, from the pockets of the unprivileged and unprotected poor. These are the masters in this land of freedom. These are our aristocracy, our scrip nobility, our privileged order of charter-mongers and money-changers! Serfs of free America! bow your necks submissively to the yoke, for these exchequer barons have you fully in their power, and resistance now would but make the burden more galling. Do they not boast that they will be represented in the halls of legislation, and that the people cannot help themselves? Do not their servile newspaper mouth-pieces prate of the impolicy of giving an inch to the people, lest they should demand an ell? Do they not threaten, that unless the people restrict their requests within the narrowest compass, they will absolutely grant them nothing?—that they will not relax their fetters at all, lest they should next strive to snap them entirely asunder?

These are not figures of speech. Alas! we feel in no mood to be rhetorical. Tropes and figures are the language of the free, and we are slaves!—slaves to most ignoble masters, to a low-minded, ignorant, and rapacious order of money-changers. We speak, therefore, not in figures, but in the simplest and soberest phrase. We speak plain truths in plain words, and only give utterance to sentiments that involuntarily rose in our mind, as we glided this morning through the *Street of the Palaces*, beneath the frowning walls of its marble structures, fearing that our very thoughts might be construed into a breach of privilege. But thank heaven! the day has not yet come—though perhaps it is at hand—when our paper money patricians deny their serfs and vassals the right to think and speak. We may still give utterance to our opinions, and still walk with a confident step through the *Street of the Palaces of the Charter-mongers*.

AMERICAN NOBILITY

A writer, of uncommon eloquence and ingenuity, has appealed, in the columns of the Evening Post, under the signature of *Anti-Privilege*, and has undertaken to prove the unconstitutionality of the restraining law, on the ground that it is a violation of that clause of the federal constitution which declares that *no state shall grant any title of nobility*. It is obvious, from the whole tenor of the article, that this is not undertaken as a mere exercise of ingenuity; but that, "just in his views or not, the writer is in earnest." We have read his remarks with attention, and profess ourselves to be of the opinion he so cogently maintains, that the restraining law is, in effect, if not in letter, a grant of titles of nobility to those whom its provisions protect in their special privileges and immunities. We

Plaindealer, December 31, 1836. Extract deleted.

cannot better appropriate a portion of our space, than by inserting an extract from this able essay.

. . . .

The author of the above new view of a very important subject has promised to continue his speculations, and we hope, for the sake of the public good which such investigations are calculated to effect, that he will redeem his pledge. We have been in the habit for a long time, of speaking very freely on the subject of the exclusive privileges of our chartered aristocracy, and have frequently, for the purpose of bringing the system into disrepute, termed those who are enjoying its advantages, the scrip nobility, and the noble order of the money-changers. The peculiar privileges which they exercise (and exercise very tyrannously at times,) we really considered, in point of fact, fully equal to those of any order of European nobility, and, in their tendency to undermine our democratic institutions, highly insidious and dangerous. But we have not before been led to reflect that the act which constitutes the exclusiveness of these rights and immunities is a grant of titles of nobility, in positive contravention of an express provision of the Constitution of the United States. We tender to *Anti-Privilege* our cordial thanks for the flood of new and useful light he has shed upon this subject.

We have heretofore looked on the restraining law as an unequal, unnecessary, and unjust restraint on the natural freedom of capital and industry. We shall hereafter look upon it with augumented abhorrence as a positive violation of the Constitution of the United States, in a respect which was meant to guard the American people from the approaches of aristocracy. We have heretofore looked upon banking incorporations, which that law encircles and protects, as possessed of privileges incompatible with the principle of equal rights, a principle which constitutes the very foundation of human freedom. We shall hereafter look upon them with increased aversion, as the possessors of actual titles of nobility, distinguished by more objectionable features than the patents of the European aristocracy; and we shall labour with renewed zeal to enfranchise the community from their degrading subjection to the noble order of the money-changers.

THE INEQUALITY OF HUMAN CONDITION

The venerable Sir Thomas More, in a work wherein he has availed himself of the convenient latitude of fiction to utter many important political maxims and opinions, which might not have been tolerated, in his days, had they been put forth in the sober guise of literal truth, has expressed numerous sentiments in regard to the errors and abuses of government, which apply with as much force and accuracy to our times and country, as to his. "Is not that government both unjust and ungrateful," he asks, "that is prodigal of its favours to those who are goldsmiths and bankers, and such others as are idle, and live either by flattery, or by contriving the arts of vain pleasure; and, on the other hand, takes no care of those of a meaner sort, such as ploughmen, colliers, and smiths, without whom it could not subsist? After the public has reaped all the advantage of their service, and they come to be oppressed with age, sickness, and want, all their labours, and the good they have done, is forgotten; and all the recompense given them is that they are left to die in great misery. The richer sort are often endeavouring to bring the hire of labourers lower, not only by their fraudulent practices, but by the laws which they procure to be made to that effect; so that, though it is a thing

Plaindealer, December 31, 1836.

most unjust in itself to give such small rewards to those who deserve so well of the public, yet they have given those hardships the name and colour of justice, by procuring laws to be made for regulating them."

Who, that knows anything of our legislation, can read this passage, without perceiving that it applies as strongly to the condition of things among ourselves, as if it had been written purposely to describe them, and not those which existed in England three centuries ago? Our government, like that against which the complaint was urged, is prodigal of favours to bankers and others, who choose to live in idleness by their wits rather than earn an honest livelihood by the useful employment of their faculties; and like that, it makes no laws conferring privileges and immunities on the "common people," who look to their industry for their support. The farmers, the labourers, the mechanics, and the shopkeepers, have no charters bestowed upon them; but the only notice they receive from the law is to forbid them, under heavy penalties, from interfering with the exclusive rights granted to the privileged few.

A very casual and imperfect survey of society, in regard to the vast disparity of condition it presents, must satisfy any reflecting mind that there is some great and pervading error in our system. If the inequalities of artificial condition bore any relation to those of nature; if they were determined by the comparative degrees of men's wisdom and strength, or of their providence and frugality, there would be no cause to complain. But the direct contrary is, to a very great extent, the truth. Folly receives the homage which should belong only to wisdom; prodigality riots in the abundance which prudence has not been able to accumulate, with all his pains; and idleness enjoys the fruits which were planted and cultivated by industry. It is not necessary to state these facts in figurative language, in order to render them worthy of serious and attentive consideration. Look through society, and tell us who and what are our most affluent men? Did they derive their vast estates from inheritance? There are scarcely a dozen wealthy families in this metropolis whose property descended to them by bequest. Did they accumulate it by patient industry? There are few to whom an affirmative answer will apply. Was it the reward of superior wisdom? Alas, that is a quality which has not been asserted as a characteristic of our rich. Whence, then, have so many derived the princely fortunes, of which they display the evidences in their spacious and elegant dwellings, in their costly banquets, their glittering equipages, and all the luxurious appliances of wealth? The answer is plain. They owe them to special privileges; to that system of legislation which grants peculiar facilities to the opulent, and forbids the use of them to the poor; to that pernicious code of laws which considers the rights of property as an object of greater moment than the rights of man.

Cast yet another glance on society, in the aspect it presents when surveying those of opposite condition. What is the reason that such vast numbers of men groan and sweat under a weary life, spending their existence in incessant toil, and yet accumulating nothing around them, to give them hope of respite, and a prospect of comfort in old age? Has nature been less prodigal to them, than to those who enjoy such superior fortune? Are their minds guided by less intelligence, or their bodies nerved with less vigour? Are their morals less pure, or their industry less assiduous? In all these respects they are at least the equals of those who are so far above them in prosperity. The disparity of condition, in a vast multitude of instances, may be traced directly to the errors of our legislation; to that wretched system, at war with the fundamental maxim of our government, which, instead of regarding the equality of human rights, and leaving all to the full enjoyment of natural liberty in every respect not inconsistent with public order, bestows privileges on one, and denies them to another, and compels the many to pay tribute and render homage to the few. Take a hundred ploughmen promiscuously from their fields, and a hundred merchants from their desks, and what man, regarding the true dignity of his nature, could hesitate to give the award of superior excellence, in every main intellectual, physical, and moral respect, to the band of hardy rustics, over that of the lank and sallow accountants, worn out with the sordid anxieties of traffic and the calculations of gain? Yet the merchant shall grow rich from participation in the unequal privileges which a false system of legislation has created, while the ploughman, unprotected by the laws, and dependent wholly on himself, shall barely earn a frugal livelihood by continued toil.

In as far as inequality of human condition is the result of natural causes it affords no just topic of complaint; but in as far as it is brought about by the intermeddling of legislation, among a people who proclaim, as the foundation maxim of all their political institutions, the equality of the rights of man, it furnishes a merited reprehension. That this is the case with us, to a very great extent, no man of candour and intelligence can look over our statute books and deny. We have not entitled ourselves to be excepted from the condemnation which Sir Thomas More pronounces on other governments. "They are a conspiracy of the rich, who, on pretence of managing the public, only pursue their private ends, and devise all the ways and arts they can find out, first, that they may, without danger, preserve all that they have so acquired, and then that they may engage the poor to toil and labour for them, at as low rates as possible, and oppress them as much as they please."

A BAD BEGINNING

The first number of a weekly newspaper, just established at Oswego, called the *Commercial Herald*, has been sent to us. Amongst leading articles there is one entitled *Loco Focos*, which professes to give an account of the principles and objects of the political party known by that name. It says—

> Their ideas of politicks and morals are drawn from the most beautiful theories that human genius has invented, and from propositions, true in themselves, but susceptible of no practical results. Hence, their tenets are founded in the false premises of a perfectibility in human nature that dispenses with all the restraints of law, and all the obligations of religion. The sweeping nature of their doctrines has brought them in contract with our whole system of legislation, and indeed with all laws human and divine. Hostile to every species of monopoly, even to the institution of marriage, they have in some respects exercised a wholesome and salutary influence upon the course of legislation.

The same paper names Shelley as "among the *authordox* writers" from whom the *Loco Focos* derive their creed, and cites a passage from the notes to *Queen Mab* as illustrative of the views of the *Loco Focos* on the subject of marriage. . . .[1]

We cannot augur favourably of a newspaper which is guilty of such sheer and coarse misrepresentation at its very outset. There is not one word of truth in these statements; they are unmitigated, unqualified slanders. We do not belong to the party, the principles of which are thus traduced, and we have

Plaindealer, March 18, 1837. Text abridged and extract deleted so as to omit references to political personalities of the day.

[1] The English Romantic poet Percy Bysshe Shelley published the long ideological poem *Queen Mab* together with notes in 1813. The ninth note was a celebrated essay against legal marriage.—Ed.

before expressed the opinion that its course of action is not in exact accordance with its principles, and not calculated to expedite the object at which it aims. But with respect to the creed which it professes, no man claiming to be a democrat can gainsay a single syllable of it. Admitting, as a political axiom, the truth of the fundamental doctrine of our government, the political equality of mankind, every article of the creed of those called *Loco Focos* has the force and certainty of a geometrical demonstration. The assertion is without a shadow of truth that they propose to dispense with the restraints of law and the obligations of religion, that they are opposed to all law, human and divine, or that they are hostile to the institution of marriage. . . .

The whole creed of those who are termed *Loco Focos* is embraced in the maxim of the equality of men's political rights. It breathes no hostility whatever to religion; has no reference to the institution of marriage; and opposes existing laws only to the extent that they interfere, either directly with men's equal rights, or indirectly, by restraints on the natural freedom of trade, which, though general in their terms, have yet the inevitable tendency of unduly fostering particular interests or classes. . . .

We have always considered the *Loco Focos* wrong in separating from the main body of the democracy, and in combining under a separate organization; because we thought the more certain, the more speedy, and the more democratick mode, of achieving the triumph of their particular principles, would have been to cooperate in general objects with those with whom they agreed in the main, constantly exercising, with vigilance and temper, their proper share of influence in the primary popular proceedings, to bring about that reformation which they desire to accomplish. But all party combinations are mere measures of *policy* to establish or maintain particular principles; and the separation of any portion of a party, therefore, on questions of difference touching cardinal principles, although it may be censurable as impolitick, can never deserve the more serious reprehension which belongs to dishonesty. It is not to be doubted that, with the mere exception of such a sprinkling as all parties contain of men governed by selfish motives, the *Loco Focos* are sincere in the creed and in the objects which they profess. They must then be considered democrats, in the strictest meaning of the word, and will naturally merge again into the great democratick party, under that best possible appellation, when it shall, by a much needed reformation of its "usages," and a lustration of its members, become worthy of its name.

THE WHIG EMBASSY TO WASHINGTON, AND ITS RESULT

. . . .

. . . The manifesto[1] takes openly the highest ground of aristocratick doctrine. It asserts, with startling frankness, the fundamental principal of that creed which rests on deep distrust of popular intelligence and virtue. It affirms that moral and pecuniary worth go together; that property is the touchstone of merit, and the only true and permanent basis of government. It in effect repeats the celebrated dogma of Mr. Webster, "Take care of the rich, and the rich will take care of the poor," a sentiment so revolting to the general sense, that he was fain to disavow it, though it was well known he had uttered it; but it is now put forth by this whig committee of

Plaindealer, May 13, 1837. Text abridged and extracts deleted.

[1] Leggett refers to the published comments of a committee of New York Whigs on a letter from President Van Buren. The President wrote in response to requests presented to him in Washington by the committee.—Ed.

no partisans with a boldness that indicates an intention of withdrawing it no more, but rather of shouting it louder and louder, as their chief and most exciting battle-cry. "In a great majority of cases the possession of property is *the* proof of merit." This is the ground on which they take their stand. They give a new reading to the old saying that "worth makes the man, and want of it the fellow." Worth with them is not moral and intellectual worth, shown by any other index than dollars and cents. He is most worthy who is worth the most money; and he the most base who is worth none. Property is the proof of merit; and according to the inevitable converse, poverty is the proof of vileness and degradation.

But property, we are told, as a general rule, cannot be acquired, in a country of free laws and equal rights, without industry, skill, and economy. This, however, is not a country of free laws and equal rights. The principle of man's natural and unalienable equality of rights is admitted in the abstract, but is widely departed from in practice. It is for endeavouring to conform the practice to the theory that the whigs raise all this no partisan clamour against Mr. Van Buren. They want a National Bank, to make the rich richer and the poor poorer; to set at naught the just influence of the poor man's equal suffrage; and place the government under the absolute control of a sordid, fluctuating, paper money aristocracy. "Property cannot be acquired without industry, skill and economy?" How, then, in heaven's name, did the pseudo rich men of the last two years acquire their wealth? Did it rain upon them from the clouds, or spring up under their feet spontaneously from the bosom of the earth? Was it an exercise of "industry, skill and economy" to lay out cities in the prairies, project railroads over mountains, and devise all sorts of impossible schemes, and then, counting upon the realization of these visionary projects, to assume the loftiest port of affluence, and riot in the most wasteful excess? Was it "industry, skill, and economy," that supplied the gorgeous equipages and sumptuous tables of the thousands, who now, overtaken by the inevitable consequences of their own folly, declaim against the specie circular, lay the blame of their wild and most immoral extravagance to the account of the government, and demand its assistance to rescue them from the bankruptcy they have brought upon themselves? Under a code of really equal laws, property would, indeed, to a certain extent, be an evidence of sagacity and prudence, but under a system of special privileges, it is as much a proof of successful gambling, as of steady enterprise employed in objects useful to mankind. Under a federal bank, property would soon become the badge of an exclusively privileged order, and poverty and vassalage the irremediable doom of the great majority of men.

We rejoice, however, that the whigs take their stand, openly and boldly, on their true distinctive principles. They now show themselves in the native hue of aristocracy. They no longer attempt to slubber over their real motives of action, or the ultimate objects which they hope to achieve. They no longer deny that a National Bank is their shibboleth and that the protection of a privileged order is the chief end of government. On this ground we are willing to meet them, and, proclaiming with equal distinctness and sincerity the principles for which we fight, we close with them in the struggle, and trust the issue to the merits of our cause. We hold that all men have equal political rights. That the sole object of government is the protection of those rights; and that whatever impairs or infringes them, whatever gives privileges to the few, which are withheld from the many, or superiour immunities, in any respect, to any particular rank or class of men, is an abuse of power, contrary to the great ends of political organization, and calling for prompt correction through the influence of equal suffrage.

"Those who believe that the possession of property is an evidence of merit *will be the last to interfere with the rights of property of any kind.*" We beg our readers to mark the terms and purpose of this pledge to the slaveholders of the south. There is no ambiguity in this part of the manifesto. The solemn promise is given by the northern whigs to the southern slaveholders, that they will respect, to the utmost extent, the rights of property in slaves, and discourage, as a cardinal measure of party, every attempt to discuss the great scheme of emancipation. The maxim, so boldly asserted, that "property is the proof of merit" includes, it seems, property in fellow beings, not less than property in things. Slaves cannot be acquired, any more than houses and lands, without "industry, skill, and economy," and he

"Is wisest, virtuousest, discreetest, best,"

who is the uncontrolled possessor of the greatest number of human creatures. The kidnapper, on the coast of Africa, with the noisome recesses of his vessel crowded with suffocating wretches, stolen from their homes and their country, must be a man of supereminent virtue and intelligence, according to the creed which recognizes property of all kinds as "*the* proof of merit;" and the craven man-seller, who drives his herd of poor negroes through the streets of the federal metropolis of this great empire of freemen, and sells them to the highest bidder under the very walls of the capitol,

———where freedom waves
Her fustian flag in mockery over slaves,[2]

is a citizen far more meritorious than the humble denizen, who, respecting the equal rights of his fellow men, and trusting solely to "industry, skill, and economy," has no proof of merit to offer that will stand the test of the whig touchstone of desert.

Mere party newspapers, of the northern and eastern states, have been endeavouring, for a long time past, to heap on their antagonists the odium of abolitionism. In that contemptible and degrading spirit of misrepresentation, which too much distinguishes the political press, they have sought, by mutual

[2] A line from Thomas Moore, London *Examiner* satirist.—Ed.

criminations and reproaches, to convince the south that the ordinary line of political demarcation also divided opinions on the question of slavery. The whigs have charged abolitionism on the democracy, and the democracy have retorted the charge upon the whigs. But we have now the formal declaration, adopted, as we are assured, by unanimous acclamation, at an immense assemblage of the whigs of this great city, that they are the friends and advocates of slavery; that they consider the possession of slaves *the* proof of merit; and that they will discourage every effort to discuss the evils of servitude. We ask of our readers to ponder this declaration. We ask of those, more particularly, to give it their most serious heed, who think with us as to the detestable wickedness and ruinous consequences of slavery. And we ask, most particularly, of those who coincide with us in regard to slavery, but differ on questions of politicks—we ask of *whig abolitionists,* to read this bill of sale which consigns them over to the task-masters of the south; which surrenders their inestimable right of free discussion; which forbids them to yearn and pray for the emancipation of three millions of their fellow men from abject bondage; but pledges that they shall witness, uncomplainingly and complacently, without raising an arm or exerting a voice, whatever enormities that meritorious class who hold their black brothers as property may choose to perpetrate on the human commodity. We ask the *American,* which has heretofore been a vigorous and efficient asserter of the sacred right of free discussion, if it consents to this sweeping measure of propitiation to the south? We ask the *Express,* which has shown some touches of human sympathy for the poor negro, and some natural horrour of the institution of slavery, if it will be a party to so base a compact? We ask of every friend of human rights, whatever may be his opinions on questions of temporary expediency, whether he will countenance this unholy league?

But let slavery and aristocracy, between which there is a natural affinity, plant their banners on the same height, and wage war with their united forces against the democracy.

Strong in the clear justice of that cause which asks for nothing but equal rights, we shall encounter the shock with unshrinking confidence, and our efforts will lose none of their energy from the reflection that, not our own freedom only, but freedom to the slave, depends on the result.

RIGHT VIEWS AMONG THE RIGHT SORT OF PEOPLE

It is to the farming and mechanick interests we must look, in these days of extraordinary delusion among mercantile men, for sound views as to the causes of the evils which distract the country, and as to the proper means of bringing affairs back to their former prosperity. If the farmers and mechanicks of the Confederacy were subject to the same periodical madness which afflicts the merchants, we should indeed think there was but too much reason to despair of the republick. But while we may look to them for such a host of sound minds in sound bodies, for such a multitude of men who, like the Roman *Mutius*,[1] are not only able and willing to act, but to suffer for their country, we shall not lose our confidence in the stability of democratick institutions.

A very sensible writer in the *National Intelligencer*, under the signature of "A Farmer," makes some excellent remarks on the state of the times. . . .

. . . .

The *National Intelligencer* speaks of the writer from whose communication we have made this extract, as, "in every sense,

Plaindealer, May 20, 1837. Extract deleted.

[1] One of the sons of Titus Adronicus in Shakespeare's play of that name.—Ed.

a country gentleman." He is a member, then, of a class on which we must mainly depend for the steady and effectual defence of the institutions of liberty, amidst the violent assaults, which, it is easy to foresee, mercantile rapacity will fiercely wage against them. To the cultivators of the soil, gentle and simple, and to the hardy followers of the mechanick arts, we turn our eyes, in these days of passion and prejudice, for that calm good sense and intrepidity, which are necessary to the protection of the great blessing of equal political rights.

The traders, as a body, are a useful class, but not the most patriotick. The spirit of traffick is always adverse to the spirit of liberty. We care not whom the remark pleases nor whom it offends; but it is a truth, which all history corroborates, that the mercantile community, in the aggregate, is ever impelled by sordid motives of action. The immediate interests of trade, not the permanent interests of their country, supply their strongest impulse. They peruse their ledger with more devotion than the Constitution; they regard pecuniary independence more than political; and they would be content to wear ignominious chains, so that the links were forged of gold.

The American people have tested, by a reduplicated experiment, continued through a long series of years, the good and evil of a federal bank, and they have seen that the evil far outweighs the good. They have seen it fail in the cardinal objects for which it was created. They have seen that it could not prevent alternate expansions and contractions of the currency, and ruinous fluctuations in commercial affairs. They have seen, also, that it could not resist the temptation to turn its pecuniary means into political channels and, through the corrupting influence of money, attempt to rule the destinies of freemen. They have seen it purchase presses, bribe publick men, and endeavour to pollute the streams of popular intelligence at the fountain head. These are facts not merely conjectured by suspicion. They rest not on the uncertain evidence of probability. They are corroborated by proofs which defy refutation, and stand indelibly recorded on the enduring archives of the federal legislature. It was for these reasons that the people decided there should be no federal bank.

But the mercantile community acquiesce not in this decision. "We must have a national bank to regulate the exchanges!" is now their cry. This is the proposition with which they meet every argument, the answer they deem sufficient for every objection. Tell them of a constitutional impediment, and they reply that they can see only the impediments to trade. Point to the political evils of a federal bank, and they talk of its financial advantages. Tell them of the danger it would threaten to liberty, and they descant on the facilities it would render to credit. An equal currency is, with them, a phrase of better import than equal rights; a uniform system of exchange a grander object than a uniform system of freedom.

Why is it that large cities are justly considered, according to the expressive metaphor of Jefferson, the sore places in the body politick? Because the sordid spirit of trade gives them their tone, and fixes the standard of their political morals. When we hear of attempts to overawe freedom of political opinion, who are the chief actors in the outrage? The sons of traffick. When the equal right of suffrage is invaded, and proscription dictates to the poor man how he shall vote under penalty of starvation, who are they that thus tyrannize over their fellow men? The merchants. What class of society now threatens tumult and insurrection, if the federal executive dares insist on the fulfilment of the laws? What class is it that warns freemen, charged with no crime but the frank utterance of their sentiments on a subject of general interest and of general discussion, to abandon their homes, and seek elsewhere a place of refuge, if they would escape immolation in the publick streets? We are forced to repeat that this audacious conduct proceeds from the mercantile community. It springs from the selfish, grovelling, debasing spirit of trade—from that spirit which venerates its desk more than the altar, its list of bank balances more than the decalogue, and its book of accounts more than the book of God.

To the farmers and mechanicks, then, we look for safety in these days of mercantile frenzy. They gain their livelihood by wholesome industry, not by maddening speculation, and they know the value of equal laws. Blacker than the clouds which lower over our shattered commerce, would be the boding tempest of the political horizon, had we no surer trust, in the midst of our difficulties, than the patriotism of those who regard the prosperity of trade more than the prosperity of their country and, like true sons of Esau, would sell their birthright for a mess of pottage.

NEWSPAPER NOMINATIONS

In our last number, when commenting on the "nonpartisan" professions of the whig travelling committee, we stated that the proceedings of that veracious body had a direct reference to an intended nomination, at no distant day, of Mr. Webster, as a candidate for the office of President. Circumstances have forced this nomination to be made, in an informal manner, at an earlier day than was anticipated. The *Evening Star,* of Thursday last, having intimated, in pretty positive terms, that Mr. Clay is entitled to the support of the aristocracy, as their next candidate for the chief executive office of the Confederacy, the *Commercial Advertiser* and the *American* of the following evening eagerly reprehended the movement of their contemporary, and protested that Daniel Webster was their man. We are sorry to observe any signs of division in the ranks of our adversaries. We should be much better pleased to see

Plaindealer, May 20, 1837.

them all unite, with one mind and heart, on a single individual; and we should be still better pleased if that individual were Mr. Webster. This would bring the strife on the true ground of antagonist political principles. It would call upon the people to array themselves under the standard either of democracy or aristocracy. It would show conclusively whether the intelligence of this country acknowledges the maxim that "PROPERTY IS THE TEST OF MERIT," or whether it still holds to the opposite maxim, "THE EQUALITY OF HUMAN RIGHTS."

The aristocratic party ought to select Mr. Webster for their candidate. They acted scurvily towards him in the last contest. To thrust him aside from the field, that they might array themselves under the petticoat banner of so poor an "available," such a mere effigy of a leader, as General Harrison, was, to say the least, mortifying treatment. They owe Mr. Webster reparation. They owe it to themselves, too, to pursue a more dignified course. Their political projects, heretofore, have been palpable confessions of inferiority. They have sought to disguise the true issue. They have seized hold of temporary and local questions. They have selected candidates, not with reference to their capacity or principles, but solely with reference to their supposed power of healing divisions, and uniting separate interests. It is time they should come out in their true characters, and avow the real objects for which they contend. Let them declare, then, their rooted distrust of the intelligence and integrity of the mass of the people; their belief that property is the test of merit, and should be the basis of suffrage; their opinion that the duty of government is to take care of the rich, leaving it to the rich to take care of the poor; and their desire, for the furtherance of these objects, to establish a federal bank, with sufficient capital to buy up men and presses, like cattle in the market. At the end of such a confession of faith, nothing could be in better keeping than the nomination of Daniel Webster for the office of President.

Mr. Webster is certainly a great man. We should oppose

him, wholly, heartily, and with all the zeal of a firm conviction that his principles are hostile to liberty. But we do not hesitate to call him a great man; a man of strong and capacious mind, much information, vigorous powers of reasoning, and an uncommon flow of stern and majestic eloquence. He is greater as a lawyer than as a statesman; but in both characters he stands in the foremost rank. We admire the energy of his faculties. When passages of his speeches come before us, separate from a consideration of the questions which elicited them, we always peruse them with delight. The pleasure they afford us is but the involuntary homage which the mind pays to a superior intellect; but it changes, by a natural transition, to an opposite feeling, when we are led to reflect upon the nature of the objects for which he is exerting his abilities. Not to assist in enfranchising his fellow-man; not to hasten that glorious day-spring of equal liberty, which is beginning to dawn upon the world; not to spread wider and wider the principles of democratic freedom, and break down the artificial and aristocratic distinctions, which diversify the surface of society with such hideous inequalities, does Mr. Webster raise his voice in the Senate-house. The dogmas of his political creed, like the dogmas of an intolerant religion, would confine the blessings of government, as the latter would those of heaven, to an exclusive few, leaving all the other myriads of men to toil and sweat in a state of immitigable degradation. This is the true end and aim of the aristocratic creed. This is the true and inevitable tendency of their measures who contend for a national bank. This is their open profession when they proclaim that property is the proof of merit, and, by the unavoidable converse, that poverty is the proof of unworthiness. For those who acknowledge such sentiments and motives, Mr. Webster is the proper candidate. He has talents and acquirements that must command respect; his personal character is unimpeached; and he has toiled long and strenuously in their service. We are glad that they are about to do all in their power to render a grateful return. The democracy will now have something to contend against, as well as something to contend for. There will be glory in overthrowing such an antagonist, as well as great gain in preserving the supremacy of their principles. With such an opponent as Harrison, we enter languidly into the contest, as a task of mere duty; with such a one as Webster, we shall rush into it eagerly, as a matter of pride as well as patriotism.

FOREIGN "PAUPERS"

In the Board of Aldermen, on Monday evening, a report was adopted, in favour of concurring in the plan suggested by the Mayor of Boston, to address a memorial to Congress on the subject of the immigration of foreign paupers. Under this name, many of the whig gentry, with our Lottery Mayor[1] at their head, seem to think every foreigner ought to be classed who has no money in his pocket. If to be without money is to be a pauper, not a few of our most lordly and aristocratick monopolists are in that category.

But while the newspapers in this quarter continue their efforts to excite popular prejudice against the poor emigrants who are seeking an asylum on our shores, and they are scoffed at as wretches underserving of succour or sympathy, we observe that a very different tone is used by the journals in the interiour. The people of the fertile west are well aware of the benefits which they derive from the labour of the hardy and

Plaindealer, July 22, 1837.

[1] New York's whig mayor, Aaron Clark, was formerly a lottery dealer. See "The Municipal Election," in Leggett, *Political Writings,* vol. II, pp. 279–281. Clark was elected because the Loco Focos split the democratic vote.—Ed.

industrious poor of Europe. They do not therefore join with our Lottery Mayor in treating these men as miserable paupers, as the offscouring of prisons and poor-houses, and wretches stained with crimes, bloated with intemperance and disease, and altogether loathsome and disgusting. They speak of them as fellow-men, as equal denizens of the great patrimony of mankind, the earth, and invite them to their own luxuriant region, where their capacity to labour will be regarded as the best sort of capital, and the moderate exercise of it will earn them a comfortable support. It would be strange indeed, in a country where millions and tens of millions of acres lie unimproved for the want of agricultural labour, if the people of the west should join in the heartless scoffs with which the aristocracy of this city greet the poor emigrant as he lands upon our shores.

The people who are daily landing here are not paupers, if the capacity and disposition to labour may exempt a man from that appellation. They are, for the most part, the sons and daughters of useful toil. They are men and women of hardy frames, accustomed to earn their living by the sweat of their brows. They are a class of which, in truth, we stand much in need. We want men to till the earth, to break up the rich soil of our western prairies, to fell the forests which shut out the light of heaven from millions of acres that might easily be made to furnish support to additional millions of fellow beings. When we depend, for the very bread we eat, on the agriculture of foreign countries; when we annually import the commodities of other lands to the extent of fifty millions of dollars beyond the sum of our surplus products; when, in many parts of the country, the fields lie untilled, and the wheels of the manufactory stand idle, for want of the assistance of labour; when these things are so, how can it be said, with any show of justice, that the people who are flocking to our shores will be a burden on our hands?

The aristocratick party seem to entertain very vague notions of pauperism. They set down as paupers, in their vocabulary, all who have no property beyond the sound minds and sound bodies which nature gives. These men are not paupers, and if they become so, it is the fault of our own laws. Let us not lay our sins, then, at their doors. We have perfect control over the matter. We are not obliged to open our poor-houses to those who are able to work; and, indeed, we believe it would be far better for the community, if we did not open them to any class of indigence or misfortune. The care of those really disqualified by nature or accident from taking care of themselves should be left to voluntary charity, not to that wretched system of compulsory charity which poor-laws enjoin. We are too reluctant, in this country, to trust the voluntary principle. We are for doing everything by law; and the consequence is that hardly anything is done well.

But with regard to these poor creatures who are flocking to our country as the boasted asylum of the oppressed of all the world, we ought to welcome them hither, not meet them with scowls, and raise a deafening clamour to excite unkindly prejudices against them, and drive them back from our inhospitable shores. For our part, we open our arms to them, and embrace them as brothers; for are they not a part of the great family of man? It is a violation of the plainest principles of morals, it is a sin against the most universal precepts of religion, to harden our hearts against these men, and seek to expel them from a land, which they have as much right to tread as we who assume such a lofty port. The earth is the heritage of man, and these are a portion of the heritors. We are not bound to support them; they must support themselves. If they are idle, let them starve; if they are vicious, let them be punished; but, in God's name, as they bear God's image, let us not turn them away from a portion of that earth, which was given by its maker to all mankind, with no natural marks to designate the limits beyond which they may not freely pass.

The glorious principles of democracy, which recognize the equal rights of all who bear the human form, forbid the intolerant spirit which is displaying itself to these friendless, homeless exiles. Democracy, which is the divine system of Christian morals applied to politicks, embraces, in its comprehensive creed of equal rights and equal duties, the whole family of man. It bids those who suffer from the oppressive governments of other countries, all hail! as they approach our shores, and welcomes them to a land, the institutions of which, founded on the true principles of human dignity, are intended to promote the greatest good of the greatest number, not the exclusive advantage of a few.

While a wretched spirit of aristocratick selfishness is endeavouring to excite the worst prejudices of the community against the houseless emigrants who are coming among us, it would be a fit employment for democratick philanthropy, on the other hand, to devise means for conveying these wanderers into the interiour of our vast country, where a soil, rich with the alluvious fertility of ages, invites them to labour, and would yield to industry a grateful return. These *paupers* would then soon relieve us from the degrading necessity of importing our bread from foreign lands; and we should find, in the reversed balance of our commercial account with other countries, that an influx of the hardy peasantry of Europe, to fill up our waste lands and cover them with harvests, is not a clog on our progress, but a new and vigorous spring in the great machinery of national wealth.

We have ourselves asked these men to our country with an emphasis of invitation which no rhetorical additions could have heightened. When we send our purveyors abroad, to gather up the harvests of other lands in order to supply our citizens with bread, we offer an inducement to foreign labour to come among us, to which no form of express invitation could give augmented force. With what propriety can we now tell them they are intruders where they are not needed, and seek to drive them away with ungracious and opprobrious taunts?

PART FIVE

The Principles of Free Trade

MONOPOLIES: I

. . . .

The Times has favoured us with a confession of faith on the subject of monopolies, and if its preaching were in accordance with its creed, there would be little ground of dispute, for it would seem by this that there is no great difference between us on general principles. The Times says:

"The Post is against all monopolies—so are we. The Post is for Equal Rights—so are we. The Post is for the suppression of small notes, and a reform of our banking system—so are we, for the last because it is needed, and for the first because the notes are an evil, and their extinction is essential to the success of one of our most important measures of public policy, the substitution of a specie currency. The Post is against legislating for the benefit of individuals, to the disadvantage or exclusion of others—so are we, and in this and on all these points, the party agrees with us."

So far, so good. We shall pass by the twaddle about "the party agreeing with us," which is mere harmless impertinence and coxcombry not worth reply. We shall pass by, too, the satisfactory and lucid reason stated by the Times for being in favour of "a reform of our banking system." We gather, then, from this confession of faith that the Times is opposed to *all* monopolies, is in favour of equal rights, believes that small bank-notes should be suppressed, the banking system reformed, and legislation for individuals, to the disadvantage or exclusion of others, should cease. One might naturally infer from all this that there is no real ground of controversy between us, and that, like many other disputants, we have been

Evening Post, November 20, 1834. Title added by Sedgwick; Roman numeral added.

arguing about nothing. But when the Times comes to explain itself, we find, notwithstanding the apparent agreement in our premises, that we differ very widely in our conclusions. It is against all monopolies in the abstract, but for them in the concrete. It is opposed to charters of incorporation in general, but advocates them in particular. It is in short against exclusive privileges as monopolies, but in favour of them as means of effecting "great objects of public utility," "developing vast resources," "stimulating industry," and so forth, which is only a repetition of the stale cant which has been used, time out of mind, by those who desired to cheat the people out of their rights for their own selfish ends.

The Times is pleased to say that we ride the doctrine of monopolies as a hobby. We might retort by saying that the Times rides it only for convenience, and just as it suits its purposes. It is "ride and tie" with it. One moment it is on horseback, pricking its ambling steed along; the next it dismounts and turns him loose to graze on the common. For ourselves, we have only to say, that if opposition to monopolies, in every form and under every disguise, is our hobby, it is because we honestly believe them to be the most sly and dangerous enemies to the general prosperity that ever were devised by ingenious cupidity. It is on this ground we have opposed them earnestly—it is on this ground we mean to oppose them, with all our ability, until the evil is arrested, or we become convinced that opposition is vain.

Though the Times professes to agree with us in the opinion that all monopolies are infringements upon the equal rights of the people, and therefore at war with the spirit of our government and institutions, it differs widely with us in its definition. It separates monopolies from corporations, and its idea seems to be that monopolies must be entirely exclusive, or they are not monopolies. There are degrees of virtue and of vice; there are degrees in every thing; but according to the Times there are none in the nature and extent of monopolies. These consist in extremes, and have no medium.

Among its exceptions are railroad incorporations, which it does not consider as belonging to the great family of monopolies. It acknowledges that a railroad may be a monopoly—"a speculation for the profit of individuals, not required by, nor likely to promote the public interest;" but, on the other hand, to meet this case, it supposes another, in order to show that a railroad company may be incorporated without creating a monopoly. Extreme cases are but poor arguments; since by carrying any right or principle to an extreme, it may be made to appear vicious and unjust. But let us examine the supposititious case which the Times has manufactured to justify its insidious advocacy of monopolies. We copy the whole passage:

"Suppose Grand Island to be inhabited by twenty people, and that their only ferry is at one end of the island. Suppose that they have no good road, and that they want a railway to transport their produce from their farms down to the ferry. No one of them is rich enough to make it, but the whole together can, provided they have an act of incorporation for the management of the joint funds, and the direction of the work. Suppose the Post to be the legislature, and that these twenty isolated proprietors apply for a charter: how would the Post reply? It would say, "there is certainly nobody concerned in this matter but yourselves, and the work would benefit you vastly, but if no one of you is wealthy enough to construct it, you must do without—you cannot have a charter, *for* I oppose monopolies, *and* every act of incorporation *is a monopoly!*"

This is all very smart and very convincing, and we only wonder that the Times did not discover that it had trumped up a case which has no application whatever to the matter in dispute. The twenty inhabitants of Grand Island, according to the case here put, constituted a complete community, having one common interest in the contemplated railroad, and all sharing equally in its advantages. They are, so far as respects this question, *a whole people,* and being thus united in one common bond of interest, the rights of no one of them would be impaired by the whole body being incorporated for any common object. This supposititious act of incorporation bears a strong analogy to the very measure of legislation which we yesterday spoke of as the proper means of effecting those objects which are now attained by partial and unequal laws. Instead of Grand Island, let us read the State of New York; and instead of an act of incorporation for a specific purpose including the whole population, let us suppose a law applicable to all purposes for which charters could be asked, under which any set of individuals might associate, and we have at once, a remedy for the evils of exclusive charters—we establish a system under which monopolies cannot exist.

But let us look a little closer at the railroad incorporation which the Times wishes to bestow on the twenty inhabitants on Grand Island. It is within the compass of possibilities that the population of Grand Island, particularly after "their resources should be developed," and "their industry stimulated," by an act of incorporation, might be increased by emigration [*sic*], or in some other way. As the charter was conferred exclusively on the twenty original inhabitants, we suppose the new comers would be denied the benefits of the railroad, unless they paid a toll, or contributed an equal proportion with the original proprietors. Would not this railroad at once become a monopoly, and as such be open to all the objections to corporations of this kind?

But we are fighting shadows. Communities cannot be incorporated except under laws equally applicable to all their members; and the idea of giving society at large exclusive privileges is an absurdity. A law which is general in its operation cannot confer exclusive privileges. The fiction of a whole community requiring an act of incorporation to accomplish an object of public utility is equally fanciful and original.

The Times further maintains that the Evening Post is an enemy to every species of internal improvement, and that the position it has taken would exclude them altogether. The Post, it says, will allow no rich man to make a road because the Post upholds equal rights, and will not permit corporate bodies to do it; of course the people must go without roads. Now all this is gratuitous assumption both of facts and consequences.

There is no necessity for either the rich man or the corporate company to make roads. The people will do it themselves; their own wants and convenience will impel them; and as their requirements and means increase, their modes of conveyance will advance accordingly. A rich man may hold all the property through which a road is to pass—but what of that? He cannot impose upon the people by making them pay to pass through it. The general law of the land points out the uniform mode of proceeding. He is remunerated by being paid the fair amount of his injury, and taxed his full share of the advantages derived from the improvement. There is here no monopoly, and there is no oppression, because every man's property is liable to similar contingencies.

But in order to justify this great system of monopoly in disguise, it is the fashion to proclaim from the housetops that communities can do nothing in their combined capacity, and that general laws are insufficient for nearly every purpose whatever. We have special laws and contrivances interfering with and infringing the common rights of individuals. We must have societies of all kinds, for every special purpose, and corporate bodies of every name and device, to do what ought not to be done, or what the community can well dispense with, or what they could as well do for themselves. Nations, states, and cities can do nothing now-a-days, without the agency of monopolies and exclusive privileges. Nor can individuals "beneficially employ capital," unless they are inspired by an act of the legislature, and a prospect of exorbitant profits, such is "the progress of the age and the march of intellect."

We need not say again that we are not an enemy of public improvements—such as are equally beneficial to the whole of that community which bears an equal proportion of the expense which they cost. But we are for putting such improvements on the footing of county roads and other municipal undertakings. The people who are to be exclusively benefitted may make them if they please, and if they do not please they may let it alone. In our opinion it is paying at too dear a rate for quick travelling through New-Jersey to purchase it at the price of depriving the citizens of that state, not members of a certain railroad company, of the right to make another railroad from New-York to Philadelphia. By such a system of legislation, the sovereign people of a whole state are deprived of their equal rights.

But it is our custom to treat all great political subjects on broad and general principles, from which alone general conclusions can be derived. A superficial or partial comparison of the advantages and disadvantages of a certain course of legislation furnishes a poor criterion from which to strike the balance; because it is wholly impossible for the ripest experience, aided by the most sagacious intellect to see and weigh everything connected with the subject of discussion. We must resort to general principles.

The question between the Times and the Evening Post, then, is not whether an act of incorporation may not be passed by a legislative body from the purest motives of public good, nor whether the public good may not in some instances be promoted by such an act. The true question is whether all history, all experience, nay, the very nature of man, does not support the position that this power of granting privileges, either wholly or partially exclusive, is not one that has always led, and, as we have thence a right to infer, will always lead, not only to corruption and abuse, but to either open or secret infringements of the sanctity of Equal Rights? This is the only question worthy of a high-minded and patriotic politician. It is not whether the practice may not occasionally lead to public, or social, or individual benefit; but whether it has not in the past been made, and whether it will not in the future be made again, the fruitful source of those inequalities in human condition—those extremes of wealth and poverty, so uniformly fatal to the liberties of mankind.

Our pen has been often employed, and we trust not wholly

without effect, in pointing out and illustrating the evil consequences of this system of bartering away the reserved rights of the great mass of the community, in exchange for public bonusses and *private douceurs,* either direct or indirect, or in furtherance of political views. This system has deranged the whole organization of society, destroyed its equilibrium, and metamorphosed a government the fundamental principle of which is equal rights to every free citizen, to one of EQUAL WRONGS to every class that does not directly share in its monopolies.

We neither wish to pull down the rich, nor to bolster them up by partial laws, beneficial to them alone, and injurious to all besides. We have repeated, again and again, that all we desire is, that the property of the rich may be placed on the same footing with the labours of the poor. We do not incorporate the different classes of tradesmen, to enable them to dictate to their employers the rate of their wages; we do not incorporate the farmers to enable them to establish a price for their products; and why then should we incorporate moneyed men (or men having only their wits for a capital) with privileges and powers that enable them to control the value of the poor man's labour, and not only the products of the land, but even the land itself?

If the Times will answer these questions, we are willing to discuss the subject, step by step, in all its important relations. But if it shall continue to lay down positions but to explain them away, like the boy who blows a bubble only for the pleasure of dissipating it by a breath, we shall not feel bound to pursue the subject in a controversial form. The weathercock must remain stationary for at least a moment, before we can tell which way the wind blows. The ship which, without rudder or compass, yaws and heaves about, the sport of every impulse of the elements, can scarcely be followed in her devious course by the most skilful navigator.

"A LITTLE FREE-TRADE CRAZY"

It gives us pleasure to perceive that the doctrines advanced by this paper, on the subject of corporate powers, have alarmed the monopolists, and that the number of our opponents is increasing. Secure in the correctness of the principle we maintain, and relying, with unlimited confidence, on the intelligence and honesty of the great body of the people, we desire only that the important question now before them should be freely and fully discussed; and shall abide the issue in the perfect assurance that it will add another and glorious triumph to the cause of Equal Rights. If the people could be deluded by the sophistry, or won by the exhortations, or swayed by the preponderance of numbers of editorial opponents of the political and politico-economical doctrines which we assert, their recent verdict through the ballot-boxes would have been a very different one from that which they happily pronounced; for it cannot be denied that, so far as the press is concerned, the odds are greatly on the side of the aristocracy. But the people judged for themselves; they could not be driven like cattle to the shambles. They cannot be driven now, but will judge for themselves again, with equal firmness and sagacity, and it is therefore we are gratified that new advocates of exclusive privileges are starting up, since their efforts in behalf of corporations will but furnish an occasion of displaying the subject in all its bearings, and showing the dangerous character of monopoly in all the disguises with which the subtle spirit of cupidity and aristocracy has arrayed it.

The Journal of Commerce thinks we are getting "a little free-trade crazy." If this is so, we shall at least have the company, in our lunacy, of some of the soundest thinkers and

Evening Post, December 13, 1834. Title added.

purest and most prudent men in our country. The malady, moreover, is spreading and we should not be surprised if the Journal of Commerce itself should be touched before long. The extension of the views entertained by the editor of that paper, on the subject of political economy, from their present limits to those which bound our own theory, would not, at any rate, be a greater change, than their reformation from the heresies of the protective system to those free-trade principles in what relates to foreign commerce which they have since ably advocated. In alluding to their former opinions we do not know but we touch on personal matters, but we do so in all courtesy, and with no thought to charge, or imply, that the conversion was not sincere and the result of careful and enlightened investigation. But in view of the fact that their sentiments on important questions have changed and are changing, and that doctrines are considered sound by them to-day which a little while ago they deemed heterodox, we should think they might have chosen a softer word to express their opinion of our fallacy than that they have thought proper to use. Assertion, however, is not argument, and the uncourteous dictum, unsupported by argument, can have no greater effect than to provoke "the fool's loud laugh."

The Journal of Commerce says, "The Post insists that all acts of incorporation, whether for Banks, Roads, Insurance Companies, or any thing else, are opposed to sound principles of political economy. We have not so learned free trade, and we do not think the Post has found its doctrines in any of the books." It is not only, nor even mainly, on the ground of political economy, that we oppose the principle of corporations, but, in a larger measure, on the broad and important political ground that it is hostile to the great democratic principle of Equal Rights. It is a happy thing for the destinies of this young and vigorous republic, that the fundamental principle of our Government is likewise the fundamental principle of political economy; and that, therefore, they who are fighting the great battle in defence of the political rights of man, are at the same time endeavouring to establish that noble science, the ignorance of whose truths and the violation of whose doctrines have been a prolific source of the burdens and oppressions under which the people of Europe groan.

They who read the pages of history with thinking eyes, will perceive that to the interference of Government with the private pursuits of individuals; to the granting of exclusive privileges to one body of citizens, and placing burdensome restrictions on others; to the giving a stimulating bounty here, and imposing a prohibitory duty there; to the withholding from whole communities the right to employ their capital or labour in a particular channel of industry, and conferring a monopoly of that privilege on some single one as a token of favour, or selling it to hide as an article of traffic—that to these, and a thousand similar violations of the principles of political economy, is to be ascribed much, very much of the misery with which the groaning nation of king-governed Europe is filled. It is there monopolies and exclusive privileges which have produced that deplorable inequality, which is the most striking characteristic of the population of Europe. It is these monopolies which have poured a mine of wealth into the coffers of the few, and stolen the last farthing from the pockets of the many. It is these which have built up lordly factories, and filled them with squalled operatives; that have extended magnificent enclosures around vast estates, and cultivated them with the toil of hired hands, who once were free-holders; that have torn down multitudes of cottages, to build one gorgeous palace in their stead; that have made a vast army and navy necessary to force the fabrics of overgrown monopolies on rival nations; that have created an enormous national debt; that have inundated the land with paper promises instead of money; and that have filled the brothels, workhouses, and prisons with prostitution, wretchedness and crime.

This is not a too highly coloured picture of the evils which Europe has brought upon herself by monopolies. The truth is rather underrated than exaggerated. Of the monopolies which have produced these disastrous effects, that of incorporations has not been the least instrumental. The Journal of Commerce thinks we do not find this doctrine "in any of the books." But if it will look into the English statute books it will find abundant proof of what we assert. It will find that they are full of laws erecting the members of every trade and calling into corporations, and granting them "privileges" by the most arbitrary restrictions. It will find that they limit the number of apprentices, fix the term of service, impose fines upon all persons exercising their calling without becoming members of the corporation, and exacting a heavy price for that privilege. If it is too tedious a task for the Journal of Commerce to pursue the investigation in that channel, let it go no further than the pages of Adam Smith. It will there find the evils of corporations set forth by a master-hand—a hand which dealt not in flourishes, but confined his sober pen to such facts, and such arguments, that his immortal work has already, in many important respects, revolutionized the policy of the world. It will find that illustrious writer sets himself sternly against the species of monopoly which the Journal of Commerce defends. Speaking of the inequalities of human condition occasioned by the policy of Europe, he says, "the exclusive privileges of corporations are the principle means it makes use of for this purpose;" and, in another place, he remarks, that "the pretence that corporations are necessary for the better government of trade is without any foundation." There are certain cases, it is true, in which he admits that charters of incorporation may be useful, but these are exceptions to his rule, and violations of his theory.

But suppose we had not found our doctrine "in the books." Does it thence follow that it is unsound! There is another thing we have not "found in the books," which the Journal of Commerce must allow has an important bearing on the question. We have not found a precedent of a government erected on the principle of Equal Rights—a government where the people rule—where the beggar and the millionary have an equal voice in public affairs, and where the aristocrat, descending from his carriage at the polls, may meet his coachman at the ballot-boxes, and see him, in the exercise of equal freedom of opinion, deposite a suffrage that may neutralise his own.

Had Adam Smith lived in our day and our country, he, too, we apprehend, would have become "a little free-trade crazy," or at least his sanity would probably have been called in question by certain journalists. He would have looked upon our country, as a kindred spirit, Jean Baptist[e] Say, has looked upon it, and would have asked, as that great political economist has asked, "Where should we expect sound doctrines to be better received, than amongst a nation that supports and illustrates the value of free principles by the most striking examples. The old states of Europe are cankered with prejudices; it is America will teach them the height of prosperity which may be reached, when governments follow the counsels of reason and do not cost too much."*

But it was the fortune of Adam Smith to draw his breath in a land where the very light of heaven is taxed to swell the resources of its unwieldy government; where deep-rooted monopolies waved their upas branches on every side of him; where the principle of exclusive privileges is interwoven with every fibre of the political fabric, where a king governs by "divine right," and where the people have no rights at all, except such as have been graciously conceded to them by their heaven-favoured rulers. His spirit, though cabined, cribbed, confined by such aristocratic bounds, yet burst from them, and taught a lesson of freedom which mankind will never forget. They listened not to him then. He spoke in a strange language and men understood him not; his voice was drowned in the interested clamour of monopolists, and they heard him not. But his teachings sunk deeply into some hearts. His words did

* See preface to the American edition of Say's Political Economy.

not pass away. His precepts are now performing their mighty work. The example of America is performing a still mightier work. He called from the vasty deep, which from time immemorial had rolled its sluggish and oblivious waves over Europe, a spirit which is teaching to mankind the true way to national wealth. The fathers of our country broke the spell that bound a sister but more powerful spirit, which, first redeeming our own land from thraldom, is now teaching to all the world the way to national freedom. These spirits are the twin-assertors of the great principle of Equal Rights—equal rights in all that relates to capital and industry; equal rights in all that relates to government. It is for this country to join their lessons, and enjoy, to the fullest extent, the two-fold blessing.

ASYLUM FOR INSANE PAUPERS

We have received a copy of a circular letter on the subject of a recommendation made by Governor Marcy to the Legislature, at its last session, that an Asylum for Insane Paupers should be erected, at the expense of the State. A select committee was charged with the subject, which reported favourably on the project; but the legislature adjourned without acting upon it. We trust they will adjourn again without acting affirmatively on any such scheme.

The taking care of the insane is no part of the business of the state government. The erecting of such an Asylum as is proposed, and the appointment of the various officers to superintend it, would be placing a good deal more power—

Evening Post, November 28, 1834. Title added by Sedgwick.

where there is already too much—into the hands of the state executive, to be used honestly or corruptly, for good or evil, as these qualities should happen to predominate in his character, or as the temptations to use his official patronage for his own aggrandizement or profit might be strong or weak. We are continually suffering, under one pretence or other, these pilferings of power from the people.

The circular to which we have alluded appeals strongly to the sympathies of its readers. It presents a deplorable and harrowing picture of the miseries endured by insane paupers in the poor-houses of Massachusetts and New Hampshire, and intimates that their condition is no better in many counties of this state. If this is so, the evil ought to be investigated and remedied; but not in the method proposed, by the erection of a splendid state Asylum. The people ought not to suffer their judgment to be led away by their sympathies. They cannot be too jealous of the exercise of unnecessary powers by the state government. The nearer they keep all power to their own hands, and the more entirely under their own eyes, the more secure are they in their freedom and equal rights.

We would have destitute lunatics taken care of, but not under the charge or at the expense of the state government. It ought to be one of the leading objects of the democracy of this country for many years to come to diminish the power of the general and several state governments, not to increase it. On the subject of legislation for paupers they ought to be particularly vigilant. In nine cases out of ten, and we believe we might say ninety-nine out of a hundred, poor-laws make more poverty than they alleviate. If the reader has ever employed himself in tracing the history of the poor-laws in England, he will not require any proof of this assertion; if he has not, he could scarcely turn his thoughts to a subject more rife with matters of serious interest.

Lunatic paupers ought certainly to be taken care of. Both charity and self-protection require this. But we would remove this guardianship as far from government as possible. Each county should certainly provide for its own; each township would be better, and if it were practicable to narrow it down to the kindred of the insane persons, it would be better still. As a general rule, all public charities, except for the single purpose of promoting education, are founded on erroneous principles, and do infinitely more harm than good. See that the people are educated, and then leave every man to take care of himself and of those who have a natural claim on his protection. We have many large charities in this community, founded in the most amiable and benevolent motives, that annually add very largely to the sum of human misery, by ill-judged exertions to relieve it.

The picture of the wretched condition of lunatic paupers, as presented in the circular before us, is certainly very touching, but legislators must not be blinded by tears to the true and permanent interests of man. They must let their feelings of commiseration take counsel of the pauser judgment. They must look at the subject in all its bearings and aspects, before they saddle the people in their collective capacity with another tax, and place the revenue so instituted at the disposal of an executive officer, who may expend it with a view to advance his private ends.

We have said that the account given of the sufferings of these pauper lunatics is touching; yet it would be easy to draw as touching a picture, and as true too, of the sufferings of sane paupers. Indeed, with many, what a horrible aggravation to their sufferings their very sanity must be,

> "Which but supplies a feeling to decay!"

The lunatics are by no means the most unhappy class of paupers, as a class. Insanity comes to many as a friend in their deepest affliction, to mitigate the tortures of a wounded spirit—to

> Pluck from the memory a rooted sorrow;
> Raze out the written troubles of the brain,
> And, with a sweet oblivious antidote,

> Cleanse the stuffed bosom of the perilous stuff
> Which weighs upon the heart.

Those who are sick and desolate; who have fallen from a high estate—fallen by their own folly, perhaps, and therefore experience the gnawings of remorse, or fallen in consequence of the ingratitude or treachery of others, may easily be supposed to experience keener anguish than the demented inmates of the same abode; since the worst pain man suffers has its seat in the mind, not in the body; and from that species of affliction the crazy are exempt. If this scheme of a grand state lunatic asylum should be carried into effect, we see no reason why next we should not have a grand state poor-house, for the reception of all paupers who had not lost their wits. Other large state charities would probably follow, and one abuse of government would step upon the heels of another. The system is all wrong from beginning to end. *We are governed too much.* Let the people take care of themselves and of their own sick and insane, each community for itself. Let them, above all things, be extremely cautious in surrendering power into the hands of the government, of any kind, or for any purpose whatever, for governments never surrender power to the people. What they get is theirs "to have and to hold," ay, and to exercise too, to the fullest extent, nor is it often got back from them, till their grasp is opened with the sword.

Our remarks are cursory and loose, perhaps, as this article has been written in the midst of more than usual interruptions. Let the reader not thence infer, however, that we have taken ground on this subject hastily; for such is not the fact. The plan recommended by Governor Marcy last winter, has frequently occupied our thoughts, and in every light in which we have viewed it has appeared to us to deserve the opposition of the democratic members of the legislature. We are for giving as few powers to government as possible, and as small an amount of patronage to dispense. Let the aristocracy advocate a strong government; we are for a *strong people.*

MONOPOLIES: II

. . . .

. . . [W]e are surprised that the Journal of Commerce does not perceive that it makes no difference in the principle of the thing whether the stock of an incorporated Company is divided into fifty dollar shares, or five thousand dollar shares. Of whatever amount the subdivisions may be, but a small portion of the community can receive any at the original allotment, and but a small portion of them could receive any, if the Journal of Commerce's favourite plan of selling the shares by auction were adopted. When the pitcher is full it will hold no more; and when the shares were all apportioned or sold, disappointed applicants could not expect to get any. The corporation would then be a monopoly enjoyed by the successful applicants; and whether their number was five or five thousand, they would possess "exclusive privileges" nevertheless, and would be the beneficiaries of unequal legislation.

It is an error of the Journal of Commerce to say, that the practical operation of corporations is to "take privileges, which would otherwise be monopolized by the rich, and divide them into such small parts, that every one who has fifty dollars may be interested, upon equal terms of advantage with the most wealthy." In practice, the operation of the thing is quite the reverse. "Kissing goes by favour," in those operations. Large capitalists get all the stock they ask for, and poor men get but a part, if any, that they solicit. There are published lists of apportionments to which we can refer the Journal of Commerce. But the fact is notorious. And moreover, it is notorious, that this pretended division of stock has even much less of

Evening Post, November 29, 1834. Title added by Sedgwick; Roman numeral added. Text abridged.

fairness and honesty about it than would seem by the face of things. Many of the applicants who get large apportionments are men of straw, mere catspaws, thrust forward to answer the purpose of some great capitalist, for whom the stock is really procured. We could name instances, if it were necessary. We have not come to this subject without being furnished with ample means of establishing our arguments. There is the very last bank that went into operation—was the stock of that incorporation divided to fifty dollar applicants? Is it not, on the contrary, a fact, that a controlling interest is in the hands of a single individual, who is represented by his puppets—we beg their pardon, his proxies—in the directory? Nor is that bank a solitary instance, as the Journal of Commerce well knows.

But if the argument were true, to the fullest extent, that "fifty dollar men" can become bankers, and life-insurers, and packet-owners, and so on, it would still not be a good argument in favour of special acts of incorporation for these several purposes; because these special acts would each embrace but a small portion of the community, and all special or partial legislation is, in its very nature, anti-republican and invasive of equal rights. Let capital and industry alone to find their own channels. This is the true principle to act upon. If any additional legislation is necessary, let it be legislation that shall embrace the whole body politic, and every variety of laudable enterprise. The "fifty dollar" argument of the Journal of Commerce might with much more propriety be put forward in support of a general law of joint stock partnerships, than in support of the everlasting iteration of special acts of incorporation, where every succeeding set of applicants are striving to get some privileges or advantages not conferred by previous charters, and, to effect their selfish and unjust ends, resorting to all the arts of collusion and corruption. Under a general law, not merely "fifty dollar men," but twenty dollar men, and one dollar men, might if they pleased place their means in the joint funds of an association to effect some great enterprise. Such a law would be the very measure to enable poor men to compete with rich. As it is, let the Journal of Commerce say what it may, acts of incorporation are chiefly procured by the rich and for the rich. What claims have your William Bards[1] or your Nathaniel Primes on the country, that our legislature should spend their time in making laws for their exclusive or particular advantage? Did we cast our suffrages into the ballot-boxes to select legislative factors for those men, or such men? Let them have their equal rights, but let them have no more.

The Journal of Commerce seems to think our reasoning involves a contradiction, because we oppose special acts of incorporations or monopolies, and yet would extend incorporations indefinitely. We have not said we would extend *corporations indefinitely;* yet if corporations were extended indefinitely, there would be no monopoly; since when every member of the community has precisely the same opportunities of employing capital and industry given to him by the laws which every other member has, there is no exclusive privilege, and no invasion of equal rights. But it is an error in terms to say that we advocate the indefinite extension of corporations, since the very nature of a corporation, is to be endowed with special privileges. We shall not dispute about words, however, if we can bring the Journal of Commerce to agree with us about principles. The act of incorporation, then, which we should desire to see passed, would be an act incorporating the whole population of the State of New York, for every possible lawful purpose to which money or human labour, or ingenuity, is ever applied, with a clause admitting to a full communion of the benefits of the body corporate, every individual who should at any future time become a member of the body politic.

[1] William Bard was president of the New York Life Insurance and Trust Company, chartered in 1830.—Ed.

REVOLUTIONARY PENSIONERS

In the proceedings of the Board of Assistant Aldermen, on Monday evening last, as reported in the morning papers, and copied into this journal, there occurred the following passage:

"Assistant Alderman Tallmadge moved that the Board now take up the report of the special committee, relative to the relief of the surviving Revolutionary soldiers residing in the city and county of New-York. . . . He moved that one hundred dollars be paid out of the city treasury on the 1st January next, to every surviving officer and soldier of the revolution in the city and county of New-York, now receiving a pension, provided the number does not exceed one hundred. He accompanied it by an eloquent appeal, in which he showed, that while we are rejoicing at the victories of the revolution, we should not forget those in their old age who achieved them."

. . . .

Let us reflect a moment what this proposition is which the Board of Assistant Aldermen have, with this single exception, unanimously adopted. Why to give away ten thousand dollars of the people's money to such of the revolutionary pensioners as reside in the city of New-York. Does not the plain good sense of every reader perceive that this is a monstrous abuse of the trust confided to our city legislators? Did we send them to represent us in the Common Council that they may squander away the city's treasures at such a lavish rate? Is it any part of their duty to make New-Year's presents? Have they any right under heaven to express their sympathy for the revolutionary pensioners at the city's cost? If they have, where is the

Evening Post, December 4, 1834. Misdated by Sedgwick. Title added by Sedgwick. Extract and text abridged.

warrant for it? Let them point their fingers to the clause in the city charter which authorizes them to lay taxes, that they may be expended again in bounties, rewards and largesses, to any class of men whatever.

Let no reader suppose that in making these remarks, we lack a proper appreciation of the eminent services rendered to this country, and to the cause of human liberty throughout the world, by those brave and heroic men who achieved our national independence. Doubtless many, very many of them, entered into that contest with no higher motives than animate the soldier in every contest, for whatsoever object undertaken—whether in defence of liberty or to destroy it. But the glorious result has spread a halo around all who had any share in achieving it, and they will go down together in history, to the latest hour of time, as a band of disinterested, exalted, incorruptible and invincible patriots. This is the light in which their sons, at least, the inheritors of their precious legacy of freedom, ought to view them; and they never, while a single hero of that band remains, can be exonerated from the obligations of gratitude which they owe. But we would not, on that account, authorize any usurpation of power by our public servants, under the pretence of showing the gratitude of the community to the time-worn veterans of the revolutionary war. Every man ought to be his own almoner, and not suffer those whom he has elected for far different purposes, to squander the funds of the public chest, at any rate, and on any object which may seem to them deserving of sympathy. The precedent is a wrong one, and is doubly wrong, inasmuch as the general regard for those for whose benefit this stretch of power is exerted, may lead men to overlook the true character of the unwarrantable assumption.

Let ten thousand—let fifty thousand dollars be given by our city to the revolutionary veterans who are closing their useful lives in the bosom of this community; but let it be given to them without an infringement of those sacred rights which they battled to establish. If the public feeling would authorize such a donation as Mr. Tallmadge exerted his "eloquence" in support of, that same feeling would prompt our citizens, each man for himself, to make a personal contribution towards a fund which should properly and nobly speak the gratitude of New-York towards the venerable patriots among them. But the tax-payer, who would liberally contribute to such an object, in a proper way, may very naturally object to Mr. Tallmadge thrusting his hand into his pocket, and forcing him to give for what and to whom that eloquent gentleman pleases. If the city owes an unliquidated amount, not of gratitude, but of money, to the revolutionary pensioners, let it be paid by the Common Council, and let Mr. Tallmadge be as eloquent as he pleases, or as he can be, in support of the appropriation. But beyond taking care of our persons and our property, the functions neither of our city government, nor of our state government, nor of our national government, extend. We hope to see the day when the people will jealously watch and indignantly punish every violation of this principle.

That what we have here written does not proceed from any motive other than that we have stated, we trust we need not assure our readers. That, above all, it does not proceed from any unkindness towards the remaining heroes of the revolution, must be very evident to all such as have any knowledge of the personal relations of the writer. Among those who would receive the benefit of Mr. Tallmadge's scheme is the venerable parent of him whose opinions are here expressed.[1] That parent, after a youth devoted to the service of his country, after a long life of unblemished honour, now, in the twilight of his age, and bending under the burden of fourscore years, is indebted to the tardy justice of his Government for much of the little light that cheers the evening of his eventful day. Wanting indeed should we be, therefore, in every sentiment of filial duty and love, if we could oppose this plan of a public donation, for any other than public and sufficient reasons. But

[1] Abraham Leggett, William's father, attained the rank of major in the revolutionary war.—Ed.

viewing it as an attempt to exercise a power which the people never meant to confer upon their servants, we should be wanting in those qualities of which this donation is intended to express the sense of the community, if we did not oppose it. We trust the resolution will not pass the upper Board.

JOINT-STOCK PARTNERSHIP LAW

The charters of several incorporated companies in this city are about to expire, and we have several times been asked if this paper, in pursuance of the doctrines we profess, would feel called upon to oppose the renewal of those charters. To this our answer is most unequivocally in the affirmative. We shall oppose, with all our might and zeal, the granting or renewing of any special charter of incorporation whatever, no matter who may be the applicants, or what the objects of the association.

But at the same time, we wish it to be distinctly understood, that we do not desire to break up those incorporated associations the charters of which are about to expire. How so? You would refuse to re-charter them, and thus they would inevitably be broken up. Not at all; as we shall explain.

It is not against the objects effected by incorporated companies that we contend; but simply against the false principle, politically and politico-economically, of special grants and privileges. Instead of renewing the charters of Insurance Companies, or any other companies, about to expire, or granting charters to new applicants, we would recommend the passing

Evening Post, December 30, 1834. Title added by Sedgwick.

of one general law of joint stock partnerships, allowing any number of persons to associate for any object, (with one single temporary exception, which we shall state in the proper place) permitting them to sue and be sued under their partnership name, to be secure from liability beyond the amount of capital invested, to conduct their business according to their own good pleasure, and, in short, to possess all the powers defined by the revised statutes as belonging to corporations. There is nothing not perfectly equitable in the principle which exempts men from liability to any greater amount than the capital actually invested in any business, provided proper notoriety be given of the extent and circumstances of that investment. If such a law were passed, the stockholders in an insurance company, or the stockholders in any other chartered company, when their corporate privileges were about to expire, would have merely to give the proper public notification of their intention to continue their business in the mode specified in the general joint-stock partnership law, and they might go on precisely the same as if their special privileges had been renewed. The only difference would be that those privileges would no longer be special, but would belong to the whole community, any number of which might associate together, form a new company for the same objects, give due notification to the public, and enter into free competition with pre-existing companies or partnerships; precisely as one man, or set of associated men, may now enter into mercantile business by the side of other merchants, import the same kinds of goods, dispose of them on the same terms, and compete with them in all the branches of their business.

There has been a great deal said about our ultraism and Utopianism; and this is the extent of it. By a general law of joint-stock partnerships all the good effects of private incorporations would be secured, and all the evil ones avoided. The humblest citizens might associate together, and wield, through the agency of skilful and intelligent directors, chosen by themselves, a vast aggregate capital, composed of the little separate sums which they could afford to invest in such an enterprise, in competition with the capitals of the purse-proud men who now almost monopolize certain branches of business.

The exception to which we have alluded above, is the business of banking. Our views on this subject were fully stated yesterday. We would not have banking thrown open to the whole community, until the legislature had first taken measures to withdraw our paper money from circulation. As soon as society should be entirely freed, by these measures, from the habit of taking bank-notes as money, we would urge the repeal of the restraining law, and place banking on as broad a basis as any other business whatever.

THE FERRY MONOPOLY

We have received from Albany a copy of the Report of the Select Committee of the Assembly on the several petitions addressed to that body, relative to the establishment of additional ferries between this city and Brooklyn. The petitioners ask that an intelligent and impartial board of commissioners may be appointed, with full powers to establish ferries between New-York and Long Island, and that the present rates of ferriage be reduced. The fact that additional means of communication between the cities of New-York and Brooklyn are very much needed, that the present rates of ferriage are exorbitantly high, and the accommodations none of the best, is too notorious for any one to deny. It is also a well known fact,

Evening Post, February 18, 1835. Title added by Sedgwick. Text abridged and subjoined extract deleted.

that numerous responsible persons have frequently and vainly petitioned the corporate authorities of this city for permission to establish another ferry, offering to bind themselves to furnish suitable accommodations, and to pay too a large sum for the desired "privilege." In consequence of the rejection of all these applications, resort has at last been had to the State Legislature.

The power of establishing ferries over the East River is claimed by the corporate authorities of this city as a franchise conferred upon them by the ancient charters, and confirmed by various subsequent acts of state legislation.

. . . .

In the difficulties which citizens now experience to obtain reasonable facilities of communication between New-York and Brooklyn, a forcible illustration is afforded of the absurd and oppressive nature of monopolies. The question how far the power to regulate this matter has been granted to the Common Council of New-York, and how far it yet resides in the legislature of the State is one which we have not qualified ourselves to answer. It seems to us, however, from an attentive perusal of the Report, and a reference to some of the authorities there mentioned, that the positions assumed in that document are sound, and that the Legislature have a primary, unalienated and supreme control over the whole matter in dispute.

Be this as it may, the common sense view of the subject plainly teaches that there ought to be no further legislative or municipal interference with the business of ferriage, than is demanded by a simple regard for public safety and convenience. We have not time to go into any argument to-day; but on this subject, as on all others, we are the advocates of the princples of *free trade*. We would put no hinderance in the way of any man, or set of men, who should choose to undertake the business of ferrying people across the river. The public interests would be best served by leaving the matter to regulate itself—or rather leaving it to be regulated by the laws of demand and supply. Free competition would do more to insure good accommodations, low prices, swift and safe boats, and civil attendants, than all the laws and charters which could ever be framed. The sheet of water which separates New-York from Brooklyn ought to be considered as a great highway, free to whomsoever should choose to travel on it, under no other restriction than complying with certain regulations for the mutual safety and convenience of all: such regulations as are now enforced with regard to private vehicles in the streets and public roads. Yet since the corporate authorities choose to turn every business that they possibly can into a source of revenue to the city, they might make a license necessary for ferry-boats, as is now done with regard to the Broadway and Bowery omnibusses. Even this tax is an infringement of those sound principles of political economy which ought to govern in the matter; but it could not be objected to in the case of ferries, while it is recognized in that of stage coaches.

In making these remarks, we are by no means forgetful of the "chartered rights" of those who now have the "exclusive privilege" of carrying people to and fro between New-York and Brooklyn. Much as we detest the principle of such monopolies, we would by no means justify any invasion of the rights duly granted to them. The public faith is pledged, and, at the expense of any temporary inconvenience, let it be preserved inviolate. But though the Corporation ought not to invade the rights which have been foolishly granted, yet as far as they still retain any control over the subject, they might restore to the community their natural rights, and leave those who wish to establish other ferries to make the best terms they can with the existing monopolies. Such a course is in reality dictated as well by selfish and local interests as by an enlarged and liberal view of the whole question. Every additional facility of access to this metropolis increases its general prosperity. We are aware that pains have been taken to create a belief that the establishment of more ferries would injuriously affect the prices of property in the upper part of the city, and that narrow and selfish opposition has been thus engendered. But we think it could be demonstrated that every additional means of communicating with Long Island will add to the prosperity of New-York. Be this as it may as respects owners of real estate, there can be no question that it is true with regard to the great body of the people.

FREE TRADE POST OFFICE

The party newspapers, both for and against the administration, contain, every now and then, statements exposing individual instances of gross abuse of the franking privilege. There can be no doubt that the franking privilege is a prolific source of many of those evils in the Post-office department which are complained of on all hands, and that a reformation of the laws on this subject is very much needed.

. . . .

But at the hazard of giving a new occasion for the charge of ultraism against this journal, we shall take the liberty to express an opinion, which we have long entertained, that the source of the evils in our Post-office system lies far too deep to be reached by any regulation or abridgement of the franking privilege, or even by its total abolition. It lies too deep, in our opinion, also, to be reached by any possible organization of the Post-office Department which it is in the power of the General

Evening Post, March 23, 1835. Title added by Sedgwick. Text abridged.

Government to establish. There are five words in the Constitution of the United States which we look upon as the grand primary source of all the evils of which the people have so much just cause to complain in relation to that particular department of the Government. We allude to the clause which gives to Congress the power *"to establish post-offices and post-roads."*

These words, in our view of the subject, ought never to have formed a part of the Constitution. They confer a power on the General Government which is liable, and almost inevitably subject, to the grossest political abuse. The abuse is one which will necessarily increase, too, from year to year, as population increases in numbers and spreads over a wider surface. The Post-office, controlled and directed by the General Government, will always be conducted with a vast deal of unnecessary expense, and, what is a consideration of far more serious importance, will always be used, to a greater or less extent, as *a political machine.*

It is not probable that the history of this Union, should it stretch out for ages, will ever exhibit to the admiration of mankind an administration under the guidance of a more faithful, energetic, intrepid and patriotic spirit, than that which happily now rules the executive councils of the nation. Yet even under the administration of a man whose integrity no arts can corrupt, whose firmness no difficulties can appal, and whose vigilance no toils can exhaust—even under the administration of such a man, what a sickening scene does the mismanagement of the Post-office not present! Remove Mr. Barry and appoint another in his place, and you will not correct, and most likely you will not even mitigate the evil. Abolish the franking privilege, and the essential defects of the system would still remain. Re-organize the whole department, and introduce all the guards and checks which legislative ingenuity can devise, and still you will not wholly remove the imperfection. The Post-office will still be a government machine, cumbrous, unwieldy, and liable to the worst sorts of abuses.

The Post-office is established by the Government for the purpose of facilitating intercourse by letter between distant places. But personal intercourse between distant places is as necessary as epistolary, though not, perhaps, to the same degree. Why then should not the Government take upon itself the support and regulation of facilities for carrying passengers as well as letters from place to place? The transmission of packages of merchandise from one part of the country to another is no less necessary, than intercourse by letter or person. Why should not Government go a step further, and institute transportation lines for the conveyance of our goods? But we shall be answered, that these objects may safely be left to the laws of trade, and that supply will keep pace with demand in these matters as in other commercial and social wants of man. Might not the laws of trade, and the power of demand to produce supply through the activity of private enterprise, be safely trusted to, also, for the carriage of letters from place to place?

If the mail establishment, as a branch of the United States Government, should be abolished this hour, how long would it be before private enterprise would institute means to carry our letters and newspapers from city to city, with as much regularity as they are now carried, and far greater speed and economy? But the objection may be raised that inland places and thinly settled portions of the country would suffer by such an arrangement. There is no place on the map of the United States which would not soon be supplied with mail facilities by paying what they were worth, and if it gets them for less now, it is only because the deficiency is levied from the inhabitants of some other place, which is contrary to the plainest principles of justice.

There are very many considerations which might be urged in favour of a *free trade view of this subject.* The curse of office hunting, which is an incident of our form of Government, and is exerting every year, more and more, a demoralizing influence on the people, would undergo a check and rebatement by the suggested change. But would you withdraw—some one may ask—the stimulus which the present post-office system furnishes to emigration, by extending mail routes through the wilderness, and thus presenting inducements for population to gather together at points which would otherwise remain unimproved and uninhabited for years? To this we answer, unequivocally, yes. We would withdraw all Government *stimulants;* and let no man suppose that the progress of improvement would be retarded by such a withdrawal. The country would grow from year to year, notwithstanding, as rapidly and more healthily than now. It would only be changing the hot-bed system to the system of nature and reason. It would be discontinuing the force-pump method, by which we now seek to make water flow up hill, and leaving it to flow in its own natural channels. It would be removing the high-pressure application of Government facilities from enterprise and capital, and permitting them to expand themselves in their own proper field. The boundaries of population would still continually enlarge, circle beyond circle, like spreading rings upon the water; but they would not be forced to enlarge this way and that way, shooting out into strange and unnatural irregularities, as it might please land speculators, through the agency of members of Congress, to extend mail facilities into regions which perhaps God and nature meant should remain uninhabited for ages to come.

There are various other points of view in which the subject deserves to be considered. But we must reserve these for another occasion.

STOCK GAMBLING

In the bill now before the legislature of this state to regulate the sales of stocks and exchange, we behold another beautiful illustration of the benefits which the community derive from our wretched system of special and partial legislation. The professed object of this bill is to prevent stock-gambling; and stock-gambling, according to our humble opinion, is a species of speculation which our law-givers, by the whole course of their legislation for years past, have done all in their power to foster and promote. If they desire now, really and sincerely, to do away with the evils of this desperate and immoral kind of enterprise, which daily displays itself to a frightful extent in Wall-street, let them adopt a more effectual method than that proposed by the bill under their consideration. Let them address their efforts to correct the cause of the evil, and the effect will be sure to be removed. Let them apply the axe to the root of the tree, and the branches will needs wither, when the source from which they derive their nourishment is destroyed.

The whole course of our legislation, in regard to financial matters, has had a direct tendency to excite a feverish and baneful thirst of gain—gain not by the regular and legitimate operations of trade, but by sudden and hazardous means. Every body has been converted into a stock speculator by our laws. Every body is seeking to obtain a charter of incorporation for some purpose or other, in order that he may take his place among the bulls and bears of the stock-market, and play his hand in the desperate game of Wall-street brag. What is the true nature of the spectacle which is presented to the contemplation of sober-minded men, every time any new company of

Evening Post, March 25, 1835. Title added by Sedgwick.

scrip gamblers is created? Do we not see persons not worth a hundred dollars in the world, running with all speed to put in their claims for a division of the stock—persons who are not able to raise even the instalment on the amount of stock which they ask, and who, in point of fact, are the mere agents of brokers and other speculators, selling the use of their names for a certain rate of premium per share on the division of stock which may be awarded to them?

A gaming spirit has infected the whole community. This spirit is the offspring—the deformed and bloated offspring—of our wretched undemocratic system of exclusive and partial legislation. To destroy the effect, and leave the cause untouched, would be as easy a task for our legislature, as to restrain an impetuous torrent while you yet leave wide the flood-gates which presented the only barrier to its course. The legislature might pass a law commanding the stream to keep within certain limits; but we doubt if its waves would recede, notwithstanding the terrors of the law—

> "They rolled not back when Canute gave command."

It is time the legislature made the discovery that there are some things which cannot be done by law. They cannot prevent the thunder from following the lightning's flash, however carefully they may word their statute, or whatever penalty they may affix to its violation. They cannot change the whole nature of man by any enactment. We doubt very much whether even the famous Blue Laws wholly deterred men from kissing their wives on occasions, particularly in the first part of their matrimonial connexion; nor do we believe they prevented beer from working on Sundays during the season of fermentation. As easy would it be, however, to effect such objects by law, as to repress the yearnings of cupidity and avarice, or stay the adventurous spirit of wild speculation which has been excited, by the penalties of a bill to regulate the sales of stock and exchange. The whole scope and tendency of all the rest of our legislation is to inflame the feverish thirst of gain, which afflicts the community; and how vain, how worse than vain, while our law-makers hold up the lure in every possible form of attraction before the public, to bid them, shut their eyes, and not attempt to grasp it!

As to the particular project before the legislature, if we understand its provisions, it is not only inadequate to the end proposed, but unjust in its bearing, and impolitic on various grounds. It proposes to destroy the use of credit in the transactions of the stock-exchange, which is much such a cure for the evil it aims to abolish as amputation of the leg would be for a gouty toe. The gout might attack the other foot, or the stomach, notwithstanding; nor would its victim be more able to resist its influences with a frame weakened by the barbarous and uncalled for mutilation he had suffered. There is no earthly reason why credit should not be used in the purchase and sale of stocks, as well as in any other species of traffic. There is no kind of business intercourse which may not be made the means of gambling, and were it even within the competency of the legislature to check the public propensity to traffic on speculative contingencies, so far as one particular species of business is concerned, the ever active disposition would immediately indulge itself in some other form of hazardous and unreal enterprise. For the real *bona fide* transactions in stock and exchange, the employment of credit is as intrinsically proper, as the employment of credit in foreign commerce, in the purchase of real estate, or in any of the various modes and objects of human dealing. The legislature might as well pass a law forbidding the citizen to deal or credit with his tailor, hatter, or shoemaker, to run up a score with his milkmen or baker, or postpone the payment for his newspaper, as to forbid a man to employ his legitimate credit in the purchase and sale of stocks.

The mere business of dealing in stocks is as respectable and useful as most others: the crime of gambling in stocks is the inevitable result of the wild and speculative spirit which springs from unsalutary legislation. When we look into the statute books, and see that more than two-thirds of all the laws passed in our state are for the creation of specially incorporated joint-stock companies; when we learn that two-thirds of these joint-stock companies were created originally, not with strict reference to their professed ultimate object, but for purposes of intermediary speculation: we must perceive that the evil to be remedied is in the legislature, not in the community; that the fountain is turbid at its head, and that it will be vain and foolish to attempt to purify it by straining the waters of a distant branch through a clumsy, filtering contrivance of the laws.

There is another view of this subject which it is important to take. By abolishing the use of credit in stock operations, you would not abolish stock-gambling, but only confine it to the more wealthy operators, and put additional facilities of fortune into the hands already favoured overmuch. You make a concession to the spirit of aristocracy. You lay another tribute at the feet of riches. You join your voice in its exaltation. You exclude from the magic circle the poor man whose capital consisted in his skill, industry, and character for sagacity and integrity, and you give it to the millionary to lord it there alone, as if his gold were better than the poor man's blood.

That we are opposed to stock-gambling and gambling, in all its forms, we need not say. But we are equally opposed to those false notions of Government which so extensively prevail in this country, and which seem to consider that every thing is to be done by law, and nothing by common sense and the inevitable operation of the laws of trade. For gambling, public opinion is the great and only salutary corrective. If it cannot be suppressed by the force of the moral sense of the community, it cannot be suppressed by statutes and edicts, no matter how comprehensive their terms, or how heavy their penalties. We have our laws against gambling now, yet establishments fitly denominated *hells* are notoriously conducted in different parts of the city, and there are various neighbourhoods where the dice-box and the roulette wheel rattle and clatter all night long. We have our laws against lotteries, too, yet what do they avail? The history of a recent instance of a man convicted of trafficking in the forbidden pursuit must convince any mind that those laws are a little more than a dead letter. And such would be the law to suppress stock operations on time. It would not do away with either the proper or improper part of the business; but it would diminish the respectability of the honest and prudent dealer, and give a more desperate character to the reckless adventurer.

WEIGHMASTER GENERAL

I

The report of the proceedings of the Legislature on Wednesday, which is copied into our paper of to-day, shows to our readers that there was a decided majority in the Assembly in favour of the bill providing for the appointment of a Weighmaster General for this city, with power to name his own deputies. This measure was passed by a strict party vote; and for the sake of creating another office to be supported out of the means of this overburdened community, those members of the legislature who were elected by the democracy, and call themselves democrats, have concurred in fastening another shackle on the limbs of trade.

There is probably not one man in our legislature so totally destitute of all knowledge of that magnificent science which is revolutionizing the world, as not to be aware that the bill

Evening Post, April 10 and 16, 1835. Title added by Sedgwick; Roman numerals added. Text abridged.

now before that body to regulate the weighing of merchandise, is an indirect tax on the people, is a violation of the principle of equal rights, is another link in that chain which folly and cunning have combined to fasten on the body politic, and by which the popular action is already so much restrained, that, notwithstanding we enjoy universal suffrage, our elections, for the most part, are rather a reflection of the wishes of the banks and of the office-holders, than of the free, unbiassed will of the people. The effect of the present bill, besides imposing an additional tax on the community, and placing harmful checks and limitations around trade, will be to institute a band of placemen in the city, who will doubtless endeavour to show themselves worthy of their hire by exerting their lungs in shouts and paeans in praise of those to whom they owe their situations. To a certain extent exertions of this kind guide the course of public sentiment, and increase its force. Independent, then, of the politico-economical objections to legislative interference of the sort now under consideration, a more momentous objection exists in the fact that such measures are directly calculated to place government on a basis other than that of the spontaneous sentiments of the people, and draw a cordon of placemen around it, more powerful than the lictors and praetorian cohorts which hedged in the abuses and corruptions of the licentious rulers of Rome.

Earnestly did we hope that our present legislature, instead of rivetting new fetters on the people, would have broken and cast away a portion, at least, of those disgraceful bonds with which the craft and ignorance of their predecessors had loaded us. But the fact is not to be disguised that our legislature, though called democratic, and elected by democrats, are in reality anything but true friends to the equal rights of the people. They represent banks, insurance companies, railroads, manufacturing establishments, high-salaried officers, inspectors of rawhides, sole-leather, beef, pork, tobacco, flour, rum, wood, coal, and, in short, almost every necessary and comfort of life. To state this more briefly, they represent monopolies and office-holders; and no wonder, therefore, that the whole course of their legislation is at the expense and to the detriment of the people at large, as they on all hands seem to be considered lawful prey.

II

. . . .

The weighing of merchandise is a matter with which legislation has nothing to do: the laws of trade would arrange that business much more to the satisfaction of all parties concerned than the laws of the state can ever do. When the Government has supplied its citizens with a measure of value, of weight, of length, and of quantity, it has done all in the way of measuring which properly belongs to Government. All your inspectors, your gaugers, and your weighers, after that, with their whole host of deputies and subalterns, are but adscititious contrivances of political cunning, to provide means for rewarding those who assisted in its elevation, or to establish a phalanx to guard it in the height it has attained.

It was our hope that our present legislature—chosen under so distinct an expression of the public sentiment against all monopolies and all infringements of the principle of Equal Rights—would exert themselves to do away the restrictions on trade and the thousand subtle contrivances for indirectly extorting taxes from the people to support useless officers; or at all events that they would not add to the number of those impositions. If we go on for many years to come, strengthening, and extending the artificial and unequal system we have for years past been building up, we shall at length find, perhaps too late, that we have erected around us an enormous, unseemly, and overshadowing structure, from which the privileged orders will have the encircled community wholly at their control, and which we cannot hope to demolish without bringing the whole fabric down with ruin on our heads.

STATE PRISON MONOPOLY

The legislature, it will be seen, have at last taken up, in good earnest, the state prison question. As this is a subject which both parties have tried their utmost to turn into a mere political gull-trap, it is not probable that any measure will be finally acted upon, before members have baited the trap with a deal of mawkish oratory, and, in so doing, expose, most thoroughly, their ignorance of the first principles of political economy.

This journal has never said much in relation to the state prison monopoly, as it is called, because a degree of importance had been given to the subject entirely disproportioned to its real merits, and demagogues had made it the theme of their vehement harangues, until an excitement was produced among the mechanic classes so strong and general, that it swallowed up almost every other question, and pervaded almost every vocation. We are as decidedly opposed to the *principle* of state prison labour as any person can be; yet we believe that the *practical evil* of the present system, on any branch of productive industry, is exceedingly trifling, and indeed almost below computation, while the result to society at large is decidedly beneficial. Nevertheless, as the fundamental principle of the system is, in our view, totally erroneous, we have never hesitated to oppose it when we deemed that the occasion called on us to speak.

One of these occasions was furnished by the publication of the report of the State Prison Commissioners, which was a weak, inaccurate, shuffling document, and was the more calculated to provoke indignation, as one of its authors is well known to have ridden himself into office on the hobby of the state prison monopoly question. It seemed to us a barefaced

Evening Post, April 28, 1835. Title added by Sedgwick.

piece of treachery for this person, after having won the suffrages of the mechanics by the incessant and superior loudness of his vociferation against the employment of convict labour in competition with honest industry, to turn round and immediately present to the legislature such a deceptive hocus-pocus report as that to which his name was subscribed.

The suggestions of the report made by the Commissioners have been embodied in the bill now before the Assembly. By this plan the prisoners are to be employed in branches of industry not yet introduced among our citizens, and among these the culture and manufacture of silk occupy a conspicuous place. We are surprised that sensible men in the legislature should not perceive that in principle, it is the same thing whether the convicts are employed in callings in which free citizens are already engaged, or are turned to others to which free citizens would naturally direct their attention in the course of a short time.

The question of the state prison monopoly, in our view, reduces itself to this: it is the exclusive employment, by Government, of a labour-saving machine, in competition with a certain portion of citizens who have no such advantage. Has Government a right to set up a labour-saving machine, and to enter into competition with any class of its citizens in any pursuit of industry? Government, it will be admitted, is instituted for the equal protection of all, in person, life, and property. These are its only legitimate objects. The confinement of criminals, so as to restrain them from perpetrating their outrages against society, is an object in which all are equally interested. The support of them in confinement is a contingent evil, and ought to be borne in the ratio of benefit conferred—that is, equally. But when the criminals are made to earn their own support by manufacturing a class of articles which a certain portion of citizens also manufacture for their livelihood, it is obvious that a fundamental principle of government is violated, since equal protection is no longer extended to all.

But the political economist may contend that the evil in this case is but temporary; that the supply will soon adjust itself to the demand; that a certain number of citizens, driven from their occupation by the introduction of convict competition, will only be obliged to turn themselves to other branches of industry; and that in a short time, the matter equalizing itself through all the callings of active life, a permanent benefit will accrue to society, in the aggregate, by reason of the increased production and diminished price of all the articles created by human labour.

If we admit this statement to be true, is it not at best an argument in favour of the state prison system on the ground that *all is well that ends well?* or that *it is right to do evil in the first instance, that good may follow?* These are principles which ought never to be countenanced in our system of political ethics. The cardinal object of Government is the equal protection of all citizens. The moment the prisoner is set to work, and the products of his labour sold, some free citizen is unequally and oppressively burdened. If this citizen is induced to forsake his now overstocked calling, and engage in some other, the competition in this new branch will operate injuriously to those already engaged in it; and this will continue to be the case, though in a gradually diminishing ratio, through all the various pursuits of active industry, until the displaced particles of society, so to speak, diffuse themselves evenly over the entire surface.

The aggregate of products manufactured by convict labour in the United States bear so small a proportion to the sum of the products of free labour, that the practical evil of state prison competition on any mechanic class is, as we have already stated, exceedingly and almost incalculably light. The final result of all labour-saving machinery (and the operation of our penitentiary system is precisely analogous with that of such a machine) is beneficial to society. An individual citizen has a perfect right to introduce labour-saving machinery, and however hard may be the effect temporarily on any number of citizens, the good of the greatest number is immediately promoted, and eventually the good of all. But when a state government sets up such a labour-saving machine, it oppresses temporarily a class of citizens, for the immediate benefit of the rest, and though the whole community will be eventually benefitted, the state has obviously, to produce this result, violated the fundamental principle of equal rights.

CORPORATION PROPERTY

The property belonging to the corporation of this city is estimated, in the Message of the Mayor which we had the pleasure of presenting to our readers a few days since, at ten millions of dollars. Of the property which is valued at this sum, a very small portion is actually required for the purposes of government. A large part of it consists of town lots, wholly unproductive. Another part consists of lots and tenements leased or rented for a trifling consideration. That part which is in the actual occupancy of the corporate authorities for public uses, is comparatively small, and smaller still that part which is actually needed in the exercise of the legitimate functions of the government.

That our municipal government should possess no property, except what is really required for the performance of its duties, seems to us so plain a proposition as scarcely to require an argument to support it. We elect our city authorities from year to year to supervise the affairs of the body politic, pass needful municipal regulations, enforce existing laws, and attend, generally, to the preservation of public order. Adequately to

Evening Post, June 3, 1835. Title added by Sedgwick.

fulfil these trusts, a building set apart for the meetings of the city authorities is necessary. A place of detention for the city criminals is necessary, and, under the present system, a place for the city paupers. These, and a few other buildings, occupying grounds of a suitable location and extent, constitute all the real estate required for the due administration of the functions of our municipal government. If our authorities, then, purchase more property than this, they either waste the money of their constituents, or buying it on credit, or paying for it with borrowed funds, they waste the money of posterity.

The government of our city is nothing more nor less than a certain number of persons chosen from year to year, by the suffrages of a majority of the citizens, to attend to those affairs which belong to all in common, or, in other words, the affairs of the community. They represent the aggregate will of the existing community in relation to those affairs; and their functions, by the very tenure of their offices, are confined within the circle of the year. It is plain, then, viewing the subject on principles of abstract right, that a government so constituted, ought do nothing which would not be approved by those from whom it derives its powers. The accumulation of unnecessary property, to the amount of millions of dollars, can never have been intended by any considerable number of voters of this city, as a duty which the city government ought to perform; and having accumulated it, to retain it seems equally averse to the plainest principles of sound policy and right.

To whom does this property belong? Not to the authorities of the city, surely, but to the citizens themselves—to those who chose those authorities to manage their affairs. If it belongs to them, and government is not a permanent existence separate from the will of the people, but the mere breath of their nostrils, their mere representative, renewed at their pleasure from year to year, it must be obvious that there can be no good reason for having that property retained in the possession of the government. It would be much better in the possession of the people themselves, since every body knows that as a general and almost invariable rule, men attend to their private affairs much better than agents attend to their delegated trusts.

Let no reader be startled at the idea we have here put forth, and suppose he sees in it the ghost of agrarianism,—that bugbear which has been conjured with for ages to frighten grown-up children from asserting the dictates of common sense in relation to the affairs of government. We have no agrarian scheme in contemplation. We are not about to propose a division of public property, either according to the ratio of taxation, or equally by the poll list, or in any other objectionable mode. But our citizens are every year called upon to pay taxes. The last legislature passed a law authorizing our corporate authorities to levy a tax greatly increased since last year. We have also our public debt, for which the property of our *posterity* is pledged, and this debt was lately swelled one million of dollars by money borrowed to be paid in 1860. Now it strikes us as somewhat unreasonable to call upon the citizens to pay taxes to defray the current expenses of the government, and to saddle posterity with an enormous debt, when the unnecessary and disposable public property now in the hands of our municipal government would wipe off the whole amount of the debt which was contracted on the credit of posterity, and defray the current expenses of the city besides for several years to come.

We would by no means dispose of our City Hall, or our Park, or our Battery, any more than we would dispose of Broadway or the Bowery. These are for the public use, for their present, daily, and hourly use, in various respects. But in the public property which the Mayor estimates at an aggregate of ten millions of dollars there will be found much which is not necessary for the purposes of Government or the health and convenience of the people. All such we would sell, and apply the proceeds to the liquidation of the public debt, and to the payment of those expenses for which taxes are now assessed. Let not the argument be used that this property will be far more valuable in a few years, and may then be disposed of to much greater advantage. If we admit the validity of this argument, it is one which may be urged to postpone the sale for half a century, and of what benefit would be the augmented amount, fifty years hence, to the present people, to whom the property in truth belongs? Society is daily, hourly, momently, changing its constituent individuals. The particles which compose the stream of life are continually passing away, to be succeeded by other particles, and the transition of these human atoms is nowhere so rapid as in the whirlpool of a great city. Many of those whose votes elevated the present municipal officers to their places, will never cast a suffrage again—some have gone to other states, some to distant lands, some to that bourne from whence no traveller returns. But others will push into their places. The social tide will still rush on. The young man will pass his probationary period and acquire the rights of citizenship; foreigners will be adopted; brethren from other portions of the confederacy will take up their abode among us. No matter, therefore, how rapidly increasing in value any portion of this superfluous public property may be, we who own it now and who next year may own it no longer, have a right to demand that it should be disposed of for our benefit, and to liquidate those debts which we have no right to leave for posterity to pay.

But we deny that there is any validity in this argument founded on the conjectural or probable rise of price. If the property improves in price, we ask whether is it better that the increase should be in the hands of the government or of individual citizens? Should the government continue to hold this property for years, through its annual successions, it is at last to be appropriated to some public purpose. If the property had been disposed of, its increased value would necessarily have been in the hands of citizens, whose capacity would in the same measure have been increased to contribute to the public expenses. The property of the citizens is at all times abundantly able to sustain any legitimate expenses of government, and all property, not required for such purposes, should remain in the people's own hands.

There is one species of public property to which we have not adverted in this article, because it does not probably enter into the Mayor's estimate, but which we could well wish were also disposed of by the public authorities, and suffered to go into the hands of private citizens. We allude to the wharves, piers and public docks, with the exception of the slips at the end of streets. Those in our view ought to be as free as the streets themselves, and the rest ought to be left in private hands. We cannot undertake to argue this subject to-day; but let those who are disposed to differ from us, reflect that we only propose to put the wharves on the same footing with houses and stores, and that the same competition, the same laws of supply and demand, which regulate the rent of the one description of property, would equally regulate the wharfage of the other.

REGULATION OF COAL

A copy of the petition of the Corporation of this city, on the subject of the law regulating the sale of anthracite coal, has been laid before us, and is worthy of a remark. The petition desires that such an alteration of the existing law may be made as shall permit the purchaser to choose for himself whether he will have his coal weighed by an appointed weigher or not. Nothing can be more indisputably reasonable than this. Those who claim that municipal authorities ought to exercise their powers for the regulation of trade, and establish inspectors,

Evening Post, September 10, 1835. Title added by Sedgwick.

gaugers, weighers and supervisors, of various kinds, to see that tradespeople do not cheat their customers in quality, strength, weight, or quantity, yet cannot, we should suppose, be so utterly blind to the natural rights of the citizen, as to require that he should not be permitted to cheat himself, if he prefers to do so.

For our own part, as our readers well know, we are opposed to the whole system of legislative interference with trade, which we wish to see left to its own laws, unfettered by any of the clogs and hinderances invented by political fraud and cunning, to extract indirect taxes from the community, and contrive offices with which to reward the selfish exertions of small-beer politicians. We should be glad to see the whole tree, root and branch, destroyed. We should be glad if the whole oppressive and aristocratic scheme of inspection and gauging, whether existing under the General Government, or that of the state, or of the city, were utterly abrogated. We should be glad to see the custom-house swept off into the sea, and the whole army of collectors, surveyors, tide-waiters, and lick-spittles, of various denominations, swept off with it—or at least compelled to resort to some other method of obtaining a livelihood. We should be glad if the inspectors of beef, flour, pork, cotton, tobacco, wood, charcoal and anthracite, and all their brother inspectors, too numerous to mention, were made to take up the line of march, and follow their file leaders into some more democratic species of avocation. The land, freed from this army of incubuses, and from the bad laws which give them being, would then blossom as the rose under the genial influence of free trade; and then it would be found, we do not doubt, from the alacrity with which the people would bear direct taxation for all the necessary purposes of government, that there was never any reason for the anomaly we have presented in resorting to indirect means for obtaining the public resources, as if the popular virtue and intelligence, on which our institutions are professedly founded, existed but in name, and the necessary expenses of government could only be obtained from the people by some method which prevented them from seeing what they paid.

But putting these ultra views, as some may consider them, entirely out of sight, there cannot be two opinions, one would think, as to the entire propriety of the request now made to the city legislature by the petition to which we have alluded. There are many persons who have greater confidence in the coal dealers than in the public weighers, and we know of no just reason why they should be prohibited by law from indulging their preference.

FREE FERRIES AND AN AGRARIAN LAW

The American, some few days since, in an editorial article, expressed itself in favour of the establishment of free ferries at the public expense. A correspondent of that paper, a day or two afterwards, proposed the establishment, at the public expense, of free carriages to carry people about the city. Both propositions were serious, not ironical. We have not the papers at hand in which they were contained, but believe we do not mistake the purport of the two articles. Now it seems to us that, the epithet *agrarian,* which the American has sometimes applied to this journal, was never so much deserved by any political theory we have advanced, as it is by that paper for the projects referred to. Let us confine ourselves, however, to that which was editorially asserted, namely, the one relative to free ferries, for which we may justly hold the American responsible. This, we certainly think can be demonstrated to be

Evening Post, October 10, 1835. Title added by Sedgwick.

agrarian, according to the sense in which that term is employed by politicians of the present day.

The agrarian law of Rome was a law to provide for the equitable division of conquered lands among those who conquered them. It was not altogether unlike our laws for the distribution of prize money; though far more just than they, according to our recollections of its provisions. But the charge of agrarianism, as applied reproachfully at the present day to the radical democracy, imputes to them a desire to throw down the boundaries of private right, and make a new and arbitrary division of property. This charge so far as relates to this journal, and so far, as we sincerely believe, as it relates to any considerable number of individuals, of any name or sect, in our country, has no foundation in truth. Of our own political doctrines we can truly say that they are in every feature the very opposite of agrarianism. They rest, indeed, on the basis of inviolable respect for private right. We would not have even the legislature take private property, except for the public good, directly, not incidentally; and then only in the clearest cases, and by rendering the most equitable compensation. We would never have it delegate that power to any private corporation, on the ground that the public good would be incidentally promoted by the doings of such a body.

But the American, in becoming the advocate of free ferries, leans to agrarianism, in the popular and justly odious sense of the word. It takes the property of A. and gives it to B. It proposes to bestow a valuable gratuity on such persons as have occasion to use the ferry, and pay for this gratuity, for the most part, with money filched from the pockets of those who never step foot in a ferry-boat. Is this not clearly unjust? Is it not to some extent, an agrarian scheme?

The American may answer us that it is but an extension of the same power, the rightfulness of which nobody ever calls in question, which is exercised by all municipal corporations in constructing streets at the public expense, for the gratuitous accommodation of all who choose to use them. Even this power in its nature is agrarian, and is submitted to by universal assent, not because it is right in principle, but because its conveniences overbalance the theoretic objections. But there is a point where the objections equal the conveniences, and to insist on any scheme which lies beyond that point, is to run the risk of being called, with justice, agrarian. Every body has more or less occasion to use the streets; and therefore every body ought to contribute towards the expense of making and preserving them. This expense is taken out of the general fund derived from taxes. The burden of taxes falls, directly or indirectly, on every body, and if not in the precise proportion of relative advantage from the use of the streets, still the difference is too slight to awaken complaint. But the case is widely different with regard to ferries. Thousands of citizens never use them at all; yet according to the agrarian scheme of the American, they would be required to pay as much for supporting them as those who cross the river a dozen times every day. They would find their advantage, the American might argue, in the greater cheapness of market commodities, the increased number of customers to the city traders, and the general improvement of the city. But this advantage would not be diffused equally, and whatever is done by legislation should tend to the equal benefit of all.

But where would the American stop? If free ferries are of advantage, why would not free markets be also? And free warehouses? And free dwelling houses? And free packet ships? And in short free from every thing? The arguments by which alone the American can support its theory of free ferries, are equally pertinent and cogent in defence of a literal *commonwealth*. Who would have thought to see the American turn so ultra an agrarian?

Now, our theory with respect to ferries is liable to no such objections. It is precisely the same as our theory with respect to banks, with respect to railroads, and with respect to every other branch of trade and enterprise. Our theory is the free trade theory. It is simply to leave trade alone to govern itself by its own laws. Ferries are as much a matter of trade, as Broadway stages,[1] or Broadway shopkeeping. Leave the subject open to unrestricted competition. Leave men to run boats where they please, when they please, and how they please, with no other restraint upon them than such municipal regulations as may be requisite for the preservation of public order—some simple rules, such as "turn to the right, as the law directs." When this course is pursued, we shall have ferry boats where they are wanted, and as many as are wanted, and no more. People will not run more boats than yield a fair profit on investment, and where competition is free there will certainly be as many. The ferries, then, between New-York and Long Island, and between New-York and New-Jersey, will be as well conducted, and as well supplied with boats, as are the ferries now between New-York and Albany.

This is our scheme: how does the American like it? The difference between us is that we are for leaving ferries to the regulation of the laws of trade; the American is for controlling them by Agrarian law.

THANKSGIVING DAY

Thursday, the fifteenth of the present month, has been designated by Governor Marcy, in his annual proclamation, as a day of general thanksgiving throughout this state. This is done in conformity with a long established usage, which has been so generally and so scrupulously observed, that we doubt whether it has ever been pretermitted, for a single year, by the

[1] That is, stagecoaches.—Ed.

Plaindealer, December 3, 1836.

Chief Magistrate of any state in the Confederacy. The people, too, on these occasions, have always responded with such cordiality and unanimity to the recommendation of the Governors, that not even the Sabbath, a day which the scriptures command to be kept holy, is more religiously observed, in most places, than the day set apart as one of thanksgiving and prayer by gubernatorial appointment. There is something exceedingly impressive in the spectacle which a whole people presents, in thus voluntarily withdrawing themselves on some particular day, from all secular employment, and uniting in a tribute of praise for the blessings they enjoy. Against a custom so venerable for its age, and so reverently observed, it may seem presumptuous to suggest an objection; yet there is one which we confess seems to us of weight, and we trust we shall not be thought governed by an irreligious spirit, if we take the liberty to urge it.

In framing our political institutions, the great men to whom that important trust was confided, taught, by the example of other countries, the evils which result from mingling civil and ecclesiastical affairs, were particularly careful to keep them entirely distinct. Thus the Constitution of the United States mentions the subject of religion at all, only to declare that "no religious test shall ever be required as a qualification to any office or public trust in the United States." The Constitution of our own state specifies that "the free exercise and enjoyment of religious professions and worship, without discrimination or preference, shall forever be allowed in this state to all mankind;" and so fearful were the framers of that instrument of the dangers to be apprehended from a union of political and religious concerns, that they inserted a clause of positive interdiction against ministers of the gospel, declaring them forever ineligible to any civil or military office or place within the state. In this last step we think the jealousy of religious interference proceeded too far. We see no good reason why preachers of the gospel should be partially disfranchised, any more than preachers against it, or any more than men devoted to any other profession or pursuit. This curious proscriptive article of our Constitution presents the startling anomaly, that while an infidel, who delivers stated Sunday lectures in a tavern, against all religion, may be elected to the highest executive or legislative trust, the most liberal and enlightened divine is excluded. In our view of the subject neither of them should be proscribed. They should both be left to stand on the broad basis of equal political rights, and the intelligence and virtue of the people should be trusted to make a selection from an unbounded field. This is the true democratic theory; but this is a subject apart from that which it is our present purpose to consider.

No one can pay the most cursory attention to the state of religion in the United States, without being satisfied that its true interests have been greatly promoted by divorcing it from all connexion with political affairs. In no other country of the world are the institutions of religion so generally respected, and in no other is so large a proportion of the population included among the communicants of the different christian churches. The number of christian churches or congregations in the United States is estimated, in a carefully prepared article of religious statistics in the American Almanac of the present year, at upwards of sixteen thousand, and the number of communicants at nearly two millions, or one-tenth of the entire population. In this city alone the number of churches is one hundred and fifty, and their aggregate capacity is nearly equal to the accommodation of the whole number of inhabitants. It is impossible to conjecture, from any data within our reach, the amount of the sum annually paid by the American people, of their own free will, for the support of the ministry, and the various expenses of their religious institutions: but it will readily be admitted that it must be enormous. These, then, are the auspicious results of *perfect free trade in religion*—of leaving it to manage its own concerns, in its own way, without government protection, regulation, or interference, of any kind or degree whatever.

The only instance of intermeddling, on the part of the civil authorities, with matters which, being of a religious character, properly belong to the religious guides of the people, is the proclamation which it is the custom for the Governor of each state annually to issue, appointing a day of general thanksgiving, or a day of general fasting and prayer. We regret that even this single exception should exist to that rule of entire separation of the affairs of state from those of the church, the observance of which in all other respects has been followed by the happiest results. It is to the source of the proclamation, not to its purpose, that we chiefly object. The recommending a day of thanksgiving is not properly any part of the duty of a political Chief Magistrate: it belongs, in its nature, to the heads of the church, not to the head of the state.

It may very well happen, and, indeed, it has happened, in more instances than one, that the chief executive officer of a state has been a person, who, if not absolutely an infidel or sceptic in religious matters, has at least, in his private sentiments and conduct, been notoriously disregardful of religion. What mockery for such a person to call upon the people to set apart a day for returning acknowledgments to Almighty God for the bounties and blessings bestowed upon them! But even when the contrary is the case, and it is well known that the Governor is a strictly religious man, he departs very widely from the duties of his office, in proclaiming, in his gubernatorial capacity, and under the seal of the state, that he has appointed a particular day as a day of general thanksgiving. This is no part of his official business, as prescribed in the Constitution. It is not one of the purposes for which he was elected. If it were a new question, and a Governor should take upon himself to issue such a proclamation for the first time, the proceeding could scarcely fail to arouse the most sturdy opposition from the people. Religious and irreligious would unite in condemning it: the latter as a gross departure from the specified duties for the discharge of which alone the Governor was chosen; and the former as an unwarrantable interference of the civil authority with ecclesiastical affairs, and a usurpation of the functions of their own duly appointed ministers and church officers. We recollect very distinctly what an excitement arose in this community a few years ago, when our Common Council, following the example of the Governor, undertook to interfere in a matter which belonged wholly to the clerical functionaries, and passed a resolution recommending to the various ministers of the gospel the subject of their next Sunday discourse. The Governor's proclamation would itself provoke equal opposition, if men's eyes had not been sealed by custom to its inherent impropriety

If such a proceeding would be wrong, instituted now for the first time, can it be right, because it has existed for a long period? Does age change the nature of principles, and give sanctity to error? Are truth and falsehood of such mutable and shifting qualities, that though, in their original characters, as opposite as the poles, the lapse of a little time may reduce them to a perfect similitude, and render them entirely convertible? If age has in it such power as to render venerable what is not so in its intrinsic nature, then is paganism more venerable than christianity, since it has existed from a much more remote antiquity. But what is wrong in principle must continue to be wrong to the end of time, however sanctioned by custom. It is in this light we consider the gubernatorial recommendation of a day of thanksgiving; and because it is wrong in principle, and not because of any particular harm which the custom has yet been the means of introducing, we should be pleased to see it abrogated. We think it can hardly be doubted that, if the duty of setting apart a day for a general expression of thankfulness for the blessings enjoyed by the community were submitted wholly to the proper representatives of the different religious sects they would find no difficulty in uniting on the subject, and acting in concert in such a manner as should give greater solemnity and weight to their proceeding, than can ever attach to the proclamation of a political governor, stepping out of the sphere of his constitutional duties, and taking upon himself to direct the religious exercises of the people. We cannot too jealously confine our political functionaries within the limits of their prescribed duties. We cannot be too careful to keep entirely separate the things which belong to government from those which belong to religion. The political and the religious interests of the people will both flourish the more prosperously for being wholly distinct. The condition of religious affairs in this country fully proves the truth of the position; and we are satisfied it would receive still further corroboration, if the practice to which we object were reformed.

MUNICIPAL DOCKS

Among the reports adopted by the Board of Aldermen at a recent sitting was one "in favour of appropriating so much space about Pike Slip as may be necessary for the accommodation of the East river steamboats, and leasing berths for the boats there for not longer than two years, such place to be called East River Steamboat Place." Another of the reports adopted was in favour of the appointment of a new set of publick officers, under the name of dockmasters, with a salary of five hundred dollars. The principle upon which these measures are founded is one entirely contrary to the genius of democratick government, and to a true theory of political economy. There is no greater reason why the docks and slips should be the property of the city government, and should be disposed of at the discretion of the Common Council, than why the store houses and dwelling houses should, in the same

Plaindealer, December 3, 1836. Title added.

way, be under the municipal control. The political objection to this is that it strengthens the government at the expense of popular rights, creates a necessity for numerous subordinate officers, and makes it more difficult for the honest unbiassed voice of the people to have its due influence over publick affairs. The economick objection is, that no code of municipal laws can ever answer the purposes of trade as well as its own laws. When the docks are owned by the people in their corporate capacity, and hired out by their municipal agents, it results, as an inevitable consequence, that there will be favouritism and partiality in the arrangement; one place will be charged at too high a rate of wharfage, and another at too low; and business will be forced from its natural direction to suit the views of speculators, or to gratify the demands of sectional rapacity. It would, in our opinion, be a wise measure of publick policy, for the corporation to dispossess itself of all property in the docks and slips, selling them to the highest bidder, with perhaps a preemption right to the owners of the contiguous lots. By such a measure a vast fund might be realized, which would go far to pay off the city debt, and would greatly diminish the burden of taxation. According to our theory of government, the more simple the principles on which it is conducted the better. When we hear of the Common Council having made a fortunate speculation in the purchase of some island or unneeded tract of land, which has risen in money price on their hands, the thought strikes us that, what the government gains, certain individual citizens must have lost; that the aggregate wealth of the community is not increased; and that it is no part of the proper duty of government to enter into competition with citizens in the business of purchase and sale. Besides, whatever increases the wealth of a government, whatever sources of revenue it obtains independent of taxation, increases its power, and diminishes the power of the people in the same ratio. This is not a result which a democrat should desire. The aristocratick theory, the main feature of which is distrust of popular intelligence and virtue, approves a strong government; but give us a *strong people* as the only certain basis of the rights of property and of social order and prosperity.

ASSOCIATED EFFORT

Some days ago, we observed in one of the newspapers, a paragraph stating that a meeting of mechanics and labourers was about to be held in this city for the purpose of adopting measures of concerted or combined action against the practice, which we have reason to believe exists to a very great extent, of paying them in the uncurrent notes of distant or suspected banks. No such meeting, however, as far as we can learn, has yet been held. We hope it soon will be; for the object is a good one, and there is no other way of resisting the rapacious and extortionate custom of employers paying their journeymen and laborers in depreciated paper, half so effectual as combination.

There are some journalists who affect to entertain great horror of combinations, considering them as utterly adverse to the principles of free trade; and it is frequently recommended to make them penal by law. Our notions of free trade were acquired in a different school, and dispose us to leave men entirely at liberty to effect a proper object either by concerted or individual action. The character of combinations, in our view, depends entirely upon the intrinsic character of the end which is aimed at. In the subject under consideration, the end proposed is good beyond all possibility of question. There is high warrant for saying that the *labourer is worthy of his hire;*

Plaindealer, December 10, 1836.

but the employer, who takes advantage of his necessities and defencelessness to pay him in a depreciated substitute for money, does not give him his hire; he does not perform his engagement with him; he filches from the poor man a part of his hard-earned wages, and is guilty of a miserable fraud. Who shall say that this sneaking species of extortion ought not to be prevented? Who will say that separate individual action is adequate to that end? There is no one who will make so rash an assertion.

The only effectual mode of doing away the evil is by attacking it with the great instrument of the rights of the poor—*associated effort.* There is but one bulwark behind which mechanics and labourers may safely rally to oppose a common enemy, who, if they ventured singly into the field against him, would cut them to pieces: that bulwark is the *Principle of Combination.* We would advise them to take refuge behind it only in extreme cases, because in their collisions with their employers, as in those between nations, the manifold evils of a siege are experienced, more or less, by both parties, and are therefore to be incurred only in extreme emergencies. But the evil of being habitually paid in a depreciated substitute for money; of being daily cheated out of a portion of the just fruits of honest toil; of having a slice continually clipped from the hard-earned crust; is one of great moment, and is worthy of such an effort as we propose.

THE COAL QUESTION

There seems to be no doubt entertained, among those who have investigated the subject, that there is a combination among the dealers in coal, in this city, not to sell under certain stipulated prices. We do not know whether this is so or not; but let us take it for granted that it is, and the question then arises, What are we to do to remedy the evil? The Albany Argus would suggest that "it might be well to inquire whether combinations to raise the price of coal, pork, flour, and other necessaries of life, are not offences against society," which require to be made punishable by law. The Journal of Commerce (a free-trade paper!) would respond affirmatively to the question, and say, "if dealers in the above articles have combined to raise prices, let the law walk into them!"

For our own part, we would neither make a new law to punish the combiners, nor . . . inflict upon them the penalty of any existing statute, or of any breach of the common law of England. . . .

. . . .

The Journal of Commerce and the Albany Argus may both rest assured that the laws of trade are a much better defence against improper combinations, than any laws which the legislature at Albany can make, judging by the specimens to be found in the statute books. When a set of dealers combine to raise the price of a commodity above its natural value, they will be sure to provoke competition that will very soon let them down from their fancied elevation. . . . Truth is truth, and though the price of fuel is enormously high, we ought not to impute all the blame to those of our citizens who deal in the

Plaindealer, December 10, 1836. Title added by Sedgwick. Text abridged.

commodity, when our own figures prove that they do not make very extravagant profits after all.

But if the blame does not lie with the coal dealers, where does it lie? We think there is no great difficulty in correctly answering this question. According to our view it lies, then, in the first place, with the legislatures of two or three states, which have given the privileges of a monopoly to certain coal companies, enabling them to fix prices by combination at the fountain head. It lies, in the second place, with those same legislatures, in giving the privileges of a monopoly to certain railroad and canal companies, enabling them to fix the rates of toll and freightage. It lies, in the third place, with Congress, which has placed so heavy a duty on foreign coal as almost to shut it out from competition with the domestic. And it lies, in the fourth place, with our municipal authorities, who increase the burden by appointing measurers of foreign coal, weighers of domestic coal, and inspectors of wood, all of whom are allowed, by law, enormous fees for a duty which they do not half perform, and which, if they performed it ever so thoroughly, would be altogether superfluous.

There is still one other cause which ought not to be omitted from the calculation; and that is, the diminished quantity of coal mined, in consequence of speculation having withdrawn labour from that employment, during the past summer, to work on railroads, to dig canals, to level hills, and fill up valleys, and, perform the various other services which were necessary to carry out the schemes projected by the gambling spirit of the times. Hence the supply is not more than adequate, at the most, to the demand; and hence those who have a monopoly of the article at fountain head ask the present enormous prices, secure that the citizens must either give them or freeze.

There is one branch of this subject in which we most cordially concur with the Journal of Commerce. That paper suggests the propriety of the institution of benevolent associations, for the purpose of procuring a large supply of coal when it is cheapest, and disposing of it, by retail, at the prime cost and charges, to the poorer classes of citizens, whose means do not enable them to buy much in advance. Such an association might do a vast amount of good, without ever expending a single dollar. Suppose, for example, a hundred citizens, of well known respectability, and sufficient pecuniary responsibility, should enter into an association for the purpose named, and should purchase a given amount of coal at six months credit, each member of the association being jointly and severally responsible for the indebtedness of the whole. The coal might then be put at such a price as, when all was sold, would yield the net cost and charges; and before the obligations of the company should fall due, the money would be in hand to discharge them. This would be a cheap charity on the part of those who engaged in it, and a most valuable one to those classes of citizens for whose benefit it would be intended.

THE CORPORATION QUESTION

One of the newspapers which has done us the honour to notice this journal, animadverts, with considerable asperity, upon our declaration of interminable hostility to the principle of special incorporation, and points our attention to certain incorporated institutions, which, according to the universal sense of mankind, are established with the purest motives, and effect the most excellent objects. The ready and obvious answer to the strictures we have provoked is, that it is the means, not the

Plaindealer, December 24, 1836.

end, which furnishes the subject of our condemnation. An act of special incorporation may frequently afford the persons associated under it facilities of accomplishing much public good; but if those facilities can only be given at the expense of rights of paramount importance, they ought to be denied by all whose political morality rejects the odious maxim that the end justifies the means. It would be a very strained and unwarrantable inference from any remarks we have made, to say that we are an enemy to churches, public libraries, or charitable associations, because we express hostility to special legislation. It would be an unwarranted inference to say that we are even opposed to the principle of incorporation; since it is only to the principle of *special incorporation* that we have expressed hostility. We are opposed, not to the object, but to the mode by which the object is effected. We are opposed, not to corporation partnerships, but to the right of forming such partnerships being specially granted to the few, and wholly denied to the many. We are opposed, in short, to unequal legislation, whatever form it may assume, or whatever object it may ostensibly seek to accomplish.

It has been beautifully and truly said, by the illustrious man who presides over the affairs of our Confederacy, that "there are no necessary evils in government. Its evils exist only in its abuses. If it would confine itself to *equal protection*, and, as heaven does its rains, shower its favours alike on the high and the low, the rich and the poor, it would be an unqualified blessing." But it departs from its legitimate office, it widely departs from the cardinal principle of government in this country, the equal political rights of all, when it confers privileges on one set of men, no matter for what purpose, which are withheld from the rest. It is in this light we look upon all special acts of incorporation. They convey privileges not previously enjoyed, and limit the use of them to those on whom they are bestowed. That special charters are, in many instances, given for objects of intrinsic excellence and importance, is freely admitted; nor do we desire to withhold our unqualified acknowledgment that they have been the means of effecting many improvements of great value to the community at large. Let it be clearly understood, then, that we do not war against the good achieved; but seek only to illustrate the inherent evil of the means. A special charter is a powerful weapon; but it is one which should have no place in the armory of the democracy. It is an instrument which may hew down forests, and open fountains of wealth in barren places; but these advantages are purchased at too dear a rate, if we give for them one jot or tittle of our equal freedom. As a general rule, too, corporations act for themselves, not for the community. If they cultivate the wilderness, it is to monopolize its fruits. If they delve the mine, it is to enrich themselves with its treasures. If they dig new channels for the streams of industry, it is that they may gather the golden sands for themselves, as those of Pactolus were gathered to swell the hoards of Croesus.

Even if the benefits, which we are willing to admit have been effected by companies acting under special corporate privileges and immunities, could not have been achieved without the assistance of such powers, better would it have been, in our opinion, far better, that the community should have foregone the good, than purchase it by the surrender, in any instance or particular, of a principle which lies at the foundation of human liberty. No one can foretell the evil consequences which may flow from one such error of legislation. "Next day the fatal precedent will plead." The way once open, ambition, selfishness, cupidity, rush in, each widening the breach, and rendering access easier to its successor. The monuments of enterprise erected through the aid of special privileges and immunities are numerous and stupendous; but we may yet be sadly admonished

———"how wide the limits stand,
Between a splendid and a happy land."

But, fortunately, we are not driven to the alternative of either foregoing for the future such magnificent projects as have heretofore been effected by special legislation, or for the sake of accomplishing them, continuing to grant unequal privileges. It is a propitious omen of success in the great struggle in which the real democracy of this country are engaged, that monopolies, (and we include in the term all special corporate rights) are as hostile to the principles of sound economy, as they are to the fundamental maxims of our political creed. The good which they effect might more simply and more certainly be achieved without their aid. They are fetters which restrain the action of the body politic, not motories which increase its speed. They are jesses which hold it to earth, not wings that help it to soar. Our country has prospered, not because of them, but in spite of them. This young and vigorous republic has bounded rapidly forward, in despite of the burdens which partial legislation hangs upon its neck, and the clogs it fastens to its heel. But swifter would have been its progress, sounder its health, more prosperous its general condition, had our law-makers kept constantly in view that their imperative duty requires them to exercise their functions for the good of the whole community, not for a handful of obtrusive and grasping individuals, who, under the pretext of promoting the public welfare, are only eager to advance their private interests, at the expense of the equal rights of their fellow-men.

Every special act of incorporation is, in a certain sense, a grant of a monopoly. Every special act of incorporation is a charter of privileges to a few, not enjoyed by the community at large. There is no single object can be named, for which, consistently with a sincere respect for the equal rights of men, a special charter of incorporation can be bestowed. It should not be given to establish a bank, nor to erect a manufactory; to open a road, nor to build a bridge. Neither trust companies nor insurance companies should be invested with exclusive rights. Nay, acting in strict accordance with the true principles both of democracy and political economy, no legislature would, by special act, incorporate even a college or a church.

Let it not be supposed, however, that we would withhold from such institutions the intrinsic advantages of a charter. We would only substitute general, for partial legislation, and extend to all, the privileges proper to be bestowed upon any. The spirit of true wisdom, in human affairs, as in divine,

"Acts not by partial, but by general laws."

Nothing can be more utterly absurd than to suppose that the advocacy of these sentiments implies opposition to any of the great undertakings for which special legislative authority and immunities are usually sought. We are opposed only to a violation of the great democratic principle of our government; that principle which stands at the head of the Declaration of Independence; and that which most of the states have repeated, with equal explicitness, in their separate constitutions. A general partnership law, making the peculiar advantages of a corporation available to any set of men who might choose to associate, for any lawful purpose whatever, would wholly obviate the objections which we urge. Such a law would confer no exclusive or special privileges; such a law would be in strict accordance with the great maxim of man's political equality; such a law would embrace the whole community in its bound, leaving capital to flow in its natural channels, and enterprise to regulate its own pursuits. Stock bubbles, as fragile as the unsubstantial globules which children amuse themselves with blowing, might not float so numerous in the air; but all schemes of real utility, which presented a reasonable prospect of profit, would be as readily undertaken as now. That active spirit of enterprise, which, in a few months, has erected a new city on the field lately desolated by the direst conflagration our history records; that spirit of enterprise, which every year adds whole squadrons to the innumerous fleet of stately vessels that transport our commerce to the remotest harbours of the world; that spirit of enterprise which seeks its object alike through the freezing atmosphere of the polar regions, and beneath the fervour of the torrid zone, displaying the stars and stripes of our country to every nation of the earth; that active spirit would not flinch from undertaking whatever works of internal improvement might be needed by the community, without the aid of exclusive rights and privileges.

The merchant, who equips his noble vessel, freights her with the richest products of nature and art, and sends her on her distant voyage across the tempestuous sea, asks no act of incorporation. The trader, who adventures his whole resources in the commodities of his traffic, solicits no exclusive privilege. The humble mechanic, who exhausts the fruit of many a day and night of toil in supplying his workshop with the implements of his craft, desires no charter. These are all willing to encounter unlimited competition. They are content to stand on the broad basis of equal rights. They trust with honourable confidence, to their own talents, exercised with industry, not to special immunities, for success. Why should the speculators, who throng the lobbies of our legislature, be more favoured than they? Why should the banker, the insurer, the bridge builder, the canal digger, be distinguished by peculiar privileges? Why should they be made a chartered order, and raised above the general level of their fellow-men?

It is curious to trace the history of corporations, and observe how, in the lapse of time, they have come to be instruments that threaten the overthrow of that liberty, which they were, at first, effectual aids in establishing. When the feudal system prevailed over Europe, and the great mass of the people were held in vilest and most abject bondage by the lords, to whom they owed strict obedience, knowing no law but their commands, the power of the nobles, by reason of the number of their retainers and the extent of their possessions, was greater than that of the monarch, who frequently was a mere puppet in their hands. The barons, nominally vassals of the crown, holding their fief on condition of faithful service, were, in reality, and at all times, on any question which combined a few of the more powerful, absolute masters. They made kings and deposed them at pleasure. The history of all the states of Europe is full of their exploits in this way; but the narrative of the red and white rose of England, of the contending houses of York and Lancaster, is all that need be referred to for our present purpose. Corporations were the means at last happily hit upon of establishing a power to counterbalance that so tyrannously and rapaciously exercised by the barons. For certain services rendered, or a certain price paid, men were released from the conditions which bound them to their feudal lords, and all so enfranchised were combined in a corporate body, under a royal charter of privileges and immunities, and were termed "freemen of the corporation." In process of time, these bodies, by gradual and almost imperceptible additions, grew to sufficient size to afford a countercheck to the power of the nobles, and were at last the instruments, not in England only, but throughout Europe, of overthrowing the feudal system, emancipating their fellow-men from degrading bondage, and establishing a government somewhat more in accordance with the rights of humanity.

But in this country, founded, in theory and practice, on an acknowledgment, in the broadest sense, of the universal right of equal freedom, the grant of special corporate privileges is an act against liberty, not in favour of it. It is not enfranchising the few, but enslaving the many. The same process which, when the people were debased, elevated them to their proper level, now, when the people are elevated, and occupy the lofty place of equal political rights, debases them to comparative servitude. The condition of things in free America is widely different from that which existed in Europe during the feudal ages. How absurd then, to continue a system of grants, for which all actual occasion long since ceased, and which are now at utter and palpable variance with the great political maxim that all alike profess! It is our desire, however, in treating this subject, to use no language which may embitter the feelings of those who entertain contrary views. We wish to win our way by the gentle process of reason; not by the boisterous means which angry disputants adopt. It has, in all times, been one of the characteristic errors of political reformers, and we might say, indeed, of religious reformers, too, that they have threatened, rather than persuaded; that they have sought to drive men, rather than allure. Happy is he "whose blood and judgment is so well commingled," that he can blend determined hostility to public errors and abuses, with sufficient tolerance of the differences of private opinion and prejudice, never to relinquish courtesy, that sweetener of social life and efficient friend of truth. In a small way, we seek to be a reformer of certain false principles which have crept into our legislation; but as we can lay no claim to the transcendent powers of the Miltons, Harringtons and Fletchers of political history, so we have no excuse for indulging in their fierceness of invective, or bitterness of reproach.

FREE TRADE WEIGHTS AND MEASURES

The American is a newspaper in which articles often appear indicating that it entertains a strong attachment to the principles of free trade, and a desire that the law of free competition should be the only law to regulate the pursuits of industry, so far as they do not interfere with the morals or order of society. It was with surprise and regret, therefore, that we read in that journal, a few evenings since, a paragraph commendatory of the tyrannical act, now under the consideration of our municipal authorities, relative to bread, and expressing a wish that it may become a law. The paragraph referred to is in the following words:

Plaindealer, December 24, 1836. Title added.

> We are adverse, on principle, to all laws regulating the quality, or price, of any article, and of course, therefore, adverse to an assize, as to the price or quality, of bread, as we are to *all* inspection laws. But policy and justice alike require that *false weights* shall not be permitted to pass current, and, therefore, we see no objection, but all fitness, in an ordinance that the loaf should be of a given *weight,* leaving it to the seller and the purchaser to arrange the *price* for themselves.

Would the American see "all fitness" in a law requiring the butchers to cut beef into one, two, and four pound pieces, or into pieces of any other stipulated weight? Would it see fitness in requiring that a quarter of lamb should be of a given weight, or that a bunch of onions should contain a certain number, and of a certain size? There is no law hindering people to buy their bread by the pound, if they choose; and there is no reason why other persons than the members of the special bread committee of the Board of Assistant Aldermen may not discover, if they think the search worth their while, the shops where the largest loaves are sold. The law does quite as much as is necessary for the protection of the community, (this is always the pretext for these arbitrary restraints on the freedom of trade) when it fixes a standard of weights and measures, and requires all persons selling by them to have them stamped and certified by a duly appointed officer. We have our doubts, indeed, whether even in going so far, it has not exceeded the proper business of legislation. We have our doubts whether it should not stop when it has simply fixed the standard, leaving buyers and sellers free to conform to it or not, as they choose. There is no inspector of yardsticks; and yet we doubt very much if people who buy by the yard do not generally contrive to get good measure. If they do not it is their own look out. We would have it the same with regard to bread. We would let the purchaser take care of himself. The law has furnished him with all the necessary appliances and means to see that he gets good weight and measure, and the rest of the affair ought to be trusted to his own shrewdness and sagacity. The familiar saying, that a man's eyes are his best chapman, contains more wisdom than our corporation ordinances; and we were in hopes to have the American's cooperation in enforcing it as a rule of publick conduct, in regard to the matter now under consideration.

ASSOCIATED EFFORT

The views which have been expressed in this journal, on the subject of associated effort, have provoked some animadversion. Among other papers that have expressed disapprobation of our sentiments is the Montreal Transcript, which has recorded its dissent in the following courteous and complimentary terms:

. . . .

The Montreal Transcript may rest assured that it is by no means our desire, on the subject of combinations, or on any other subject, to throw dust into the eyes of our readers. If we even possessed such power of argument and such felicitous command of language as it ascribes to us, and could easily make the worse appear the better reason, we trust we should be governed by too just a sense of the duties and responsibilities of our vocation, ever to lend ourselves to the support of errour, for the sake of displaying our ingenuity, or the copiousness of our logical resources. What we have said on the subject of combination we fully believe is the true doctrine; but we are inclined to think, from some of the phrases in the foregoing paragraph, that the Montreal paper under-

Plaindealer, January 14, 1837. Extract deleted.

stands our remarks in a wider sense than they we[re] intended. On one point it is plain that we are misapprehended.

The maxim that *the end justifies the means* is one which we utterly repudiate. Not only did the Plaindealer never avow nor act upon that sentiment; but it cannot be found in anything written by its conductor, in any other medium of communicating with the publick. We hold that the saying is in direct opposition to the soundest and most obvious principles of morals, and ought never to be countenanced, in any possible circumstances, nor for the attainment of any possible object. The means must justify themselves; or no end, however desirable, and no exigency, however pressing, can wholly excuse their being employed. In the case adverted to, we considered that a combination on the part of those who suffer from the fraudulent practice of paying operatives their wages in depreciated paper would be justified, not as an exception to a general rule, but as in entire conformity with the universal, invariable, and immutable rule of right. It is on this ground, and on this alone, that we wish the propriety of our counsel to be judged.

The broad and comprehensive position we maintain on the subject of combinations is this: that the means are proper in themselves; and that it is the end alone which, in any case, is obnoxious to censure. We hold that both the principles of free trade, and the plainest principles of natural equity require, that men should be left at liberty to pursue by concert, if they choose, any object they have a right to achieve by individual action. The safety of the community against extortionate and intolerant combinations is sufficiently insured by the effect of competition and the influence of publick opinion.

It seems to us that the Montreal Transcript, in making an exception in favour of a combination of operative mechanicks against the extortionate and fraudulent practices of employers, surrenders the whole ground of argument. The admission is fatal to the position it assumes. It is equivalent to an acknowledgement that the propriety or impropriety of a combination depends on the character of the object which it is sought to accomplish. This is precisely the ground we maintain. We assert the right to combine, but do not defend the abuse of that right; as, in the same way, we assert the right of free discussion, but shall never be found among the apologists of an intemperate and pernicious exercise of that right.

But if we admit that the line may be distinctly drawn (which it cannot be) between combinations for a good purpose, and combinations for a bad purpose, the question then comes up whether we would make those in the latter category punishable by law. We answer no. We would punish by law those persons who undertook to achieve by combination, what it would be punishable by law to undertake to achieve by separate unconcerted action, and no others.

The Montreal journalist might suppose a variety of cases in which the community would be great sufferers from a combination of persons to effect certain objects, which never could be effected by spontaneous individual action. We should then answer him by supposing cases in which the action of a single extortionate individual, without transcending his undoubted legal rights, might be productive of great evil; and we should further show that the steady influence of publick opinion is the best law to regulate the conduct of associations and individuals in both classes of cases. A combination of a hundred wealthy men might, under peculiar circumstances of season, monopolize all the provisions in this city, and refuse to sell a starving inhabitant a mouthful of food, unless he paid its weight in gold. A single individual without wealth, a poor fisherman, for example, might have it in his power to rescue a hundred men from certain death at sea, and might refuse to do so, unless each promised to pay him his weight in gold for the service. The fisherman does not do so, because publick opinion, composed of the general sentiment of humanity as applicable to the subject, his own notions of humanity included, is a supreme law to regulate his conduct. The hundred rich men, in the same way, do not monopolize all the food, and retail it at a dollar an ounce, because they are restrained by the same supreme law.

The Montreal Transcript will yet discover, we hope, that it egregiously misapprehends the real tendency of our doctrines. We are quite willing to admit that combinations to regulate prices are, for the most part, very foolish and expensive undertakings, and, in familiar phrase, cost much more than they come to. But this very fact furnishes a reason why the combiners should be left to themselves. If they have a taste for expensive amusements, let them indulge themselves; for those who pay the piper surely have a right to dance.

All that we have here said is comprehended in a very brief sentence, which was once, a long time since, uttered by the leading men of the mercantile community of France, when they were asked by the minister what they desired the government to do to promote their interests. Their reply, though it consists of but three words, comprises a whole volume of political wisdom. It was, *Laissez nous faire.*

SALE OF PUBLICK LANDS

> Will the editor of *the Plaindealer* oblige us by an exposition and application of his free trade principles, as they may or should be adapted to the sale of the Publick Lands? More concisely, will he inform us whether he does or does not deem a restriction of the sales of publick lands to actual settlers on the same, constitutional, salutary and proper?

The above is from a weekly contemporary print, published in this city, called *the New Yorker.* Without acknowledging any

Plaindealer, January 14, 1837. Title added.

right which that or any other journal has to catechize us on subjects on which we have offered no opinions, we yet have no objection whatever to answer the question put to us.

Free trade we take to consist in the buyer and seller being left to make their own bargain; it would therefore be no violation of principles of free trade for the Government, which is the seller in the case stated, to ask any price, or make any conditions it thought proper, in disposing of the publick lands. So much for the free trade part of the question.

The constitutionality of such a restriction as is stated depends upon the fact whether there is or is not any clause in the Constitution of the United States stipulating the mode and terms of sale in regard to the publick lands. The Constitution of the United States says that "the Congress shall have power to dispose of, and make all needful rules and regulations respecting, the territory or other property belonging to the United States." As there is here no limitation of power as to the mode or terms of the sale of the publick lands, we should think the constitutionality of the restriction about which we are asked could not be doubted.

With regard to the propriety of the restriction, the question, in our view, should be decided by a careful consideration of it solely as it will tend to promote the greatest good of the greatest number. That this object would be most certainly effected by that mode of disposal which would lead to the largest amount of actual settlement upon, and cultivation of, the publick lands, we do not doubt.

Having thus been drawn out to express our views on this subject, which we certainly had no desire to withhold, may we take the liberty to ask the New Yorker a question? We understand it to be in favour of special legislation in regard to banking, insuring against losses from fire and the perils of the sea, &c. Will it be good enough to inform us why the business of manufacturing gilt ginger bread and sugar whistles is not as much entitled to be protected by special charters and the provisions of a restraining law, as that of bankers and insurers?

MANACLES INSTEAD OF GYVES

The *American*, some days ago, in an article on the subject of the laws relative to pilots, proposed the following as the features proper to be embraced in a new law on the subject:

. . . .

We see, also, by the newspapers, that a committee of merchants have drawn up a scheme, which embraces similar provisions. It proposes to have appointed, by legislative authority, a Board of Commissioners, whose business it shall be to superintend the whole pilot system, to examine candidates, appoint and license pilots, and attend to the enforcement of a multitude of minute and complicated arrangements.

It seems to us that this scheme merely recommends *manacles instead of gyves;* that it is a mere substitution of one kind of fetter for another. It would diminish the burden, but does not propose to cast it off entirely. It mitigates the evil, but does not go to the extent of abating it. It enlarges our bounds, but does not give us freedom. Is not the piloting of our vessels, in and out of our harbour a simple matter of trade? Then why not leave it to be governed by the laws of trade? Why should it be a matter of political regulation? Why should control of the subject be left to a body of legislators, nine-tenths of whom cannot, in the nature of things, be supposed to have any knowledge concerning it? Why should it not be submitted to the operation of those principles, which, in all the affairs of trade to which they have ever been applied, have invariably been found of adequate efficacy?

The ocean, beyond the limits of our jurisdiction, has its bars and rocks and quicksands; yet no difficulty is experienced in finding persons of sufficient knowledge and skill to guide

Plaindealer, January 21, 1837. Extract deleted.

commerce through all its dangers, without asking legislative supervision, or requiring those entrusted with the important business to be authenticated by official appointment. It seems to us if the business of piloting a vessel were left equally free from political interference, with that of navigating it across the ocean, the result would be greatly to the advantage of all concerned, directly or indirectly, except those only who fatten on the unearned fruits of monopoly, and those who derive an undue political influence from the power of dispensing official patronage.

If there were no law regulating the number of pilots, it would be fixed by that law of trade which adjusts the supply to the demand. The compensation would also be adjusted, in the same way, by the amount of competition; as the wages of masters and mates of vessels, and of seamen, for any given voyage, or as the prices of any other service or commodity, are now fixed. Ignorant and unskilful persons might engage in the business; but competition here again would remedy the difficulty. It would naturally lead those possessing the requisite qualifications to obtain the best sort of credential which, under any circumstances, they could possible have, namely, a certificate, duly authenticated, from a board consituted by the underwriters and merchants. It might lead, also, to the formation of rival joint stock pilot associations, of sufficient capital to afford ample pecuniary guarantees against loss by the carelessness or ignorance of those employed. The insurers, also, would devise a code of regulations for their own security, the tendency of which would necessarily be to promote the interests of commerce, for the interests of commerce and of the insurers are identical.

We do not like to speak with unbecoming positiveness on this subject, lest we incur an application to ourselves of the sentiment of Pope, that "fools rush in, where angels fear to tread;" yet we must say that, after a good deal of meditation on the subject, and an examination of it by such tests as our knowledge supplies, we have arrived at the conviction that the business of piloting might as safely be left to the principles of absolute free trade, as any other business wh tever. If there were no law to regulate the subject, it may be said, an extortionate pilot might, under peculiar circumstance, exact an exorbitant compensation, and refuse to act unless it were paid. A physician, or surgeon, too, might be brought to the bedside of an affluent patient under circumstances which required instant medical or chirurgical aid, and refuse to administer the potion or the knife, on which all hope depended, without being previously paid an enormous remuneration. If the common sentiment of mankind, in the one case as well as the other, were not sufficient to prevent the attempt of such extortion, could a jury be found that would ratify the compulsory bargain?

If the laws of trade would of themselves lead to the best results in regard to piloting, we think no one will dispute that it would then be clearly proper to separate the subject from political control. We are of those, who, as a principle of abstract political doctrine, desire to confine government to the fewest possible offices. Those who differ from us in political creed, and, as an abstract principle, desire to strengthen the powers and multiply the functions of government, will yet admit that it is desirable to retrench power in the hands of its present possessors. Thus, on the one ground or the other, we should count upon the cooperation of both the democracy and the aristocracy, to bring about the emancipation of trade, in the respect of which we speak, if it could be shown that the simple principle of competition is adequate to all the purposes which the law now vainly attempts to enforce. That it is so we do not entertain a doubt; and the opinion is sustained by every species of analogical reasoning to which it can be subjected. The experiment could not, at any rate, place our commerce in worse peril than it is exposed to by our present system; and, in that view of the subject, is it not worth a trial?

THE MEANING OF FREE TRADE

In our last number but one, we replied to some questions put to us by a weekly contemporary print, the *New Yorker*, on the subject of the conditions proposed, in Mr. Walker's land bill, to be annexed to the sale of publick lands. The views we there expressed do not meet the approbation of our querist, who enters into a discussion of them at so great a length, as forbids alike our copying the article entire, and our replying to all the points of the argument. Some of them, however, shall receive such attention as our limits permit us to bestow. Our definition of *free trade*, that it consists in the buyer and seller being left to make their own bargain, does not seem to satisfy the *New Yorker*, which confesses that it has heretofore looked on the term as expressive of a much wider signification. We quote the passage:

> "Free trade," says our enlightener, "we take to consist in the buyer and seller being left to make their own bargain." Indeed! In the plenitude of our ignorance we had given a much wider signification to the phrase. Let us illustrate: Suppose on the next day that the new tariff bill before the House of Representatives is under discussion in Committee of the Whole, Mr. C. C. Cambreleng should propose an increase of the duty on iron imported to one hundred per cent, except iron intended for the construction of railroads, which should be admitted free of duty. There would doubtless be evinced what is called a "sensation," and some member, ignorant, like us, of the true import of the term, might accuse the honourable gentleman of an abandonment or violation of the principles of free trade, for his consistent support of which he has long been distinguished. "You mistake," replies the commercial representative, with a compassionating smile; "free trade consists in the buyer and seller being allowed to make their own bargain; and as I propose no restriction of this liberty, my free

Plaindealer, January 28, 1837. Title added.

trade consistency is unimpeachable." The caviller, rebuked, instructed, and satisfied, would of course humbly acknowledge his errour. Now, if it be true that free trade has no further import than this, we must of course stand corrected. But we have hitherto understood that the law which authorizes so many pilots and no more to conduct vessels into the harbour of New York, (though allowing shipmasters to "make their own bargains") and the law which forbids the keeping of offices of discount and deposite by individuals or voluntary associations (though allowing depositers and the banks to "make their own bargains") are violations of the principle of free trade. As such, we have advocated their unqualified repeal; and we have thought the strenuous and efficient hostility of the *Plaindealer* to these and many kindred restrictions was based on a like conviction. We appeal, then, to the common sense of the reader to bear us out in the assertion that the passage of a law restricting the sales of publick lands to those only who would bind themselves to settle upon and cultivate the same, would be a measure of the same generick kind with those which, under such sounding titles as "the American system," "protection to domestick industry," &c. &c. have encountered the unremitting and ardent hostility of the editor of the *Plaindealer* for years past. It is a system of cobbling, and forcing, and discriminating, designed to supersede one of real and palpable free trade.

And again, after expatiating at some length on the difficulties which it supposes would be experienced in carrying the provisions of Mr. Walker's land bill into effect, and the presumed evil consequences which would result from them, the *New Yorker* says:

We do not assert that the *Plaindealer* sees all this as we do; but we do believe that it cannot give an hour's consideration to this system of restriction to actual settlers without being convinced that it is not a free trade system. It surely cannot believe that an act providing that a blacksmith might buy publick lands, but a physician must not—that a Kentuckian might have lands at fifty cents per acre, while a Pennsylvanian should not have them at any price—would be consistent with the broad and distinctive principles which it has hitherto maintained. And yet it affirms as much in its sweeping assertion that it would be no violation of the principles of free trade for the government to make any conditions it thought proper.

If Mr. Cambreleng should be guilty of the silly conduct which the *New Yorker* has taken for one of its illustrative hypotheses, he certainly would commit a very egregious violation of the plainest principles of free trade; simply because he would not, in that case, leave the buyer and seller free to make their own bargain, but would seek to thrust a prodigious legislative barrier between them. The buyers, in the case supposed, are the workers and consumers of iron in this country; and the sellers are those who deal in the article in Great Britain. The trade between them is free, when no legislative hindrances, of any kind, are interposed by a third party. Congress, in this case, is that third party; and the buyer and seller are not left alone to make their bargain; but the third party steps in with its conditions, which are of as imperative obligation on the purchaser, as those of the seller.

In the other case adduced, that of the pilots, the errour is the same. The buyers are those who have occasion for the services of pilots; and the sellers are those who have such services to dispose of. The trade between them would be free, if each party were left to make its own bargain, without legal limitation or restraint. But the legislature is a third party, and says to those needing the aid of the pilots, you shall not be free to make your own bargain, but, will you, nill you, you must take a pilot of my appointing, or at all events, whether you take one or not, you must pay as if the service were actually rendered. And it says to the pilots, you shall not be left free to charge that rate which the demand for your services and the amount of free competition might warrant, but you shall always, be the circumstances what they may, and be the service relatively worth more or less, have liberty to charge, and power to enforce your demand, according to certain immutable rates, which are hereby established. This is not free trade, because this is not leaving the buyer and seller free to make their own bargain. They are both under the necessity of deferring to a third party, who makes the bargain for them.

So also in the other case which has been chosen as of analogous force, that of the law which forbids all except specially chartered corporations from keeping offices of discount and deposite. It is an errour to say that the depositers and the banks are free to make their own bargains. The depositers are not free, because the law restricts them to a certain limited number of companies, and says, in effect, you shall not deposite your money except with A, B, or C, and none but A, B, and C, are authorized to discount your note. You shall not, therefore, make your own bargain; but you shall be subject to the conditions which the shutting up of the business of discount and deposite in such narrow bounds, by counteracting the effect of competition, will necessarily impose upon you. Here, as in the other cases, a third party interposes between buyer and seller; and consequently they are not free to make their own bargain, or, in other words, their rights of free trade are violated.

Our antagonist is mistaken in supposing that we should consider a law in relation to the publick lands, exactly and particularly designating the classes and descriptions of persons who might and who might not buy those lands, a violation of the principles of free trade. We should certainly consider it a very absurd law, but absurd on different grounds from those imputed. There are many modes in which government may abuse its powers besides by violating the principles of free trade; as there are many ways in which a man may commit crime, without taking the life of a fellow being. If a person should be proved guilty of forgery, the jury would hardly be instructed to bring in a verdict of wilful murder; and so, if the government should impose very silly conditions upon itself with regard to the publick lands, we should not pronounce it guilty of violating the freedom of trade. The government has the sole and absolute right of disposal of the publick lands, under but one limitation: that of disposing of them for the general welfare. The conditions which it imposes upon itself, or the terms which it annexes to the sale, may be unwise, and subversive of the professed object; but cannot properly be considered a violation of free trade, any more than could the conduct of the proprietor of the *New Yorker,* if he refused to sell his paper except to a particular class of purchasers, or to none, except for their own exclusive use, and on the express condition that they would not resell. If a third party, the legislature for example, imposed these conditions, they would be a violation of free trade, inasmuch as they would come between buyer and seller, and would not leave them free to make their own bargain. But it is no more a violation of free trade for the seller to say, I will not sell except on certain terms, than for the buyer to say, I will not buy, except at a certain price.

The *New Yorker,* it seems, is less of a monopolist than we had been led to suppose. It says:

> Having uniformly advocated the unqualified repeal of the Restraining Law, the removal of all kindred restraints, and the reform of our banking system generally, we feel that we are unjustly ranked with the advocates of chartered monopolies. All the restriction on banking we desire is, simply the restriction of the right of issuing paper as money to those alone (whether individuals or companies) who shall establish before a proper tribunal that they are unquestionably able to redeem a certain amount of paper whenever called upon, and such a constant supervision over them as shall ensure their continued solvency. As to insurance, we do not regard such a supervision as so necessary, but we think it would be found salutary. We want no charters, (unless the above is a charter,) no distribution of stock, no exclusive privileges, no restrictions, except the restriction of the power of coining paper money to those who are able to redeem it.

This shows, whatever erroneous notions the *New Yorker* may entertain as to the definition of the *term* free trade, that it has made greater advances towards the *thing,* than many journals which make a more boastful display of their economick knowledge. We trust a little further investigation will satisfy it that the salutary restrictions, which it is now in favour of having imposed by legislative authority, would be much more certainly and efficiently imposed by the laws of free trade. They would be the natural and necessary consequence of unrestricted competition.

GAMBLING LAWS

Mr. Cutting lately introduced a bill into the Assembly, which, it will be seen, has been passed in that house, for the more effectual punishment of crime. The first section of the bill is in the following words:

> The keeping of a gambling house by any person in the city of New York, shall be, and hereby is declared, a misdemeanour, and indictable as such; and upon conviction thereof, the offender shall be subject to a fine, not exceeding five hundred dollars, or to imprisonment not exceeding one year, or both, in the discretion of the court before whom the same is tried.

We do not believe that a law of this kind is the best method of preventing gaming. There have always been laws against gaming in this city; yet they have slumbered on the statute book, mere dead letters, while gambling has been pursued with a degree of openness scarcely inferiour to that of the licensed gaming houses in New Orleans. Our readers are aware that we belong to that class of persons who do not believe in the omnipotence of law to effect every conceivable object of reformation. The law of publick opinion, if left free to act, would, in a vast multitude of cases, be found more

Plaindealer, January 28, 1837. Title added.

efficient, than a penal statute. We believe that gaming is one of the vices which would be much more effectually restrained, if left entirely to the salutary influences of publick opinion, than it ever can be by legislative interference. If laws on the subject are highly penal, they are not enforced; and if slightly penal, they are ineffectual: and, in both cases, they forestall and render sluggish and inoperative the publick sentiment, which otherwise, we think, we would be found an active and efficient agent in restraining the vice.

A legislature is always badly set to work in manufacturing crime. To risk money in a wager is not a crime *per se,* whether the wager be on the result of a race, on the fate of a lottery ticket, on the turn of a dicebox, or on any other like contingency. It is folly, perhaps, in all cases, and it becomes crime and madness in some; but to draw the line between allowable folly and criminality, in a matter of this kind, is rather the office of publick opinion, than of the law.

But Mr. Cutting's bill does not go to the extent of punishing gaming, but merely to punish those who afford facilities to gamblers, to punish the *keepers* of gaming houses. It is one of the heaviest charges against the law, that it spreads a flimsy net to catch small offenders, while it weaves no meshes strong enough to hold the larger ones. The poor wretch who gets drunk on threepenny gin is sent to bridewell[1] or the watch-house, while the judge who sentences him daily inebriates himself with impunity on Madeira or Champaigne. The keeper of the shilling faro table is lodged in prison, and mulcted in a heavy fine; while the dashing coterie of rich and fashionable blacklegs, who support their own *hell,* under the thin disguise of a club house, and nightly allure spendthrifts to their ruin, have passage free. Mr. Cutting knows dozens of conspicuous individuals in this city, who, to all intents and purposes, and to the worst intents and purposes, keep gambling houses, that would not be touched by his bill, if it should be passed into a law.

[1] That is, to prison.—Ed.

To suppress vice in part is perhaps better than not to suppress it at all; but the objection we urge to the proposed law, and to all such legislation, is that it does not really promote its ostensible object. If the legislature had spent as much time in framing penal statutes against intemperance, as it has wickedly spent, for years past, in framing grants of special charters, it could not possibly have effected the reform, in that respect, which publick opinion has accomplished. We would leave the vice of gambling to be corrected in the same way.

FREE TRADE POST OFFICE

A bill, it will be seen, is now before Congress, reported by the Post Office Committee, the object of which is to carry into effect the recommendation in the Postmaster General's last annual report, on the subject of epistolary communication between the inhabitants of this country and Great Britain. . . .

. . . .

. . . [I]t is not improbable that the bill will have been passed into a law before these remarks are presented to our readers. It is therefore with no expectation of arresting or changing, in the slightest degree, the course of action on the subject, that we choose it as the theme for our speculations in the present article; but merely because it may answer a useful purpose to invite the reader's mind to a consideration of what constitute the proper functions of political government, and how far the principle of unrestricted competition may be safely left to form its own laws and supply the wants of society.

Plaindealer, February 4, 1837. Text abridged and extract deleted.

Everybody must admit that the Post Office, as a branch of the Government, is an institution obviously and inevitably liable to the most prodigious abuses. Under the present system, there are some twelve or fifteen thousand postmasters, holding their appointments directly from one man, and removable at his mere will. Nearly all this numerous army of postmasters, at least a full myriad of them, have subordinates under their control; and if we include in the estimate the contractors, drivers, carriers, and the various other persons more or less dependent for support on the enormous system, it will probably yield an aggregate of not much less than half a million of persons under the immediate direction, to some extent, of a single individual, seated at the head of the federal government. Can any one be so blind as not to perceive, at a glance, that this is a monstrous power, at all times susceptible of being exerted, with the most dangerous effect, for the advancement of objects hostile to the true interests of the people? We do not ask the question with reference to the present, or the past, or any future administration, or with particular reference to any event which has occurred or is likely to occur; but simply in reference to the subject in the abstract, and to the aspect it presents under all the changes and fluctuations of party affairs.

It is not only the vast means of undue influence which the present system gives to a single federal officer, in enabling him, to some extent, directly to control the suffrages of a numerous body of organized dependents; but the facilities it furnishes for the rapid and simultaneous diffusion of political intelligence which it may be desired to circulate, for the obstruction of that of a contrary tenor, and for the exercise of all the arts of political espionage, also render the Post Office, as a branch of government, a dangerous institution. If this is a danger not necessary to be incurred; if the duties which it performs are a matter of trade which might safely be left to the laws of trade; and if the transmission of our letters and newspapers, from place to place, might be submitted, with salutary results, to the operation of the same principles which now secure the carrying of our merchandize and our persons, there are many who will readily admit that the free trade system, as tending to simplify the offices of government and restraining its powers, would be better than one of political regulation. We are ourselves strongly inclined to the belief, that if the clause in the federal charter which gives to Congress the control of the Post Office had never been inserted, a better system would have grown up under the mere laws of trade. The present system, let it be conducted as it may, can never, in the nature of things, be wholly free from political abuses, and is always in danger of being converted into a mere political machine. The abuses which are its inevitable incidents, will necessarily increase from year to year, as the population swells in numbers, and spreads over a wider surface. It must always, managed by political intermediaries and rapacious subordinates, be attended with a vast amount of unnecessary expense; and this expense must be drawn from the people by a method of taxation in utter violation of their equal rights.

Should the history of this Confederacy stretch out for ages, it will probably never exhibit to the world the spectacle of a chief magistrate combining more exalted qualities than distinguish him who now occupies that lofty station. Sincerer patriotism and more unbending integrity no man can ever possess. Sagacity, firmness, restless activity, and unceasing vigilance, are also among his characteristics. Yet even under his administration, what numerous and not unfounded complaints have vexed the ears of the people of the errors and mismanagement of the Post Offices! Much of the clamour, beyond all question, arose out of party motives, and had no reasonable foundation; but much, on the other hand, was prompted by real delinquency, and was little exaggerated beyond the warrant of truth. If these abuses have existed during the administration of Andrew Jackson, it is not probable that they will not recur under future Presidents. They are inseparable from the system. It is a government machine, cumbrous, expensive, and unwieldly, and liable to be perverted to the worst of uses.

On what principle is the line drawn which separates the matters which are left to the laws of trade, from those which are deemed to require political regulation? The Post Office is established for the purpose of facilitating intercourse by letter between different places. But personal intercourse, though less frequently necessary, is not less positively so, than communication by correspondence. The intertransmission of merchandize is as necessary as either. Why should the government confine its mediation to the mere carrying of our letters? Why not also transport our persons and our goods? These objects, it will be answered, are readily accomplished by the laws of trade, and may therefore properly be left to individual enterprise. But what constitutes this the precise point where the laws of trade become impotent, and where individual enterprise needs to be substituted by political control?

If the clause of the Constitution under which the Post Office establishment exists were struck from the instrument to-morrow, is any one weak enough to suppose that the activity of commerce would not soon supply a system of its own? Modes of conveyance would be instituted at once; they would speedily be improved by the rival efforts of competition; and would keep pace, step by step, with the public demand. It may be said that places far inland and thinly inhabited would suffer by the arrangement. The solitary squatter in the wilderness might not, it is true, hear the forest echoes daily awakened by the postman's horn, and his annual letter might reach him charged with a greater expense than he is now required to pay. But there is no place on the map which would not be supplied with mail facilities by paying a just equivalent; and if they are now supplied for less, it is because the burden of post office taxation is imposed with disproportional weight on the populous sections of the land. But there is no reason why the east should pay the expense of threading with the mail the thick wildernesses of the west, or of wading with it through the swamps and morasses of the south. This is a violation of the plainest principles of equal rights.

The subject of a free trade Post Office presents many considerations which it would be tedious to the reader to pursue to the end in all their ramifications. It is enough for the present that we lay before him a theme of meditation, which will exercise his ingenuity, and afford a not unprofitable incentive to thought. We open the mine, and leave him to trace its various veins of ore. Some of these lay obvious to view. The curse of office-hunting, for example, an inseparable incident of popular government, every year exercises, and in a ratio of prodigious increase, a pernicious influence on the political morals of the country. Under a free trade system of post office business this epidemic evil would necessarily be abated in a vast degree. But would you withdraw, it may be asked, the stimulus which our post office system, by extending mail routes through the wilderness, furnishes to emigration; which provokes a spirit of enterprise to explore the wilds of the west, and to plant colonies in the interminable woods and on the boundless prairies; which causes towns and villages to spring up where the wolf howled and the panther screamed but the week before; and covers with the activity of social life and industry the desert which, but for the impulse furnished by the government, would continue desolate and solitary for ages?

We have no hesitation to answer in the most direct and unequivocal affirmative. All government bounties, of every shape and name, are as much opposed to our notions of the proper freedom of trade, as government restraints and penalties. We would withdraw all government *stimulants*, for they are bad things at best. But let no man suppose the progress of improvement would be thus retarded. Its direction might be changed; but its advance would be unobstructed. The country would continue to grow, from year to year, not less rapidly and more healthfully than now. Instead of the forcing system, which exhausts the soil, and brings forth only sickly and immature productions, we should merely adopt one of nature and of reason. We should merely leave water to flow in its proper channels, instead of endeavouring to compel its current, without reference to the laws of gravitation. The boundaries of population would still continue to enlarge, like ripples on a sheet of water, circle beyond circle; but they would not be forced into unnatural irregularities, and to shoot out this way and that, according to the schemes of politicians and speculators, who, through interested agents in the halls of Congress, should choose to open roads and penetrate with the mails into places which, if left to the natural course of things, would sleep for centuries in the unbroken solitude of nature.

The project now before Congress, to which we adverted in the outset of this article, is liable to no objection, in our view, except that it adds new complication, and gives greater extent and firmness to the post office system under its political organization, thus rendering more distant and feeble our present slight prospect of economic reform.

FREE TRADE, TAXES, AND SUBSIDIES

. . . .

The *New Yorker* has no warrant for saying that, according to the opinions expressed by this journal, a reduction of the tariff to such an *ad valorem* duty as would merely supply the means of defraying the current expenses of the government "would be just no free trade at all." It would certainly not place trade in a state of absolute freedom; but it would be such an enlarge-

Plaindealer, February 11, 1837. Title added. Text abridged and extract deleted.

ment of its bounds, such a relaxation of its fetters, as might well deserve to be spoken of as comparative freedom. We are in favour of absolute freedom of trade in banking; yet we consider the limited repeal of the Restraining Law, although it does not restore to the community their natural rights, in their fullest integrity, a great triumph of free principles, nevertheless. We rejoice at every successive victory obtained, because it carries us nearer to the goal. In war, every advantage over your enemy is, to some extent, a triumph of the principles you maintain, though there may be other battles yet to fight, and other victories to achieve, before the whole object embraced in the ground of quarrel can be accomplished. In religion, every convert whom you bring to kneel at your altar is a triumph of your creed; though its perfect success is not established till the whole world acknowledges its truth. The same remark holds good in relation to science, to art, and to every variety of subject. The gradations of legislative interference with trade are innumerable. Any law which creates an intermediary condition between absolute freedom and absolute restriction is a fetter upon trade. But these fetters may be as light as the pinions on the heels of the feathered Mercury, or they may be as heavy as the chains which bound Prometheus to his rock.

It is a mistake to say that theoretick free trade consists in the equality of duties. It consists in levying no duties at all. It consists in leaving the parties to trade—the buyer and seller—perfectly unrestrained by the conditions of a third party. The amount of revenue necessary for the purposes of government should be derived through a system of taxation that would rest with equal proportional burden upon all, and not merely upon the consumers of foreign merchandize. The man who is clad in deerskins, whom the forest and lake supply with animal food, and whose own field yields him whatever else the necessities of nature demand, should no more be exempt from proportional taxation, than he who flaunts in silks, whose blood is warmed with the spices of the east and the wines of the south, and whose table groans beneath the weight of imported luxuries. Taxes, to the extent of the necessary expenses of government, laid by a rule of universal equality, are no infringement of the principles of free trade; because trade cannot exist without organized government, and organized government cannot be supported without taxation. But the moment government says to the citizens, you who are engaged in one branch of trade, or you who consume one description of commodity, shall pay taxes; and you who deal in another branch of traffick, or consume articles of a different description, shall not be taxed; it obviously violates the proper freedom of trade, as well as the great democratick principle of equal rights.

The *New Yorker* has very imperfectly acquainted itself with our views, if it is not aware that a system of bounties is as much opposed to them, as a system of prohibitory or protective duties. Would it be free trade if the government should say to the Postmaster, you may carry the *New Yorker*, and the other weekly newspapers, free of postage; but you must allow the *Plaindealer* one cent for every number which passes through your hands? Would this not be a direct interference on the part of the government with the weekly newspaper trade? Would it not be saying to those concerned in it, you shall not be left free to make your own terms with your subscribers, but shall be compelled to make such a charge as will enable you to meet an onerous and unjust tax, imposed on the whole community, for the special benefit of one exclusively privileged newspaper? When the government allows a bounty, it devotes, for the benefit of an individual or a class, money derived from the whole community, under the pretence that it was to be expended for the benefit of the whole. Such legislation is objectionable on precisely the same grounds of political justice and economy that may be urged against discriminating duties.

We do not "hesitate or turn recreant" in regard to any subject. We are for applying the principles of political economy to every possible subject which they embrace in their widest latitude of correct interpretation. But it is one thing to condemn political regulation, when, in a matter of trade, the government, as a third party, interferes between the other two, the buyer and seller; and another to withhold condemnation, when those political regulations are merely the rules which one of the two parties, the seller, sets down for his own guidance.[1]

MEEK AND GENTLE WITH THESE BUTCHERS

It will be seen, by our paragraph under the proper head, that Mr. Brady introduced a proposition into the Board of Aldermen last Wednesday evening, the object of which is graciously to permit all butchers to sell meat in their own shops, provided they take out a license, at an expense of fifty dollars, and enter into some sort of security that they will open only a single shop. This proposition is not to be considered as containing the views of its mover as to the degree of freedom which the citizen should be permitted to enjoy in the business of dealing in meat; for that individual has distinguished himself, for a good while past, as the earnest opponent of the unjust and arbitrary restraints and limitations which are imposed on that branch of traffic, giving a monopoly to a few, and forcing the citizen to pay a price much greater than would be asked, if competition were left free to regulate the supply to the demand. But the resolution of Mr. Brady was probably framed

[1] Leggett here refers to the question of the federal government selling western land only to settlers. See "Sale of Publick Lands" and "The Meaning of Free Trade" above, p. 350 and p. 355.—Ed.

Plaindealer, February 18, 1837.

with reference to his prospect of success in any measure tending towards an enlargement of the bounds of the butchers' monopoly; and in that view of it he is entitled to thanks for the measure. But what a sorry picture does not this proceeding exhibit to us of the ignorance and tyranny of our municipal legislators! It is solicited, as a measure of freedom, that a free citizen, as free and intelligent as any member of the Common Council, may be permitted to follow a respectable and useful calling, provided he brings proof that he faithfully served the full term of apprenticeship to that branch of business, gives bonds that he will pursue it only within a specified limit, and pays into the public treasury a large sum of money for the gracious permission which the fathers of the city vouchsafe to him! Can any thing be a greater outrage of common sense than these stipulations? Can any thing be in more palpable and direct violation of the most obvious natural rights? Can any thing, even under the despotic government of Czars, Autocrats, and Grand Seignors, be more arbitrary, unequal, oppressive, and unjust? The prohibitions and restrictions within which butchers are circumscribed, may, with equal warrant of propriety, be drawn round other callings. There is as much reason why the Common Council should take upon themselves to regulate your private affairs, reader, or our own. They may, with equal grace, ordain that no carpenter, or tailor, or hatter, or shoemaker, shall open a shop, except he served a regular apprenticeship to the business, gives bonds that he will open but one, and pays a large bonus into the general coffers for "the blessings of liberty," in that case extended to him. Doctors, lawyers, merchants, and ministers of the gospel, are not less liable than butchers to this municipal supervision and control; and there is quite as much reason, in relation to every one of those vocations, why it should be limited and regulated by the Common Council, as there is in the case of butchers. We hope that among those who have undertaken this business on free trade principles, there are some citizens spirited enough to resist the present ordinances, and defy the inquisitorial power which attempts to tyrannize over them. We should like to see the question tried whether we are, in fact, mere serfs and vassals, holding our dearest privileges but by the sufferance of our municipal servants, or whether we are in truth freemen, possessed of certain inalienable rights, among which is that of pursuing, unmolested, and in our own way, any calling which does not interfere with the rights of others, subject only to the impositions of an equal tax.

THE CAUSE OF HIGH PRICES, AND THE RIGHTS OF COMBINATION

. . . .

The *New Era* does not differ from us in opinion as to the general and pervading cause of high prices. It considers the *bank monopoly system* as the fruitful mother of most of the financial ills under which the community labours, and looks to the complete enfranchisement of trade as the great legislative panacea which alone can effectually cure the complicated disorders of the body politick. But in regard to the late flour riot, it seems disposed to extenuate the conduct of the mob, on the ground that the merchants whose storehouse was invaded had actually monopolized an immense quantity of flour, having been enabled to do so by loans from the State Bank.

. . . .

. . . We admit the facts of the *New Era*, at the same time that we reassert the opinion first expressed by us, that the riot was both causeless and disgraceful. In admitting its facts, however,

Plaindealer, March 4, 1837. Text abridged and extracts deleted or abridged.

we must not be understood as asserting them; for we know nothing, except from the statements of that journal, either as to the quantity of flour held by the mercantile house which it names, or the particular nature or source of its bank accommodations. But assuming that the *New Era* speaks only upon accurate information, we receive its allegations as true, and still refuse to mitigate the strength of our censure, or extenuate the conduct of the mob.

It is no offence against society for a flour dealer to purchase as much flour and grain as he thinks he can readily dispose of to advantage, or can afford to retain in his possession until the consumers shall accede to his demands. It is no offence against society to borrow funds to enable him to accomplish this object; and none to borrow them from a bank. And it is no offence against society for a bank to lend a flour dealer money, any more than it would be to lend it to any other person, in any other branch of business. Nay, if the purpose for which the money was required was communicated to the officers of the bank as the ground of the application, they might still lend it, without committing the slightest offence against society. The sole consideration which is obligatory upon the bank is that of the pecuniary responsibility of the borrower. The object for which the funds are required, further than as it affects that consideration, should not weigh with them a pin's weight.

If the transaction then, in none of its particular features, was an offence against society, it could not become such in its aggregate aspect. The people might well deplore that they had so long permitted their legislative servants to go on, chartering one monopoly after another, until the whole money business of the community, instead of being left open to the wholesome influence of unbounded competition, was placed under the exclusive control of a comparatively few specially privileged individuals, having the power to regulate, according to the dictates of folly or cupidity, the precise channels in which the streams of credit shall flow. But they would surely have no right to assail, either the bank, for lending its money to whom it pleased, or the borrower, for availing himself of its disposition in his favour. To do so would be a causeless outrage; since neither of the parties had transcended its clear, indisputable rights.

The mere fact that the merchants whose warehouse was attacked had more flour on hand than all the other dealers, only shows that they conducted the business on a larger scale. If they asked higher prices than other dealers, they would obtain no custom. If their influence over other dealers caused them all to raise their prices to the same level, and that was above the general level of value, in other places, as fixed by the relations of supply and demand, or any other cause, they would but provoke immediate competition from abroad; for it is the nature of all commodities of traffick to flow *upwards* to the highest level, as much so as it is the nature of water to flow *downwards* to the lowest. But if we suppose, for the sake of the argument, (a thing that would not be possible in fact) that the influence of these same flour dealers extended to every other flour dealer in the country, and their prices fixed the universal standard of price: or, to simplify the matter still more, if we suppose that they were the sole owners of all the flour in the United States, they would still have a right to fix their own price; and whatever that might be, it would afford—great extenuation, we admit—but no justification of a riot.

We take this extreme hypothesis to illustrate our views. Publick opinion in this country is the supreme law. Publick opinion, expressed without tumult, would, in the case supposed, supply an adequate remedy for the evil; but expressed through the means of tumult would defeat the very end proposed. Publick opinion, in such a case, would make a spontaneous, unanimous, and irresistible call on the legislative agents of the community, to take the subject of grievance into their own hands. The flour of a single monopolist, which he was holding from a starving people, would be seized by due process of law; it would be *"private property taken for publick use;"* and *"a just compensation,"* estimated by an equitable comparison of the amount of supply with the amount of demand, would be awarded to the owner. In such a case, the conservative principle, the universal principle of self-preservation, which resides in communities, not less than in individuals, would be fairly called into exercise. It would be an analogous instance with those which are perpetually occurring in times of warfare, but of much stronger obligation. It would be adequate to the end proposed, the relief of the community, according to some just scheme of supplying their wants; whereas, should an unruly mob attempt to achieve the same object by the means of tumult, the effort would but end in the destruction, or most partial and unequal distribution, of the food for which they were famishing, and thus aggravate distress, and place it beyond the reach of alleviation.

Thus, even in the extremest hypothesis which can be framed, we pronounce sentence against tumult. But in the case which really occurred there does not seem to have been the slightest provocation. It does not appear that the flour dealers, whose premises were invaded, had given the smallest occasion of offence to the community. They had a large quantity of flour, and held it at a high price. But they had not "*monopolized*" flour, even so far as this city is concerned, and according to the *New Era's* own showing—which "proclaims fearlessly" the names of half a dozen extensive dealers in flour, whose stores were "jammed to bursting, on every floor, with barrels of flour collected from our native mills and fields," and which promises to name more. If the persons singled out as the objects of mob vengeance charged more than others for their flour, purchasers would only have to leave them, and draw their supply from some of those bursting storehouses. If they all charged alike, the fact would be evidence of one of two things: either that the price was fixed by the relation of the supply to the demand, or by combination. If by combination, rivalry would be provoked from abroad, and this would relieve the community. But the *New Era* may answer that the combination was universal. The burden of proof for such a position would rest upon itself; but we do not hesitate to meet it. Our answer then is, that a universal combination to sustain prices at the point fixed by the relations of supply and demand is perfectly justifiable: and a universal combination to raise them above that point is impossible in the nature of things. The extent and diversity of the interests engaged in the traffick, the varieties of character, and the natural rivalry of trade, forbid it. Even where the parties to such a league or compact are few, and all centered in one narrow circle of business, it is found impracticable to maintain it for any length of time. There are continual violations of faith; there are continual evasions of the terms of agreement, under the impulse of that strong, natural, irradicable spirit of competition which constitutes the mainspring of trade. Despite all the covenants that might be entered into, the price of flour would inevitably adjust itself according the demand, as compared with the supply; according to that principle which furnishes the universal scale of value, the instant price transcends the absolute cost of production under the most favourable circumstances.

It is a happy thing for mankind that this principle does thus invariably operate; because it furnishes a warning to the improvident, checks the profusion of the wasteful, teaches frugality to the extravagant, and arouses a wholesome spirit of economy and foresight in the whole population. If an inadequate supply were not instantly revealed by the tell-tale index of price, a community might run on in profusion and wastefulness, until famine suddenly seized them in his bony clutch. But the mercury in the chrystal tube does not more surely indicate the temperature of the air, than the price of any general staple of a country does the relation of supply and demand. It not only furnishes a warning against thoughtless improvidence at the present time, but supplies a stimulus to competition for the time to come, and induces enterprise to engage in that field which had been imperfectly cultivated before. The events of this year will teach a useful lesson, to be practised the next. Agriculture, admonished of its folly in deserting the plough, to follow in the deluded train of crazy speculation, will return, with renewed industry, to its proper toil. Our fields will smile again with waving harvests; our rivers will glisten with the snowy canvass that wafts the products of the teeming earth to the marts of commerce; and labour will go cheerfully about his work, full fed on nourishing food, which the abundance of supply will have placed amply within his means.

That the present price of flour is the result of the inadequacy of the crop, and not of combination, is a fact perfectly demonstrable, notwithstanding all the allegations which have been uttered to the contrary. It is but little beyond the general average of price; which, in itself, is convincing proof. But independent of this, all the elements which enter into the computation are of a notorious character. The amount of flour raised in the entire country is ascertainable from publick sources, and to a surprising degree of accuracy. The amounts exported and imported are likewise readily ascertained; together with the average amount of consumption by the stationary population, and the average increase of consumers. If a consideration of these elements shows that there is not in existence that quantity of flour which will be in demand before another crop can be brought into market, the price naturally and necessarily adjusts itself according to the scale of deficiency. The effect of this probably is to place flour immediately and entirely beyond the reach of one class of purchasers; and each successive rise diminishes the number of competitors. We may easily carry out the process in our minds, until the stock should be diminished to the last loaf, and none but the wealthiest could enter into the rivalry which the precious food would occasion. In all this, we cannot perceive that immediate injustice is done to any portion of society; while the remote effects of the rise of price in proportion to the diminution of supply are of the happiest kind in averting a recurrence of the evil.

But let us suppose that other views prevailed, and that the dealers in flour were compelled to dispose of it at the same rates which were asked during the most abundant seasons. And let us suppose, too, that this forced cheapness had not the natural effect of causing thoughtless and wasteful expenditure. Still, the time would soon come when the entire stock would be exhausted, and the whole community alike would be without that description of food. It would be very hard that they should be without flour; but whom could they blame? Whom should the mob attack? What description of rights of property should now become the object of outrage? The exhaustion of flour was occasioned by the deficiency of the crop; the deficiency of the crop by the withdrawal of labour from agriculture to other pursuits; the withdrawal of labour by the rage for speculation; the rage for speculation by the sudden expansion of the paper currency; and the sudden expansion of the paper currency by exclusive legislation. Shall any of these intermediate causes of the evil, or shall the great first cause, legislative folly and rapacity, become the object of tumult and violence? Clearly no! The people have the matter perfectly in their control, by the mere influence of peaceful opinion, expressed in the constituted modes. The duty of the press, then, is neither to justify nor extenuate outrage; but to point out, calmly and dispassionately, the prolifick fountain of the evils which oppress the people, and to arouse the publick mind to such action as shall put an end, utterly and forever, to that entire system of exclusive legislation, which is in direct hostility to the rights of man, to the fundamental maxims of our government, and to the great cause of social order and happiness.

The right to combine we have heretofore treated as an indispensable attribute of the freedom of trade; but the *New Era* contests the position, in an article devoted exclusively to that topick. We copy it entire.[1]

[1] Here abridged.—Ed.

. . . .

> . . . An individual has a right to stand still in the street from the rising to the going down of the sun; but a multitude have not, because they would obstruct the free passage and business of others. So every flour merchant, in a beleagured city, whose inhabitants are wan with famine, may demand what price he likes for his precious commodity; but a combination of these merchants to demand even the same price, would be an overt act against the commonweal, and an impediment to free trade. And so each one of the tailors who were prosecuted a short time since in one of our criminal courts, might lawfully have demanded any rate of wages he chose, and have withheld his labour until his condition of exchange had been complied with; but when they all united to accomplish that which was no more than the warrantable object of each, they were indicted for "a conspiracy to injure trade and commerce," and the charge being proved by their overt acts, they were convicted and punished.

. . . .

. . . The notions here expressed against the right to combine, are entertained by other intelligent journals, and very extensively among thinking men in the community. Yet we are satisfied that they are founded in errour, and that their natural tendency, if made a motive of political action, will be to institute the most oppressive and intolerable evils of legislation. The position which we maintain is, that men have a perfect natural right to do by combination, what they have a right to do by separate, unconcerted action; and that any laws to limit or abridge that right are necessarily arbitrary and tyrannous. Nay more, we are disposed to regard the principle of combination as the great natural bulwark of the rights of the poor and the oppressed, and, indeed, in many cases, as the only means which weakness has of resisting the aggressions of power, simplicity of craft, and unprotected labour, of the grasping selfishness of the rich.

The instances which are adduced in the foregoing article are easily answered. No man has a right to combine with others to do what he has not a right to do by separate action. He would not, therefore, have a right to combine to obstruct the streets, because he would not have a right to do so in his own individual person. His right to stand in the street from morning to night rests on the fact that his doing so does not obstruct it. But if you suppose a case where the standing in the street becomes a positive inconvenience to the publick, the individual so blocking up the way would be liable to be removed as a nuisance, and punished for committing it. The instance of the beleaguered city comes within that category of cases over which society, in its corporate capacity, has absolute control. The property of the flour dealers, in such an event, would be taken, not because of their combination, but because it was necessary to the publick preservation. It would be taken in virtue of that power which is inherent in all governments, of taking private property for publick use, when the exigences of state requires it. The case of the tailors, so far as they were punished merely for combination, was an exceedingly hard one, and violently outraged the universal publick sense of justice. So fa[r] as punishment was awarded to them for a breach of the peace, in attempting to overawe others by coercive measures, it was fully deserved. Two persons have a natural right to combine; but they have no right to compel a third to join their combination, or punish him for refusing to do so.

The position that, because money is an article of merchandize, the chartered money-changers have an unlimited right either to retain it in their own hands, or to ask what terms they please for it, is unsound; simply because such conduct would be in positive violation of their charters, and would forfeit all the privileges—abundantly large—which they really do possess under them. If the position were asserted of those who deal in money without a charter, it would undoubtedly be true, putting the usury laws out of question, as we trust they will, before many years, be put out of existence. But the *New*

Era is mistaken in this: that the evil of which it complains, in terms not stronger than are warranted by its enormity, is chargeable to a combination of the banks, or any subordinate combination to which the banks supply the means of mischief. It is chargeable to those who institute those banks, who confer on them their special and exclusive privileges, and shut up all competition in the narrow and tyrannous bounds of ignorant and unjust legislation. We do not by any means deny that, if the whole monetary power of the country, or the whole and exclusive right of pursuing any other important branch of business, were conferred, by the supreme legislative authority, on a limited number of associations or individuals, a combination among those associations or individuals might be productive of the most disastrous effects. But we should charge those effects, not to the principle of combination, but to the hideous and paralysing principle of monopoly legislation. We should attempt to remedy the evil, not by erecting ineffectual dams and barriers against the desolating tide where it was hurrying along in swollen and irresistable fury, inundating the land with its waters of bitterness, but by tracing it to its source, and demolishing the monstrous impediments placed there by ignorance and fraud, to prevent its winding through its thousand natural channels, and force the whole volume with destructive rapidity in one particular direction. The principle of combination should not be charged with those evils which result from legislative restrictions upon competition. Let the *New Era* try the question by instances in which that principle alone operates, unmixed with legislative interference, in the shape either of bounties or impositions, and we think it will arrive at the same conclusion with ourselves.

We concede to our opponent, fully and freely, and have often so argued before, that combinations, for the most part, are exceedingly silly, and end in loss and discomfiture to those who combine. But this is a matter for the parties to judge of for themselves, and does not affect the question of right. The owners of all the packets to Liverpool, for example, have a perfect right to combine, and fix their own terms of freight and passage. If their combination was so regulated as not to require more for freight or passage than a fair return upon their investment of capital, they would not, by combining, provoke competition, any more than if each individual acted separately and for himself. Neither would the publick have any reason to complain. But the moment this combination produced the natural effect of increasing the demands beyond a just compensation, or diminishing the excellence of the accommodations, the public would complain, and the complaint, exciting the attention of ever ready enterprise, would lead rival competitors to establish opposition lines of packets. It would be precisely the same with money and credit, if those who deal, or who would deal in money and credit, instead of being circummured in the narrow limits of a pernicious system of legislation, were left solely to the government of the laws of trade. A few capitalists of vast wealth might combine together to raise the rate of usance; but all capital could not possibly be drawn into such a league, and competition would speedily demolish the baseless fabrick of avarice and cupidity. Even if such a league could be so extended as to embrace all the capital in the country, it would only provoke competition from abroad; and if it could be so extended as to embrace all the capital in the world, it would only provoke labour to form a counter combination.

What is combination? It is a mere league of trade between two or more individuals. It is a modified form of partnership. Every partnership is, indeed, a combination, and much more positive and stable, than those temporary and imperfect compacts now under consideration. The *New Era* would not deny the right of two or more individuals to form a partnership for any purpose of trade. Yet such a partnership might embrace the capitalists in the business of lending money; or the coal merchants in the business of selling coal; or the flour dealers in the business of selling flour. Where then would be the remedy of the community? In those simple principles which always govern trade. In the simple fact, that profit is the object of trade, and that, in order to insure it, price must bear a just proportion to the relations of supply and demand.

Combination is one of the great means by which the highest interests of society are promoted. What is it that raises the wages of the printers in your office to something like a tolerable equivalent for their patient toil? Is it the spontaneous liberality of their employers? Is it individual action? If they trusted to the efficacy of either of these, we fear their labour would be sadly unrequited. No, it is combination. It is the influence of associated effort and mutual coöperation. What is it that increases the pittance of the day labourer in some sort of proportion with the monstrous advance of other things, and enables him scantily to appease the cravings of hunger? It is combination, less effectual, in his case, because planned with less intelligence, and acted upon with less obedience to the terms of the compact, but still of sufficient efficacy to mitigate the evils which he would otherwise endure. What is it that has, in a great degree, banished the curse of intemperance from the land, and snatched myriads of human beings from all the complicated horrours it entails? Again we say, combination, the bulwark of the rights of the poor and lowly, and a powerful instrument in the hands of the good. It is an efficient weapon against the oppressor; but, like the sword bestowed by the good genius in the fairy tale, it shivers into fragments when drawn against the oppressed.

OMNIPOTENCE OF THE LEGISLATURE

In one of George Colman's metrical oddities,[1] that writer advances the bold opinion that,

——What's impossible can't be,
And never, never comes to pass.

This seems, however, to be a great mistake. The wisdom of modern legislation is continually performing impossibilities. The laws of physics and metaphysics, of mind and matter, are every day abrogated by the laws of man, and the march of improvement is so rapid, that it would scarcely be surprising if the whole system of things should shortly be taken wholly under the control of our lawgivers.

Judge Soule, of our state legislature, has lately made a great step towards that consummation. He has introduced a bill to fix the value of money, under every variety of financial circumstances, at precisely seven per cent. a year, and he has framed its provisions with such profound sagacity, that money lenders and money borrowers will never attempt to evade them. This will be glad news to those who are at present paying three per cent. a month.

The notable project of Judge Soule provides that bonds, bills, notes, assurances, all other contracts or securities whatsoever, and all deposites of goods or other things whatsoever, whereupon or whereby there shall be received or taken, or secured or agreed to be reserved or taken, any greater sum, or

Plaindealer, April 1, 1837.

[1] George Colman (the younger) was an English playwright and author of comic verse whose *Poetical Works* were published in their first American edition in 1834. —Ed.

greater value, for the loan or forbearance of any money, goods or other things in action, than the legal rate of seven per cent. per annum, shall be void; and any bond, bill, note, assurance, pledge, conveyance, contract, and all evidences of debt whatsoever, which may have been sold, transferred, assigned or indorsed upon, for or upon which any greater interest, discount or consideration may have been reserved, obtained or taken than is provided in the first section of the said title shall be absolutely null and void; and no part of any such contract, security or evidence of debt, shall be collectable in any court of law or equity. It also declares every violation of the provisions of the act to be a misdemeanor, subjecting the person offending to fine or imprisonment, or both.

There was a certain philosopher who spent his life in bottling moonbeams. Judge Soule seems to belong to the same school.

The Astronomer in Rasselas,[2] by a long and attentive study of the heavenly bodies, at length discovered the secret of their governments, and qualified himself to direct their courses, and regulate the seasons. "I have possessed for five years," said he to Imlac, "the regulation of the weather and the distribution of the seasons: the sun has listened to my dictates, and passed from tropic to tropic by my direction; the clouds, at my call, have poured their waters, and the Nile has overflowed at my command; I have restrained the rage of the dog-star and mitigated the fervours of the crab. I have administered this great office with exact justice, and made the different nations of the earth an impartial dividend of rain and sunshine. What must have been the misery of half the globe, if I had limited the clouds to particular regions, or confined the sun to either side of the equator!"

Judge Soule has now taken upon himself an office not less important in the financial system, than that of the learned astronomer in the planetary. He is for dividing the rain and

[2] *Rasselas* (1759) is a tale by the English critic and essayist Samuel Johnson.—Ed.

sunshine of the money-market with an impartial hand, and giving equal portions to borrower and lender. In doing this he perhaps may be thought to carry the principle of equality to an undue extent, since it places all borrowers on a level, whatever the difference in the nature of the security they offer, or in the precariousness of the objects to which the loan is to be applied. But Judge Soule is too much of a philosopher to regard such slight circumstances of difference. He looks down on the money-market from such a height as reduces both bulls and bears to uniformity of stature.

The Astronomer, in Rasselas, confessed that there was one thing, in the system of nature, over which he had not been able to obtain complete control. "The winds alone," said he, "of all the elemental powers, have hitherto refused my authority, and multitudes have perished by equinoctial tempests, which I found myself unable to prohibit or restrain." We are afraid that the astronomer's worthy prototype in our legislature will also find there is likewise one thing which is beyond his authority. Judge Soule will yet discover, we imagine, that the interest on money is as variable as the winds, and that as the latter sometimes whisper in zephyrs and sometimes rave in tempests, so the former, in spite of all his efforts will sink down and almost die away, and at others swell and rage to the tune of three per cent. a month.

It is a matter of astonishment to us that any man, having sense enough to recommend him to his constituents for a seat in the legislature, can be so blind as not to see that usury laws are essentially and necessarily unjust and arbitrary. The value of money depends on a thousand very varying contingencies, as much so as the value of any other commodity. A failure of our chief articles of export, either as to quantity or price, immediately increases the demand for money, and at the same time decreases the security of the borrower. An abundant crop and large prices have, as certainly, the opposite result. This is a difference which affects whole communities. The differences which distinguish individual borrowers are not less obvious. One has ample security to offer; another has none. One needs money to aid him in a pursuit which promises certain profit; another needs it to prosecute an enterprise of exceeding hazard, which, if successful, promises a large return, but if unsuccessful, leaves no hope of re-payment. One borrower, has health, activity and prudence; another is infirm, indolent and rash. Judge Soule is for making up a Procrustean bed for all alike, without reference to the variety of form and stature. We recommend him to the muse of *Croaker*, as a fit subject for poetic honours, and in the meanwhile apply to him a stanza addressed by that writer to a great leveller in another line:[3]

Come, star-eyed maid, Equality!
  In thine adorer's praise I revel,
Who brings, so fierce his love to thee,
  All forms and faces to a level.

[3] "Croaker" was a pseudonym used by Joseph Rodman Drake and Fitz-Greene Halleck for a series of satirical poems which appeared in the *Evening Post* in 1819. The stanza quoted is from "The National Paintings: Col. Trumbull's 'The Declaration of Independence'" by Drake.—Ed.

PART SIX

Literary Property

RIGHTS OF AUTHORS

. . . .

The whole question of the propriety of an international copyright law, or a copyright law at all, resolves itself, we think, into the enquiry whether such a regulation would promote the greatest good of the greatest number. This is the principle which we conceive constitutes the basis of the most important rights of property. They are artificial rights, not rights of nature. They are created by laws, not merely confirmed by them. This is obviously the case with regard to that species of property which the political institutions of all civilized countries regard with peculiar deference, and secure with particular care, and to which the distinctive appellation of *real estate* is given. The right of property in land, like the right to breathe the vital air of heaven, is, by nature, common to all mankind; and the only just foundation of individual and peculiar rights is furnished by the law of the land. Locke, who goes as far as any writer in tracing the right of property to inherent causes existing anterior to political institutions, does not maintain that any thing gives to an individual a distinct and exclusive right to land, except in as far as by occupying it and mixing his labour with it, it becomes his own in such a sense that you cannot take it away without also taking the fruits of his labour, which, he contends, are his own by nature. Paley, on the contrary, in his book on Relative Duties, considers the law of the land the only real foundation of territorial property.

But let us, in conformity with the opinions of Locke and other accredited writers, concede that men have a natural right of property in the productions of their own industry and skill; that the mechanic, for example, has an exclusive right to the article he manufactures; the fisherman to the fish he catches;

Plaindealer, January 27, 1837. Text abridged.

and the fowler to the birds he shoots. To the same extent the author has an exclusive natural right of property in the book he composes; that is, he has a natural right to the manuscript, so long as he chooses to retain it to himself. The process by which the mechanic fabricates a particular article is his property, so long as he keeps it secret. The peculiar arts of the fisherman and fowler are their property, in the same way, until they communicate them. And the thoughts of the author are his property, equally, until he publishes them to the world. In all these cases, alike, so far as natural rights are concerned, they then become common property. Every body is at liberty to imitate the article manufactured by the mechanic; to practice the artifices of the fisher and fowler; and to copy the book of the author. Any further exclusive or peculiar property in them has no other foundation than the law.

The right of exclusive property, of the exclusive use and benefit of the fruits of one's own labour, is the great and secure foundation of social order and happiness. Without it, man would never rise above a semi-barbarous condition; and in those communities where it is most securely guarded, we invariably find the highest degree of moral and intellectual refinement, the greatest general prosperity, and the most advanced condition of all the arts which sustain and embellish life. But we would have it understood, in passing, that this important and fundamental right is violated as fatally by unequal laws, by laws which give peculiar facilities for the acquisition of wealth to the few, and deny them to the many, as by those more obviously arbitrary edicts, which directly and openly deprive the labourer of his reward. The true security of the right of property consists in equal legislation.

If we are correct in the position assumed, that the exclusive natural right of an author to his production, like that of a mechanic to the fashion or device of his table or chair, extends no further than to his immediate copy, the question for society then to determine is, whether it is proper to create and guard this right by legal enactments; and the decision of it, in our view of the subject, should rest solely on the consideration of the effect it would have on the interests of the great mass of mankind, or, to repeat Bentham's phrase, it should be decided according to the principle of "the greatest good of the greatest number." It is entirely within the competency of the law to make a literary production property, either absolutely and in perpetuity, or in a qualified sense, and, for a limited period of time. If government should choose to do neither, but leave the published book as free to be copied, as a new device in cutlery, a new style in dress, the author would be without reasonable ground of complaint, since he entered into the vocation without the prospect of any other advantage, than what necessarily and inalienably belongs to the opportunity of the first use of the fruits of his labours.

But if the law undertakes to establish a certain kind of property in the productions of authorship, "in the fruits of intellectual exertion," to use the language of our correspondent, it must fix the limit somewhere; and those intellectual labourers excluded from the vineyard, (and there would necessarily be many such) would then have some reason to complain of partial legislation. The farmer who, by a long and careful study of the processes of nature, discovers an improved method of tillage and culture, by which he can make his field yield a harvest of twofold abundance, ought surely not to be excluded from the category of those who benefit mankind by the fruits of intellectual exertion; yet the neighbouring farmer, who ploughs the adjoining field, copies his mode of tillage, and no one ever thinks of instituting a law to give the first a right of property, and secure to him the exclusive advantages of his discovery. The artist who spends days and nights of patient intellectual toil in devising tasteful and symmetrical patterns for the lace worker and silk weaver, sees the fruits of his intellectual labour copied as soon as they are exhibited; and does not dream of asking the security and advantage of any peculiar legal rights. The natural advantage of the inventor, that he is first in the market, presents a sufficient stimulus to exertion, and secures, in most cases, an adequate reward.

If the principle of copyright were wholly done away, the business of authorship, we are inclined to think, would readily accommodate itself to the change of circumstances, and would be more extensively pursued, and with more advantage to all concerned than is the case at present. It is very much the fashion of the day to deride and decry cheap publications. We are not of the number who can join in the censure. The great good which the invention of printing originally effected, was to diffuse literature, and make books accessible to myriads, who were precluded from them before, by reason of the enormous prices at which manuscript copies were sold. What the first rude efforts of the printing-press were, in comparison with the slow and painful manipulations of the cloistered scribe, the art of cheap printing of the present day is to that art as it was practised by our fathers. It is spreading literature over the entire land. It is penetrating with it into every nook and corner of society. It is offering its golden fruits, ay, richer than gold, to the poor and ignorant, as well as to the rich and educated. It is awakening millions of human beings to a sense of their birthright; to acknowledge that they are God's creatures, and not beasts that perish. We are the friend of cheap literature, for it is the friend of humanity, and is exercising an important influence in the illustration of the most interesting problem of morals, the infinite perfectibility of man. If there were no copyright laws, all literature would take a cheap form, and all men would become readers. It would take a cheap form to preclude competition; and it would be widely diffused because of its cheapness. Instead of an edition of two, or three, or five thousand copies, which never constitute, as a general rule, the maximum of a popular author's success, twenty, thirty, and perhaps a hundred thousand would be readily disposed of. Let us withdraw our attention, for an instant, from a contemplation of the interests of authors, to consider those of mankind at large. Who can fail to see how vastly the general benefit would be promoted? What a noble spectacle an entire nation of readers would present! With what intelligence and order would not its affairs be conducted! And if knowledge is power, what a vast influence it would exercise in the counsels of nations, and in directing the destinies of mankind!

But there is no need that we should throw the interest of authors out of sight in this consideration. On the contrary, we believe the benefit to themselves would be in an equal ratio with that to the community at large. If they were left without the protection of a copyright, their business would assume new forms. They would connect themselves, in schemes of extensive publication, with those whose facilities would put competition at defiance. The advantage of a first copy is in itself incalculable. With publishers of large capital, whose measures are wisely taken, it is worth more than ordinary copyrights. The Harpers, if we are correctly informed, pay British writers, for a duplicate copy in advance of publication in London, as much as some of the copyrights of some of the most favoured authors at home will command. Nobody attempts to reprint the Penny Magazine and Penny Cyclopoedia upon Jackson; simply because, having by arrangement with the British publishers, the benefit of a first copy, he puts it in so cheap a form, and prepares so vast an edition, that competition is intimidated, as it has everything to lose and but little to gain.[1] The advantages of a first sale, when the preparatory steps are duly and discreetly taken, are prodigious. They constitute the author's natural and inalienable right; and we repeat our strong conviction that if he were left alone, the interest of both author and public would be most effectually promoted.

If we are right in the view we have taken of this subject; if

[1] William Jackson, of New York, was the American publisher to whom Leggett here refers; the British publishers were the Society for the Diffusion of Useful Knowledge. Jackson sold his *Penny Magazine* for three cents and carried on the business from 1833 to 1841.—Ed.

it can be shown that the present system is wrong in itself, as tried by the greatest good principle; the argument in favour of the extension of the copyright law, so as to embrace the authors of other countries, falls to the ground. It is the same argument which we constantly hear used in favour of extending the grants of special charters. But if an evil exists in our system, it is the duty of good citizens to endeavour to abolish it, not to make it an excuse for instituting other evils. Our correspondent says truly and eloquently, that there is no ground on which our Congress can be bound to act according to a decision of the House of Lords, nor on which they are not at liberty, setting authority and precedent aside, to revert to the first principles of justice and expediency. Our institutions are founded on a maxim widely different from the fundamental principle of other governments; and it is proper that our legislation should be marked by an equally distinctive character. It is for this young and vigorous republic to set an example to the nations of the old world; and after those glorious principles of equal liberty which constitute the basis of our political fabric, we hardly know a measure which would tend in a larger degree to promote the best interests of mankind, than the enfranchisement of the press from the exclusive privileges of authorship.

THE RIGHTS OF AUTHORS

Able pens are wielded against us on the subject of literary property. But as we have no end to answer which is not equally that of truth, we insert the arguments of our antagonists with

Plaindealer, February 11, 1837. Text abridged.

as much readiness as our own, certain that the ultimate result of discussion, in this, as in regard to every topic within the embrace of human reason, must be the establishment of sound principles. . . .

. . . .

It is true that too many of those whose genius has rendered them immortal, have employed their noblest efforts to embellish the solid structure which tyranny erects on the prostrate liberties of man. The two divinest bards, that ever addressed their strains of undying harmony to the enraptured ears of mortals, were the flatterers and upholders of aristocratic pride, and the scoffers of the rights of the people. Homer and Shakspeare "licked absurd pomp," and taught men to regard as a superior order of beings those whose only claims to preeminence were founded in rapine and outrage. But when we look back through the bright list of names which English literature presents, we do not find this censure to be of general application. He from whom the remark is derived, as to the potent influence of those who frame a nation's ballads in forming the national character—sturdy old Andrew Fletcher of Saltoun—did not address himself to a caste; he addressed himself to the people, and stood forward ever the eager and intrepid champion of their rights. Milton did not address himself to a caste, but to mankind; and Marvell and Harrington were animated in their writings by the single and exalted motive of improving the political condition of their race.

But we need not contest the sentiment to which we have offered this brief reply, since it does not touch our argument. It is for the very purpose that "the Republic of Letters" may be upheld by *the people,* and that it may be composed *of* the people, that we desire to see the principle of literary property abrogated. We do not wish to deny to British authors a right; but we desire that a legal privilege, which we contend has no foundation in natural right, and is prejudicial to "the greatest good of the greatest number," should be wholly annulled, in relation to all authors, of every name and country. Our position is, that authors have no natural right of property in their published works, and that laws to create and guard such a right are adverse to the true interests of society. We concede at once, and in the fullest manner, that if the propriety of establishing a right of property in literary productions can be shown, the principle ought to be of universal application; that it ought not to be limited to any sect, or creed, or land, but acknowledged, like the plainest rights of property, wherever civilization has extended its influence. An author either has a natural and just right of property in his production, or he has not. If he has, it is one not to be bounded by space, or limited in duration, but, like that of the Indian to the bow and arrow he has shaped from the sapling and reeds of the unappropriated wilderness, his own exclusively and forever.

With regard to the influence which British literature exercises in forming the popular mind and character in this country, we see no cause to fear unfavourable results, if American literature, to which we naturally look to counteract the evil tendencies of the former, is not excluded, by reason of the incumbrance of copyright, from an equally extensive circulation. Leave error free to flow where it listeth, so that truth is not shut out from the same channels. Give both an equal opportunity, and who can doubt to whom will belong the victory? "Who knows not," says John Milton, "that truth is strong, next to the Almighty? She needs no policies, nor stratagems, nor licensings, to make her victorious. Those are the shifts and the defences that error uses against her power." It was under the influence of British literature exclusively, and in many instances of education obtained in British colleges, that our national independence was asserted and achieved; and it would be strange, indeed, if we should be rendered now unmindful of its value, by the tawdry and sickening aristocracy which bedizens the pages of British novels and romances. "The men who write the ballads" are not those whom a copyright stimulates into the exercise of their powers; and if they were, the Americans, thank heaven! are not the people whom ballads move with irresistible influence. We go to our political affairs, as mathematicians go to their abstruse labours; with their intellectual energies screwed to too high a pitch, to be shaken from their purpose by the sounding of brass or the tinkling of cymbals.

We turn now to a consideration of the article of our correspondent, who has ingeniously erected his structure of logical arguments on a foundation furnished by ourselves. Our position that an author has an exclusive natural right of property in his manuscript, was meant to be understood only in the same sense that a mechanic has an exclusive natural right of property in the results of his labour. The mental process by which he contrived those results are not, and cannot properly be rendered, exclusive property; since the right of a free exercise of our thinking faculties is given by nature to all mankind, and the mere fact that a given mode of doing a thing has been thought of by one, does not prevent the same ideas presenting themselves to the mind of another and should not prevent him from a perfect liberty of acting upon them. The right which we concede to the author is the right to the results of his manual labour. The right which is claimed for him is the right to the ideas which enter into his mind, and to which he gives a permanent and communicable form by writing them down upon paper.

But when we pass from corporeal to incorporeal property, we immediately enter into a region beset with innumerable difficulties. The question first naturally arises, where does this exclusive right of property in ideas commence? The limits of corporeal property are exact, definite, and always ascertainable. Those of incorporeal property are vague and indefinite, and subject to continual dispute. The rights of corporeal property may be asserted, without the possibility of infringing any other individual's rights. Those of incorporeal property may obviously give rise to conflicting claims, all equally well founded. If you catch a fish in the sea, or shoot a bird in the forest, it is yours, the reward of your patience, toil, or skill; and no other human being can set up an adverse claim. But if you assert an exclusive right to a particular idea, you cannot be sure that the very same idea did not at the same moment enter some other mind. This is obviously and frequently true with respect to single thoughts, and it will readily be conceived that it may happen with respect to a series. Language is the common property of all mankind, and the power of thought is their common attribute. Shall you then say to a person who has expressed certain ideas in certain words, you shall have an exclusive right of property in those ideas so expressed, and no other human being shall ever use the same sentiments, without incurring a penalty for his tresspass?

If the author has a natural right of property in the ideas of his mind, once committed to paper, it is a right which ought to be universally acknowledged, and he should be allowed to enjoy exclusively the profit of the use of his property in every civilized nation of the world. But where does this right commence? How many ideas must be joined together before they constitute a property? If a man construct an edifice, every brick or board of the entire fabric is his. He may sell it, or lend it, or convert it to what use he will; but no one can take it against his consent without committing a robbery. Is the author's edifice of ideas equally his, in its component materials, as well as in their aggregate combination? Every sentence, perhaps, contains an idea, so natural that it is likely to occur to many minds, and expressed in such obvious language, that the same terms substantially would probably suggest themselves to all. His work is made up of such sentences. In what then consists his right of property? Is each particular sentence a property? Or do they not become property until joined together?

But the subjects of books are various. Some are flights of imagination; some are records of facts. In one, history relates her sober details; in another, science demonstrates his abtruse propositions. In all these, intellectual labour is exerted; but is the fruit of that intellectual labour property in all cases alike? Are the meditations of the poet property in the same sense with the calculations of the mathematician; and has each an exclusive right to the results of his labour? Before you answer this in the affirmative, you should reflect that the processes of mathematical calculation are the same throughout the world, and that the end aimed at by them is also identical. A book of mathematics is a book of calculations, conducted according to certain invariable and universally acknowledged principles; and though to compose it requires perhaps intense intellectual exertion, yet it calls for no original ideas or discoveries. Two mathematicians, one in France, for instance, and the other here, may easily be supposed toiling through the same processes at the same moment, and accomplish results exactly the same. Which has the exclusive right of property in his production? Which shall be permitted to publish his book, and proclaim to the other, and to all the world, I alone am invested with the rights of authorship?

Many of the most interesting and valuable works are mere records of discoveries in experimental science. But two philosophers may at the same time be engaged, in different parts of the world, in the same series of experiments, and may both hit on the same result. The discovery, as mere property, is only valuable perhaps through the medium of publication; yet shall the right of publishing be restricted to one, and if the other presume to tell the same philosophical facts, shall he be considered a species of felon? The law of patents rests confessedly on the same principle as the law of copyright. They both pretend to have natural and obvious justice for their foundation. The inventor of a new application of the principles of mechanics claims a right of exclusive property in the fruit of his intellectual labour, not less than the writer of a poem or a play. Yet some of the most valuable inventions which have ever been given to mankind have been produced simultaneously, by different minds, in different parts of the world. It is uncertain to this day to whom men are indebted for the application of the magnetic needle to navigation; and the honour of the discovery of the art of printing is yet a matter of dispute. While Franklin was pursuing his electrical experiments in Philadelphia, the philosophers of Paris were engaged in similar investigations, and with similar success. Rittenhouse, when he planned his complicated and ingenious *Orrery*, knew not that such an instrument had already been completed, which was destined to perpetuate the name of its inventor.[1] Newton and Leibnitz each claimed the exclusive honour of their method of fluxions; and many more instances might be adduced, if we had leisure to pursue the subject, of such jarring and incompatible claims to exclusive property in the fruits of intellectual labour. The cases we have stated will sufficiently show that there cannot be, in the nature of things, a positive and absolute right of exclusive property in processes of thought, which different minds may be engaged in at the same moment of time. Two authors, without concert or intercommunion, may describe the same incidents, in language so nearly identical that the two books, for all purposes of sale, shall be the same. Yet one writer may make a free gift of his production to the public, may throw it open in common; and then what becomes of the other's right of property?

The remarks which we have thus far offered go merely to assail the position of the natural right of property in ideas, as existing anterior to law, or independent of it. It is essential to the establishment of such a natural right, that it should be shown to be distinct property, which absolutely and wholly belongs to some one individual, and can belong to no other than he. The labour of your hands belongs to you; for no other individual in the world performed that labour, or achieved its particular results. But the labour of your mind can produce only ideas, which may be common to many minds, and which

[1] David Rittenhouse, American astronomer and instrument maker, was anticipated by Charles Boyle, the fourth earl of Orrery, in the invention of a gear-driven device for illustrating the relative movements of the bodies in the solar system.—Ed.

are not susceptible of being distinguished by marks of peculiar property. Another person falling, under similar circumstances, into the same mood of cogitation, may produce ideas—not merely similar—not another set of perfect resemblance to the first—not a copy—but identically the same. There is an inherent difficulty in fixing limits to incorporeality. The regions of thought, like those of the air, are the common property of all earth's creatures.

We do not offer the crude observations which we have here made as a full answer to our correspondent's argument; for we mean to reserve the question for a more deliberate and careful discussion in another number. But we merely put them forth as some of the reasons which lead us to deny that the author and inventor have any property in the fruits of their intellectual labour, beyond that degree in which it is incorporated with their physical labour.

RIGHT OF PROPERTY IN THE FRUITS OF INTELLECTUAL LABOUR

We have provoked such odds against us, in the contest on the subject of the rights of property in intellectual productions, that we do not know but that it would be "the better part of valour" to quit the field incontinently. To emulate the conduct of the bold knight whose determined heroism is recorded in *Chevy Chase,* and who, when his legs were off, "still fought upon his stumps," might seem, in such a dispute as we engaged in, rather censurable obstinacy, than praiseworthy courage. Or if it provoked a smile, it would probably be one, not

Plaindealer, February 25, 1837.

of approbation, but of that kind which we bestow on the logical prowess of Goldsmith's *Schoolmaster,* who could argue after he was vanquished,[1] as *Bombastes Furioso* continues to fight after he is killed.[2]

There is one motive, however, which might not be without some weight with us to persist in the controversy, even after being convinced we had espoused the wrong side. If our doing so would continue to draw such writers into the field as we have heretofore had to contend with, we should not be without excuse; as their forcible reasoning and perspicuous style would far more than counterpoise the influence of our erroneous opinions, exert what ingenuity we might to establish them.

But we choose to deal ingenuously with our readers. We took up arms to battle for the truth, and shall lay them down the moment we find we have inadvertently engaged on the side of her adversaries. That we are shaken in the opinions we have heretofore expressed, we freely admit. The idiosyncracies of style, to use the term aptly employed in the eloquent communication annexed, are marked with such distinctness, that a bare phrase of three or four words, from a writer of admitted genius, is often so characteristic and peculiar, as to indicate its source at once, even to those who have no recollection of its origin, but who judge of it as a connoisseur does of a painting.

How far this peculiar mode of expression can be considered property on the principles of natural justice, is the question in dispute. We are not entirely convinced that we have taken wrong ground on this subject; yet we by no means feel so confident of the correctness of our opinions as we did when we put them forth. One thing seems to us, and has all along seemed, very clear: if the author has a natural right of property

[1] This is likely a reference to the title character in Oliver Goldsmith's novel *The Vicar of Wakefield* (1776).—Ed.

[2] In William Barnes Rhodes's long-popular mock-heroic burlesque *Bombastes Furioso* (1810) the title character is killed in a fight but revives to join in the finale.—Ed.

in the products of his intellectual labour, it ought to be acknowledged as extensively as the capitalist's right of property in his money, or the merchant's in his goods. It is a common law right, not a right by statute, maugre all decisions to the contrary. If, on the other hand, his right is derived from a law founded on views of expediency, instead of the principles of natural justice, we revert to our first position, that the greatest good of the greatest number would be more effectually promoted by the total abrogation of copyright property.

Let the claim of natural right be established, and we should be among the last to invade it; but concede that the question rests on any other basis, and we think we should have no great difficulty in showing that the general welfare would be advanced by abolishing the principle of exclusive property in written compositions, as it is never asserted in those which are merely spoken.

INDEX

This book is set in Caslon 540, a modern typeface based on the famous fonts of the engraver and type founder William Caslon (1692–1766). The earlier legal restrictions on English printers had made them dependent on Dutch sources for types well into the eighteenth century. Caslon naturally modeled his designs on the Dutch forms, introducing his own improvements in fit and proportion. So many variations on Caslon's originals have been produced since his time, combining tradition with individuality, that it is difficult to classify Caslon as an old-style or transitional typeface.

Printed on paper that is acid-free and meets the requirements of the American National Standard for Permanence of Paper for Printed Library Materials, Z39.48-1992. ♾

Book design by Hermann Strohbach,
New York, New York
Cover and jacket design by Erin Kirk New,
Watkinsville, Georgia
Editorial services by Harkavy Publishing Service,
New York, New York
Typography by Typoservice Corporation,
Indianapolis, Indiana
Printed and bound by Thomson-Shore, Inc.,
Dexter, Michigan